Lecture Notes in Computer Science 2753

Edited by G. Goos, J. Hartmanis, and J. van Leeuwen

Springer

Berlin
Heidelberg
New York
Hong Kong
London
Milan
Paris
Tokyo

Frank Maurer   Don Wells (Eds.)

Extreme Programming and Agile Methods – XP/Agile Universe 2003

Third XP Agile Universe Conference
New Orleans, LA, USA, August 10-13, 2003
Proceedings

Springer

Series Editors

Gerhard Goos, Karlsruhe University, Germany
Juris Hartmanis, Cornell University, NY, USA
Jan van Leeuwen, Utrecht University, The Netherlands

Volume Editors

Frank Maurer
University of Calgary, Department of Computer Science
2500 University Drive NW, Calgary, Alberta, T2N 1N4 Canada
E-mail: maurer@cpsc.ucalgary.ca
Don Wells
4681 Brockham Way, Sterling Heights, MI 48310, USA
E-mail: don@extremeprogramming.org

Cataloging-in-Publication Data applied for

A catalog record for this book is available from the Library of Congress

Bibliographic information published by Die Deutsche Bibliothek
Die Deutsche Bibliothek lists this publication in the Deutsche Nationalbibliographie;
detailed bibliographic data is available in the Internet at <http://dnb.ddb.de>.

CR Subject Classification (1998): D.1, D.2, D.3, F.3, K.4.3, K.6

ISSN 0302-9743
ISBN 3-540-40662-X Springer-Verlag Berlin Heidelberg New York

Springer-Verlag Berlin Heidelberg New York
a member of BertelsmannSpringer Science+Business Media GmbH

http://www.springer.de

© Springer-Verlag Berlin Heidelberg 2003
Printed in Germany

Typesetting: Camera-ready by author, data conversion by PTP-Berlin GmbH
Printed on acid-free paper   SPIN: 10930663   06/3142   5 4 3 2 1 0

Preface

XP Agile Universe 2003 is the third conference in a series running in North America and attracting participants from all over the world who are interested in the research, development and application of agile software processes. Agile approaches value people and interaction over processes and tools – moving software engineering from the process-oriented software development approaches of the 1990s towards people-oriented approaches that we are starting to see more and more in this decade. Agile approaches stress a holistic view of software developers as being involved in analysis, design, implementation and testing activities, while more traditional, tayloristic approaches separate these tasks and assign them to different "resources." Tayloristic approaches create knowledge-sharing problems as information gathered by one person needs to be handed over – usually in the form of documentation – to the next person in the chain. Agile approaches reduce the number of hand-offs and, thus, decrease the amount of required documentation for knowledge sharing.

While deemed a novelty only a few years ago, agile methods are now becoming established in the software industry and are being applied in more and more application domains. While agile approaches move into the mainstream of software organizations, we are only now beginning to understand their benefits, areas of applicability, and also their dangers. This year's conference will increase this understanding and provide a better base for industry practitioners as they assess the effectiveness of agile methods in their environment. Researchers will use the work presented to create conceptual models of agile approaches that allow us to find new insights and steer future research.

Submissions to this year's conference mirror the breadth and the depth of agile approaches. Thirty-five technical papers were submitted while the conference proceedings now include 17 high-quality contributions (49% acceptance rate). Every submission was reviewed by at least three program committee members. The committee was a mix of industry practitioners and researchers. Papers submitted by program committee members were refereed separately to ensure objective feedback. Some papers were shepherded by committee members who spent quite a bit of effort to helping the authors improve their submissions. Our special thanks go to these shepherds: Hakan Erdogmus, Tom Kubit and Randy Miller.

The proceedings consist of six sections that reflect the breadth of the submissions.

The section "Becoming Agile" discusses how agile approaches can be introduced into new environments. The papers deal with extending the scope of agile methods towards larger and more distributed teams, teams involving multiple stakeholders, success stories of agile methods, and the boundaries between agile and more traditional, tayloristic approaches.

The next section, "Agile Methods and Processes," includes papers on the rules of and reflections on Extreme Programming, ISO certification while being agile, and indicators, instead of metrics, that can be used to help agile teams.

The section on "Agile Testing" discusses how test-driven approaches can be used in the context of database application development and with JNI, how system testing as well as user interface testing can be integrated into agile methods, and contains the test automation manifesto.

While agile approaches value people over tools, most agile teams use some tools anyway. The section on "Tool Support for Agile Teams" looks into new developments in this area. It discusses tools for scaling agile methods as well as for project coordination support. Another paper empirically analyzes distributed pair programming.

The "Educator Symposium" section includes recent developments on the introduction of agile methods into academic education. Papers in the section where peer reviewed by the Educator Symposium committee.

The "Workshop" section contains very brief overviews on the workshops that will be held at the conference.

No conference can be successful without volunteers who contribute their time to the endeavor. We want to thank all our program committee members who reviewed papers and provided valuable feedback to the authors. Specifically, we would like to thank Brian Button, Grigori Melnik and Don Reifer – all of whom spent a huge effort in helping to set up the conference program.

While the technical contributions included in this book represent an important part of the program, no conference is successful without the effective interaction among its participants, their sharing of knowledge and experience. To enable this, the program contained specialized workshops, a broad variety of tutorials, and the open-space sections. All these provided ample opportunity to interact and bring together experts and beginners in agile methods.

We hope that you enjoyed the conference.

May 2003   Frank Maurer
                                                                                        Don Wells

Conference Committees

Program Committee

Co-chairs: Frank Maurer, Don Wells
Tutorials Chair: Brian Button
Workshops Chair: Grigori Melnik
Panels Chair: Ken Schwaber
Educators Symposium Chair: Don Reifer
Open Space Chair: Ann Anderson
BOF Coordinators: Bill Wake

Program Committee Members:

Scott Ambler	Jim Highsmith	Grandville Miller
Ann Anderson	Chet Hendrickson	Don Reifer
Dave Astels	Scott Henniger	Linda Rising
Ken Auer	Andy Hunt	Ken Schwaber
Mike Beedle	Ron Jeffries	Forest Schull
Barry Boehm	Bil Kleb	Jeff Sutherland
Jim Coplien	Tom Kubit	Dave Thomas
Ward Cunningham	Manfred Lange	(Pragmatic
Aldo Dagnino	Tim Mackinnon	Programmer)
Noopur Davis	Michele Marchesi	Dave Thomas (Bedarra)
Armin Eberlein	Brian Marick	Jim Tomayko
Jutta Eckstein	Robert C. Martin	Arie Van Bennekum
Hakan Erdogmus	Pete McBreen	Chris Wege
Michael Feathers	Todd Medlin	Frank Westphal
Steve Fraser	Steve Mellor	Laurie Williams
John Grundy	Gerard Meszaros	William Wood

Educator Symposium Committee

James Caristi	Ed Gehringer	J. Fernando Naveda
David West	Rick Mercer	Joe Bergin

Organization Committee

Chair: Angelique Martin
Student Volunteers Chair: Rick Mercer
Sponsors/Exhibits Chair: Lance Welter
Marketing, Communications Chair: Stanley Jordan
Website Master: Micah Martin

Conference Sponsors and Partners

XP Agile Universe would like to thank the following:

Galaxy Class Sponsors:
Object Mentor, Inc.
Microsoft
RADSoft

Star Class Sponsors:
RoleModel Software
Agile Logic Nola Computer Services

Satellite Class Sponsors:
Tek Systems

Media Partners:
Agile Alliance
Cutter Consortium
Software Development Magazine
Louisiana Technology Council

Table of Contents

Tool Support for Agile Teams

Educator Symposiums

Workshops

Rebalancing Your Organization's Agility and Discipline

Barry Boehm[1] and Richard Turner[2]

[1] University of Southern California
Los Angeles, CA 90089-0781
boehm@usc.edu
[2] The George Washington University
Washington, DC, 20052
Rich.Turner@osd.mail

Abstract. In these days of rapid change, many organizations find that their current balance between using agile and disciplined methods is not what it should be. (We realize that "disciplined" is not the opposite of "agile," but it is our working label here for methods relying more on explicit documented knowledge than on tacit interpersonal knowledge). In a forthcoming book [1], we have analyzed many organizations' experiences with agile and disciplined methods, and have elaborated our previous characterization [2] of the "home grounds" in which agile and disciplined methods have been most successful. This analysis has enabled us to determine five critical decision factors that organizations and projects can use to determine whether they are in either the agile or disciplined home grounds, or somewhere in between. These five decision factors are size, criticality, personnel, dynamism, and culture. In this paper, we set the context by characterizing the agile and disciplined home grounds. We then define the five decision factors and their rating scales; provide a stepwise approach for assessing your organization's or project's location in the decision space and developing a strategy for rebalancing its agility and discipline; and illustrate its use with a representative organizational example.

1 The Home Grounds for Agile and Disciplined Methods

Table 1 summarizes what we have characterized as the "home grounds" for agile and disciplined methods – the sets of conditions under which they are most likely to succeed. The more a particular project's conditions differ from the home ground conditions, the more risk there is in using one approach in its pure form and the more valuable it is to blend in some of the complementary practices from the opposite method.

Most of the entries in Table 1 are self-explanatory, but the concept of "Cockburn levels" of development personnel deserves further explanation. Alistair Cockburn has addressed levels of skill and understanding required for performing various method-related functions, such as using, tailoring, adapting or revising a method. Drawing on the three levels of understanding in Aikido (Shu-Ha-Ri), he has identified three levels of software method understanding that help sort out what various levels of people can be expected to do within a given method framework [3].

F. Maurer and D. Wells (Eds.): XP/Agile Universe 2003, LNCS 2753, pp. 1–8, 2003.
© Springer-Verlag Berlin Heidelberg 2003

Table 1. Agile and Disciplined Method Home Grounds

Characteristics	Agile	Disciplined
Application		
Primary Goals	Rapid value; responding to change	Predictability, stability, high assurance
Size	Smaller teams and projects	Larger teams and projects
Environment	Turbulent; high change; project-focused	Stable; low-change; project/organization focused
Management		
Customer Relations	Dedicated on-site customers; focused on prioritized increments	As-needed customer interactions; focused on contract provisions
Planning and Control	Internalized plans; qualitative control	Documented plans, quantitative control
Communications	Tacit interpersonal knowledge	Explicit documented knowledge
Technical		
Requirements	Prioritized informal stories and test cases; undergoing unforseeable change	Formalized project, capability, interface, quality, forseeable evolution requirements
Development	Simple design; short increment; refactoring assumed inexpensive	Extensive design; longer increments; refactoring assumed expensive
Test	Executable test cases define requirements, testing	Documented test plans and procedures
Personnel		
Customers	Dedicated, collocated CRACK* performers	CRACK* performers, not always collocated
Developers	At least 30% full-time Cockburn level 2 and 3 experts; no Level 1B or -1 personnel**	50% Cockburn Level 2 and 3s early; 10% throughout; 30% Level 1B's workable; no Level -1s**
Culture	Comfort and empowerment via many degrees of freedom (thriving on chaos)	Comfort and empowerment via framework of policies and procedures (thriving on order)
* Collaborative, Representative, Authorized, Committed, Knowledgable ** These numbers will particularly vary with the complexity of the application		

We have found these levels extremely helpful in creating a rating scale for our Personnel decision factor. We have taken the liberty here to split his Level 1 to address some distinctions between agile and disciplined methods, and to add an additional level to address the problem of method-disrupters. Our version is provided in Table 2.

Level -1 people should be rapidly identified and reassigned to work other than performing on either agile or disciplined teams.

Level 1B people are average, less-experienced, hard-working developers. They can function well in performing straightforward software development in a stable situation. But they are likely to slow down an agile team trying to cope with rapid change, particularly if they form a majority of the team. They can form a well-performing majority of a stable, well-structured disciplined team.

Table 2. Levels of Software Method Understanding and Use (After Cockburn)

Level	Characteristics
3	Able to revise a method (break its rules) to fit an unprecedented new situation
2	Able to tailor a method to fit a precedented new situation
1A	With training, able to perform discretionary method steps (e.g., sizing stories to fit increments, composing patterns, compound refactoring, complex COTS integration). With experience can become Level 2.
1B	With training, able to perform procedural method steps (e.g. coding a simple method, simple refactoring, following coding standards and CM procedures, running tests). With experience can master some Level 1A skills.
-1	May have technical skills, but unable or unwilling to collaborate or follow shared methods.

Level 1A people can function well on agile or disciplined teams if there are enough Level 2 people to guide them. When agilists refer to being able to succeed on agile teams with ratios of 5 Level 1 people per Level 2 person, they are generally referring to Level 1A people.

Level 2 people can function well in managing a small, precedented agile or disciplined project but need the guidance of Level 3 people on a large or unprecedented project. Some Level 2s have the capability to become Level 3s with experience. Some do not.

2 The Five Critical Decision Factors

Now that we have a common understanding of home grounds and personnel capability, we can develop our balancing criteria. Table 3 describes five major decision factors involved in determining the relative suitability of agile or disciplined methods in a particular project situation. These factors are the project's size, criticality, dynamism, personnel, and culture factors. A project which is a good fit to agile or disciplined for four of the factors, but not the fifth, is a project in need of risk assessment and likely some mix of agile and disciplined methods.

The five factors are summarized graphically in Figure 1. Of the five axes in the polar graph, *Size* and *Criticality* are similar to the factors used in Cockburn to distinguish between the lighter-weight Crystal methods (toward the center of the graph) and heavier-weight Crystal methods (toward the periphery). The *Culture* axis reflects the reality that agile methods will succeed better in a culture that "thrives on chaos" than one that "thrives on order," and vice versa.

The other two axes are asymmetrical in that both agile and disciplined methods are likely to succeed at one end, and only one of them is likely to succeed at the other. For *Dynamism*, agile methods are at home with both high and low rates of change, but disciplined methods prefer low rates of change.

The *Personnel* scale refers to the extended Cockburn method skill rating scale discussed earlier, and places it in a framework relative to the complexity of the application. This captures the situation where one might be Level 2 in an organization developing simple application but Level 1A in an organization developing highly-complex applications. Here the asymmetry is that while disciplined methods can work well with both high and low skill levels, agile methods require a richer mix of higher-level skills [4].

Table 3. The Five Critical Agility/Discipline Decision Factors

Factor	Agility Considerations	Discipline Considerations
Size	Well-matched to small products and teams. Reliance on tacit knowledge limits scalability.	Methods evolved to handle large products and teams. Hard to tailor down to small projects.
Criticality	Untested on safety-critical products. Potential difficultiies with simple design and lack of documentation.	Methods evolved to handle highly critical products. Hard to tailor down to low-criticality products.
Dynamism	Simple design and continuous refactoring are excellent for highly dynamic environments, but a source of potentially expensive rework for highly stable environments.	Detailed plans and Big Design Up Front excellent for highly stable environment, but a source of expensive rework for highly dynamic environments.
Personnel	Requires continuous presence of a critical mass of scarce Cockburn Level 2 or 3 experts. Risky to use non-agile Level 1B people.	Needs a critical mass of scarce Cockburn Level 2 and 3 experts during project definition, but can work with fewer later in the project—unless the environment is highly dynamic. Can usually accommodate some Level 1B people.
Culture	Thrives in a culture where people feel comfortable and empowered by having many degrees of freedom.	Thrives in a culture where people feel comfortable and empowered by having their roles defined by clear policies and procedures.

For example, a disciplined project with 15% Level 2 and 3 people and 40% Level 1B people would initially use more than 15% Level 2 and 3 people to plan the project, but reduce the number thereafter. An agile project would have everybody working full-time, and the 15% Level 2 and 3s would be swamped trying to mentor the 40% Level 1Bs and the remaining Level 1As while trying to get their own work done as well.

By rating a project along each of the five axes, you can visibly evaluate its home-ground relationships. If all the ratings are near the center, you are in agile method territory. If they are at the periphery, you will best succeed with a disciplined approach. If you are mostly in one or the other, you need to treat the exceptions as sources of risk and devise risk management approaches to address them.

3   A Stepwise Approach for Balancing Agility and Discipline

The steps below provide a simple recipe for balancing agility and discipline. Be sure, however, that you perform them in consultation with your key stakeholders.

1. Use Figure 1 to assess where your projects currently are with respect to the 5 key axes. If you have different organizations with different profiles, make separate assessments. Also, assess the likely changes in your organization's profile over

the next 5 years. Key stakeholders to consult include your users, customers, developers, suppliers, and strategic partners. Key future trends to consider include:

- the increased pace of change and need for agility;
- the increased concern with software dependability and need for discipline;
- your ability to satisfy your stakeholders' evolving value propositions, and to keep up with your toughest competitors;
- the increasing gap between supply and demand for Cockburn Level 2 and 3 people;
- your ability to cope with existing and emerging technical challenges such as COTS integration, evolving Internet and Web capabilities, distributed and mobile operations, agent coordination, and multi-mode virtual collaboration.

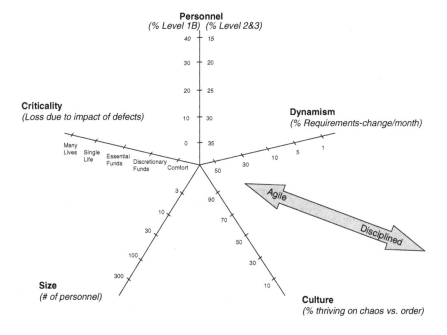

Fig. 1. Dimensions Affecting Method Selection

2. If your assessments show you comfortably in the agile or disciplined home ground now and in the future, your best strategy is to embark on a continuous improvement effort to become the best you can at agility or discipline. To start such an effort, the best next steps are:

   a. Convene a representative working group of key stakeholders to assess alternative agile or disciplined improvement approaches and recommend an approach that best fits your situation.

     b.   Identify a reasonably tractable project, staffed with capable and enthusiastic people, to be trained in using the approach, to apply it, and to develop a plan for both dealing with problems encountered and for extending the approach across the organization.

     c.   Execute the plan for extending the approach, always including evaluation and feedback into continuous improvement during and after each project.

3.   If your Figure 1 assessments leave you mostly in the agile or disciplined home grounds, but with some anomalies, treat the anomalies as risk factors to be added to the charters of the groups performing steps 2a-c. Examples of potential anomalies are:

     a.   Operating mostly in a disciplined home ground, but in an increasingly dynamic marketplace.

     b.   Operating with agile fix-it-later developers with a growing, increasingly enterprise-integrated and dependability-oriented user base.

     c.   Finding that your technical people are successfully adapting to dynamism, but that your contract management people are not.

The first two anomalies can be addressed via risk assessment and managerial techniques. The third would involve a more specialized approach to change management in the contracting organization, but done with their collaboration and the support of upper management.

If you have several organizations and several profiles, it is best to prioritize your approach to work on those you believe are most important and likely to achieve early successes. An exception is if there are projects in crisis that need, and are receptive to, significant help and redirection.

4.   If your Figure 1 assessments leave you with a highly mixed agility-discipline profile, you need to develop an incremental mixed strategy to take you from your current situation to the one you have chosen as a goal. For example, suppose that your organization primarily does 50-person, essential-funds critical projects with a mix of 20% Level 2 and 3 and 30% Level 1B personnel, with dynamism rapidly increasing from 5%/month to 10%/month, a culture only 30% oriented toward thriving on chaos, and a corporate steady-state goal to do all software internally. This profile is shown in Figure 2.

In this case, you would like to function internally like the successful ThoughtWorks discipline-extended XP lease management application team described in [5, 6, 7]. If your staffing profile had 30% Level 2 and 3 and 10% Level 1B people and your culture was 70% toward thriving on chaos, then you could apply their recommended processes and succeed internally. Unfortunately, your current staffing profile and culture make this infeasible.

One option for you would be to start on a long-term internal effort to upgrade your staff and change your culture. But a quicker and less risky approach to rebalance your agility and discipline would be to enter a strategic partnership with an agile methods company to serve as near-term trainers, co-developers, and mentors for your staff. This would expedite an initiative to bring as many of your Level 1A people up to Level 2 as possible, and to bring as many of your Level 1B people up to Level 1A, at least in some niche area. The agile methods company people could also serve as change agents in making your organizational culture more thrive-on-chaos oriented.

In other cases, you might be a growing pure-agile company with a need to add more discipline to accommodate larger and more critical products. You could employ a similar strategy with a disciplined services company to rapidly rebalance your operations, staff profile, and culture.

5. Your organization should complement whatever agile/disciplined balancing options it pursues with sustained effort to improve your staff capabilities, value-oriented capabilities, and communication capabilities. It is also important to track your progress with respect to your plans and apply corrective action whenever new opportunities come up. A good checklist for staff capabilities is the People CMM [8]. A good starting point for value-oriented capabilities is *Value-Based Software Engineering* [9, 10]. A good mechanism for tracking multi-criteria, multi-initiative programs is the Balanced Scorecard technique [11].

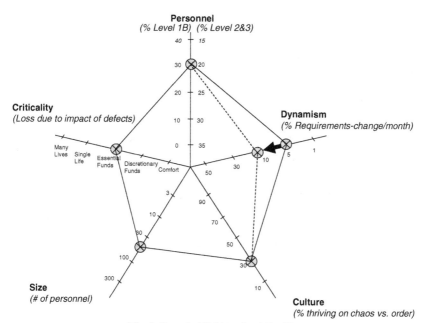

Fig. 2. Sample Highly-mixed Profile

4 Summary

We have defined a set of criteria and a process for using them to help organizations plan how to balance their agility and discipline. By looking at the current profile and comparing it with the desired profile, a gap analysis can show the critical areas where the organization needs to change. An illustrative example provides some specific guidance on how to apply the process.

Biographies

Barry Boehm is the TRW Professor of Software Engineering at USC, and Director of its Center for Software Engineering. He is a Fellow of the ACM, AIAA, IEEE, and INCOSE, and a member of the National Academy of Engineering.

Richard Turner is an Adjunct Professor of Engineering Management at The George Washington University, and Deputy Director for Science and Technology of the Department of Defense Software Intensive Systems Office.

References

1.   B. Boehm and R. Turner, Balancing Agility and Discipline: A Guide for the Perplexed, Addison Wesley, 2003 (to appear).
2.   B. Boehm, "Get Ready for Agile Methods, With Care," IEEE Computer, January 2002, pp. 64–69.
3.   A. Cockburn, Agile Software Development, Addison Wesley, 2002.
4.   J. Highsmith, Agile Software Development Ecosystems, Addison Wesley, 2002.
5.   A. Elssamadisy and G. Schalliol, "Recognizing and Responding to 'Bad Smells' in Extreme Programming," Proceedings, ICSE 2002, pp. 617–622.
6.   A. Elssamadisy, "XP on a large Project: A Developer's View," in Extreme Programming Perspectives (Marchesi et al. ed.), Addison Wesley, 2003, pp. 387–397.
7.   G. Schalliol, "Challenges for Analysts on a Large XP Project," in Extreme Programming Perspectives (Marchesi et al. ed.), Addison Wesley, 2003, pp. 375–385
8.   B. Curtis, W. Hefley, and S. Miller, The People Capability Maturity Model, Addison Wesley, 2002.
9.   B. Boehm, "Value-Based Software Engineering," ACM Software Engineering Notes, March, 2003.
10. B. Boehm and L. Huang, "Value-Based Software Engineering: A Case Study," IEEE Computer, March 2003, pp. 21–29.
11. R. Kaplan and D. Norton, The Balanced Scorecard: Translating Strategy into Action, Harvard Business School Press, 1996.

Extreme Programming: Growing a Team Horizontally

Carla Fredrick

Retek Inc.
950 Nicollet Mall
Minneapolis, MN 55403
612-587-2278
Carla.Fredrick@retek.com

Abstract. There is a great deal of skepticism surrounding whether or not the Extreme Programming (XP) methodology has the potential to work for large-scale projects. This paper highlights two software development projects that used XP. The projects were similar but the implementation, decision-making and functional requirements varied considerably. This paper documents the advantages and disadvantages of XP experienced in these projects, highlights how the process regarding team growth evolved and matured, and discusses the lessons learned.

Keywords: extreme programming, XP, developers, hard fast rules, requirements, horizontal, vertical, Junit tests, stories, shunted tests, lurk, velocity, refactoring, persistence requirements, customer team

1 The First Project

The project team had two main objectives: 1) to make the client happy with a quality product that fulfilled their requirements and 2) to pilot XP as a methodology that can be implemented company-wide. To satisfy these objectives, developers were dedicated to learning, analyzing, and changing the way we did things. We began with strict procedural rules and stuck with them long enough determine whether or not they were effective. When the team had questions, we consulted XP books and websites to find potential solutions.

The first project had two clients with similar functionality in mind, but with different requirements and business needs. We were given the challenge of building a base product that would work for both of these clients. A couple of the main differences between the two sets of requirements were: one had a custom database, the other did not; one required minimal hits to the database, the other wanted real-time accuracy. These are significant differences, but there were enough functional similarities that some basic foundation code could be written first and used for both.

Some initial decisions were made regarding how to approach the different databases and how to structure the code. One decision was to use Jakarta Struts and JavaServer Pages™ for the user interface and to use a serialized database and mock data to simulate a database until further persistence requirements were gathered from both clients. These decisions allowed the team to be oriented horizontally along the J2EE tiers of the application. Instead of coding a functional area vertically – from user interface to database – we looked at the code of a specific tier, or layer. The J2EE 3-

F. Maurer and D. Wells (Eds.): XP/Agile Universe 2003, LNCS 2753, pp. 9–17, 2003.

tier architecture includes the user interface tier, the business logic or service tier, and the database tier) [4][5]. Looking at the code this way allowed us to be able to focus efforts on making similar code reusable and to implement patterns, or reusable solutions to recurring problems [7].

1.1   Growing the Team

We needed to add developers to the team to handle the number of stories, or scenario-based requirements, that were being introduced to the labs. There is a natural slowdown in a project when new people are added. New developers are not familiar with how things work and as prescribed by XP, they are required to pair with another team member. With pairing, not only does the new team member have a learning curve, but also someone else is slowed down in the process. However, there are benefits to this training. With hands-on learning and one-on-one coaching, most new people learn more quickly and accurately. Additionally, a new team member will ask basic questions that may constructively challenge the way things are currently being done.

We alleviated some of the time that a new developer might take from the lab by first having them "lurk" for an iteration. While lurking, they could ask questions, watch pairs work, and poke around in the code, but not do any actual work. This way, when they started pairing with developers, they have some familiarity with the code. This proved to be an effective way to get people started in the lab with less impact on the current velocity, or how fast the team can program. [3]

How efficiently a lab writes code is directly related to the number of developers in the lab. Velocity for a lab tends to top out at ten developers. It is thereby suggested that a way to scale a team past ten is to break a team into two labs (five developers each) and grow each lab up to ten developers [1]. We decided to create a new lab that would be in charge of just database work. There were many reasons for this. One was because of the already explicit and consistent interface that evolved from the serialized database. Another reason was that we had two clients and needed twice as many specific database accessors. Thirdly, the data access layer could take on the performance requirements.

1.2   Integrating the Development

Our first attempt was to have a separate group that was closed off from development in the lab. The initial lab was a good size and had good chemistry so nobody was taken from this lab to staff the new lab. This approach did not alleviate any work from the development team. Though, the Java developers were not required to write SQL, they now had to communicate every requirement change to the new team. There was too much room for error, so some adjustments were made. Developers from the initial lab were moved into the new database lab. So the new lab had both SQL-fluent people and Java-fluent people where neither was fluent in the other's skill set. By pairing, we hoped that each other's strengths would pull the code in a positive direction. In theory, this is a great idea because as time went on, the SQL people would learn Java and the Java people would learn more SQL. In the reality of our project, the two groups did not mesh well. Because of this, and a need for additional help on gathering requirements, people were shuffled once more. The database lab then consisted of all Java developers from the original lab. The SQL people would help when needed to writing SQL but would work more on gathering requirements. They also worked on testing the application. Because they had knowledge of how the database worked, they were the right people to look at the application to make sure it was selecting and updating data correctly.

The interface between the service layer and the database layer became a contract that was crucial to maintaining good, reusable code. The interface forced all of the business requirements to be housed within the service layer, so both clients could use the service code and plug into different data access layers. If any logic were allowed into the database layer, it would have to be implemented twice, once for each client.

Separating the code also meant separating the tests. Tests that go against the database take longer than tests that use serialized data. So, by separating the labs, the service lab benefited by saving a few minutes every time the tests were run. Similarly, the service lab would not be affected when the database was down for maintenance, updates or table changes. The separation also gave all developers more physical space in the lab and more importantly, it relieved some of the responsibilities from each lab. Nobody in the service lab would have to worry about which tables to call, where performance would be a problem, or which Java patterns to follow for the database layer any more. Likewise, those tasks became the sole responsibility of the database lab. This also means there is less to teach a new developer coming into the lab, so they will become acclimated sooner.

It was a hard and fast physical and procedural separation between the labs and the code. At the end of each business day, the service layer would package their code and pass it to the database lab. The database team would not have access to modify the packaged code at all. The following morning, the first task of the day for the database lab was to resolve all of the conflicts the new code brought to the database code. These conflicts were typically brought on by a change in the interface between the tiers or layers. The service layer made the change and now the database code would have to support it. The stories introduced by the client were complete once the database layer finished implementing the code to support this interface. Upon a story's completion, the service code and database code were deployed to a testing environment. The testers would test the application from front to back and report any bugs in the system. The bug would be tracked down and resolved in the appropriate lab.

Once this process was in place, things worked quite efficiently. Getting to that point, however, was not a simple task. Each day the labs would write code that would need to be synched up with the other lab the next day. To accomplish this, we wrote scripts that would help integrate the two repositories of code.

1.3   Managing Client Needs

As development continued the two clients' needs were drifting farther and farther apart. With two clients, two sets of business requirements, two schedules, and additional resources needed to fulfill demand from two clients, another new lab was needed. This new lab was considered custom to a single client and worked on an additional functional area that was not required by the other client. The new lab however, still needed the changes that the initial lab was doing. To accommodate this, the service lab continued to package code for the database team, the database team would continue to package code for the testing team, but in addition they would deploy the code to the custom team who would add functionality to the "base" code.

The process was both good and bad. Because the base service lab was the driving force, they controlled everything and the other, more subsequent labs, could not change the object modeling that the base lab was creating. The service lab benefited because they did not care what the other labs were doing. The database lab and custom lab, however, sometimes needed a change to happen in the service layer but they didn't have access. They would have to request it of the service lab. For people that were used to being able to go in and make the changes they needed, this took some getting used to. But, it was clear that the only way to make the code service three different labs' objectives was to have one lab responsible. The custom lab was invisible to the base lab. This allowed the vertical separation to occur. In this case, where the new functional area needed to remain completely separate from the rest of the code, vertical separation makes sense. The custom lab was able to release the product to the client without impacting the base lab. When the base lab's work started winding down, it made sense to combine the database and service/UI labs back into one lab. The support people joined the single lab, to get a feel for how things are done, help with the last iterations of work and to be comfortable taking over.

At our largest, we were 36 developers strong (6 of which were dedicated performance people), with a customer and testing team of 15 members. Looking back, the project was a success. There were a lot of growing pains, but overall we made good decisions and at the end of the project, we had the process down and surprised ourselves at the velocity we were able to achieve. But most importantly, the clients were happy.

2   The Second Project

A new and bigger XP project had been underway for many months when our first project came to an end. Their approach was different than ours because they had different base requirements and a staff of 65. Only a handful of team members were experienced Java developers and even fewer had XP experience. Their initial approach started with four full labs that shared a common code repository. "Coaches" would float between labs in an attempt to spread knowledge and to keep things uniform. The practices of XP were heavily customized to resemble more traditional methodologies; for example, pairing was optional, code was owned, and testing was minimal.

The four labs were divided by functional area and each lab worked vertically. The lab environment allowed for good communication for functional requirements but little was discussed from a technical perspective. The requirements were maintained within the lab but were not documented. Since everyone was in one room, the communication could flow freely; however, with requirements traveling by word-of-mouth, there was more room for error and inconsistency between technical implementation and requirements among labs. Additionally, since requirements were not documented, they started changing.

When five of us from the first project joined this project, it had been significantly reduced in size (down to one lab of about 12). Things were not going well and the client was not happy. The development team was using a variation of XP and all communication had broken down. Because each team member was working vertically, there was little communication between team members. New development had completely stopped, and the team was focused on fixing bugs. The code was difficult to read because it was a conglomeration of many different coding styles. No rules had been enforced, so people had their user interface call the database, others coded everything in a service class, and yet another wrote numerous classes that were all identical with the exception of the title. Nobody seemed to talk to anybody else to see if they could share code. If an existing object didn't quite fit their needs, they created a new one, or at times, changed the one that already existed, not bothering to see if the change broke any body else's code.

2.1 A New Lab

We joined the team by pairing with people, trying to get them to follow some of the practices we found worthwhile from the previous project. It took us some time to get our bearings and start making actual changes to the methodology, though. The first step was to understand how willing the team was to change what they had been doing for almost a year. There was definite support for change, but there was fear too. People had grown comfortable in their silos of knowledge and were not necessarily willing to let someone else touch what they had worked so hard on. In some circumstances, people felt threatened when their decisions were questioned and alternative approaches were suggested. However, the desire for change eventually outweighed the fears and frustrations. With the push from management, we broke the team into two labs, a database lab and a service/UI lab. We made pairing and test first programming mandatory practices, and we tried to implement patterns within layers.

The biggest challenge was that the team did not have a hard separation between the three layers of architecture. On the first project, the serialized database that made a lab separation relatively easy to make. Building a serialized database is easy when you start that way. However, when a year of development has not been serialized, it is not feasible to retrofit this approach. The decision was made to use the FIAT (Factory Interface Adaptor Test) Pattern. A pattern internally developed to "test in isolation" (based of ObjectMentor's Shunting pattern [8]). This refactoring was one that could be done incrementally. Refactoring is a process of changing a software system in such a way that it does not alter the external behavior of the code, yet improves its internal structure [2]. When a functional area was being worked on, it would be refactored to use the new test pattern instead of calling the database. If any old tests existed in the area, they were recycled so that business requirements would not be lost.

The first project made a decisive separation in the code from the beginning. The process of creating a packaged bundle of code from the service lab to the database lab required a significant deal of overhead and maintaining completely separate code repositories was deemed unnecessarily strict. So instead, the labs separated into different rooms and the team reached an understanding that database people could modify only database classes and nobody from the service/UI layer is allowed to touch those classes. Within a couple of months, the database lab had refactored and reworked the code to a state where additional work could be tasked out and completed very efficiently. In fact, they were so efficient that they kept running out of work.

2.2   Additional Changes

The bulk of the work that needed to be completed was split between the UI and the service areas. Since management continued to push more and more developers onto the team, it made sense to split the service and UI into separate labs. The labs could be broken up even further because there were two separate user interfaces being developed. Because the database lab continued to be ahead of the game and sitting idle from time to time, we decided to combine the service and database labs.

All of the change created additional problems. With many new faces and work being cranked out at a pace faster than people were used to, stories were being completed with missing requirements. Tasks were divvied out and people completed them, but pieces were missing and not realized until the front end was in place and the application could be tested from front to back. The story would then look complete with lots of bugs when actually there were entire pieces of functionality missing.

Two processes were introduced to correct this. First a "design team" was defined. This team consisted of the coaches from each lab. The design team is in charge of tasking out the stories before they came into the lab and they would help track them throughout development, similar to the "Team Coordination Layer" described by Ron Crocker [6]. Any problems implementing the design would have to go through the design team so that appropriate changes could be cascaded throughout the related tasks and repercussions could be caught upfront and not as bugs later. Secondly, cached data was introduced as a way to mock out the database side and test things out fully through the service layer. This more front to back testing would assure that significant things were not left out.

The process changes that have been implemented have helped grow the team to 40 developers and has enabled the team to post increasingly higher and higher velocity each iteration. Changes are continually being made to try to produce the correct mix to assure fast, quality production of code. A lot of process changes have enabled this project to turn itself around. There are sure to be even more changes.

3   Lessons Learned

Between the two projects, we can see what worked well and what did not. It is our goal to minimize mistakes in the future and use our experience to create a model of XP that can scale and be successfully applied to many more projects. Most of the people that were involved in both projects believe that XP is a good approach to software development and hope to continue on projects that work in this fashion. To do so we need to improve the process with the lessons we have learned.

3.1   Lesson 1: Horizontal Separation Is Faster

Separating labs horizontally creates better code and faster development than separating the labs vertically. When developers code vertically, the team is weaker. They become functional exerts. They are the only people who know that area and they feel a strong connection to the code. The XP principle of "collective code ownership" tends to be violated.

Additionally, if one group works solely on a functional area, good architecture and code re-use are sacrificed. Working on a single functional area encourages greater code complexity. If instead, the group works across all functional areas but focuses on the user interface layer, all developers in that group will have exposure to each functional area. Additionally all functional areas will look alike. It will be easier for developers to come up to speed on a new area, because that area will feel just like everything else. For example, all of the data access classes are written by one group of people. Therefore, database specific utilities and patterns are created and used throughout the code. This creates great uniformity in each layer, which make it easier to read and implement new functionality.

Another plus when separating by architectural layers is that the scope is smaller per layer and there are fewer patterns to understand. New developers can be productive sooner. There is also an inherent division of skills between layers. Some developers' strengths lie in object modeling, others in database and others in the user interface. These skills can be harnessed and utilized when the project is separated this way.

Creating strict layers also gives the benefit of code reuse and flexibility. If we have a requirement to have the application run against a different database, we can rewrite the database layer with minimal effect on the rest of the application. Similarly, if a more lightweight user interface is desired, we have the flexibility to change the UI with little impact to the rest of the application.

3.2   Lesson 2: Pairing Works

When the team is not dedicated to pairing, the benefit of reuse, clean code, self-documented code, and thorough Junit tests is lost. It is important to remember that the principle of pairing came about because XP takes good software development practices to the extreme. Code review creates good code therefore constant reviewing (pairing) will create better code [3]. If this practice is dropped, even partially, the old methodology of formal code reviews does not take its place. So no code review is done and bad code more easily slips through the cracks.

Pairing enables a natural knowledge transfer. It is rewarding when someone comes into our lab and asks who can answer a question about a certain functional area. We all can. When code is written this way, even the most complex business problems can be easily figured out. Additionally, pairing leads to less code ownership. Code ownership makes people defensive – people take it personally when someone suggests their code does not work. When developers are less connected to the code, they are willing to admit when something could be improved. When code is written well, the entire lab can take pride in knowing they've created something that is easy to use and works well.

3.3   Lesson 3: Hard and Fast Rules Are Good

On the first project we implemented a practice that we called the "3 times" rule [2]. If a change did not fit into a pattern quite right, we noted it as an exceptional case, talked about it, and worked it into the pattern. The second time we came across something that did not fit, we again, continued using the pattern. The third time however, is reason to refactor. By this time it was clear what the exceptional cases were and we had three examples to use as we worked on the change in the pattern. The "3 times" rule gave our patterns and decisions a chance, while not ruling out the possibility of change. Additionally, after having used the patterns, the team has a clearer picture of the benefits and shortfalls of the pattern.

Strict rules prevent teams from letting their code fall down a "slippery slope". The second project experienced this by not enforcing pairing. There were many rules outlined for the team, but because pairing was optional, developers became functional experts with a high level of code ownership. Moreover, since many of the developers were not experienced Java or XP developers, they were unable to follow the rest of the rules outlined for the project without a pair.

3.4   Lesson 4: Design Team Promotes Connectivity within between Labs

XP labs have shown best the productivity in labs that have no more than 12-15 developers. A lab works as a single unit and communication between the team members needs to be complete and thorough. When a group gets too large, communication falls apart. Having a team of people that help organize the design and the tasks helps regulate the work getting done and creates a point person to which concerns and problems can be raised. This point person works within the design team to make forward moving decisions. Since all of the design decisions are made by a small group of people, they are made uniformly and with every layer in mind.

4   Conclusion

Our first project grew organically with XP in mind. It separated labs horizontally when they got too big. The developers were dedicated to pairing and following all of the rules of XP. The first project was successful. The second project, started with a larger team that was separated into labs by vertical slices. Pairing was optional and the other rules were not enforced. The second project is currently implementing a more true XP methodology into the project and shifting the vertical focus to a horizontal one. The project is trying to get on the XP course but it is still suffering from the mistakes made by going too fast without solid rules or utilizing downtime to make the process more efficient.

XP is an evolving methodology. It has the potential to become the methodology of the software industry. One of the only things holding it back is the question of whether or not it can scale. We are currently gathering data with regards to if and how it can scale to a sizable project. Hopefully this paper will serve as a tool that others can use to prove its ability to do so.

5   Information and Questions

For more information or comments about the paper or the FIAT pattern, contact Carla.Fredrick@retek.com.

Acknowledgements. This paper reflects the work and efforts of everyone involved on the projects. Additional contributions by Tani Kalweit, Tom Cox, Marc Carlson, and Chris Fredrick.

References

1. Beck, K., Fowler, M. *Planning Extreme Programming* (2000), 118.
2. Beck, K. *Extreme Programming Explained:Embrace Change* (2000), 21. 90
3. Bond, M. *SamsTeach Yourself J2EE in 21 Days.* (2002), 16.
4. Broemmer, D., *J2EE Best Practices* (2003), 11.
5. Crocker, Ron. "The 5 Reasons XP Can't Scale and What to do About Them." XP Conference May 20–23, 2001 Villasimius, Italy.
6. Fowler, M., et al. *Refactoring Improving the Design of Existing Code* (xvi, 58).
7. Grand, M. *Patterns in Java: Volume 2* (1999), 1.
8. Meade, E., Website: http://www.objectmentor.com

Agile Planning with a Multi-customer, Multi-project, Multi-discipline Team

Karl Scotland

Development Team Leader, BBC Interactive
karl.scotland@bbc.co.uk

Abstract. Most XP literature refers to teams that work on a single project, over a number of months, for a single customer using a narrow range of technical disciplines. This paper describes the agile planning techniques used by a team that works on multiple projects, for multiple customers, using a wide range of multiple disciplines. The techniques described were inspired by the agile practices of XP and Scrum. A small case study of a project shows how the team is able to collaborate with their customers to deliver maximum value under tight conditions.

Keywords: Agile, XP, Scrum, Planning, Releases, Iterations, Stories, Wiki, Interactive TV.

1 Introduction

The development team is a small group, currently seven strong, developing enhanced TV (eTV) services for the BBC. The range of deliverables includes content entry tools, content transformation processes, and Set Top Box (STB) applications. Services are required to be compatible for broadcast in the UK on the digital satellite (DSat) platform, and the digital terrestrial (DTT) platform.

1.1 Projects

The team works on a large number of very short projects, typically of a couple of weeks in length. This means that the workload is unavoidably chaotic. The short time-frame of each project means priorities must be robustly managed both within projects and across them. In addition, there is little opportunity to get into a rhythm during a project. The solution is to treat all projects as a single ongoing project.

A further complication is that the team works in a domain in which they have little control over milestone dates. Some projects have absolutely immovable delivery dates, such as a major sporting event like Wimbledon, while other projects have unknown delivery dates, due to the nature of channel scheduling. In either case, they must always be in a position to deliver something that is acceptable to broadcast. On the DSat platform, services are also required to be tested by the platform operator. Testing slots are limited, and must be booked eight weeks in advance, adding a further constraint to planning.

F. Maurer and D. Wells (Eds.): XP/Agile Universe 2003, LNCS 2753, pp. 18–24, 2003.

1.2 Customers

The large number of projects worked on naturally means that the team deals with a variety of different customers. The majority of these customers are internal producers - the people with editorial responsibility for creating the services. They are currently located on the same floor as the technical team, and are hence always easily accessible.

Graphics designers and operational support engineers, and the technical team itself are also considered to be customers on occasions, with requests for particular design and navigation, deployment or strategic implementations. To manage the numerous producers all vying for technical resource, a creative director is responsible for prioritizing work, and ensuring that the producers speak with one voice. This is a role comparable to the King in Ron Jeffries' Petition the King metaphor [1].

Increasingly, the team is working with producers from other divisions within the BBC, located at other sites. On order to manage the decrease in accessibility, an internal producer is usually appointed to be a 'proxy', representing the main producer, and to provide a local point of contact. The main producer is also encouraged to be on-site as often as is necessary to keep the communications and feedback as high as possible, and to enable them to learn the complexities of the domain where appropriate.

1.3 Disciplines

The interactive TV domain requires the team to use a wide range of skills. These are predominantly:
- OpenTV – an object oriented C based API used for DSat
- MHEG5 – best described as a cross between a markup language and assembly language used for DTT
- Perl – used for content processing and transformation.
- HTML and related web languages – used for simple content entry and publishing tools.
- C++ - used for more complex content entry and publishing tools.

This diverse range of skills, some of which are very specialized, means that maximizing the teams productivity can be challenging. There is a danger of being too dependant on gurus, causing a bottleneck in development and a truck-factor[1] of one. As well as using agile planning techniques to manage this, other XP [2] practices such as pair programming and open workspace are used in order to be able to deliver flexible amounts of software across the different disciplines.

2 Release Planning

Release planning takes place three or four times a year as the culmination of commissioning rounds. This is a process through which the various divisions of the BBC can submit proposals for services that they would like the team to build. Over the course

---

[1] The number of team members who have to be hit by a truck before the project is in crisis.

of a day at most, these proposals are whittled down into a simple, high level, long term plan, which is put together in Excel. This plan allows the blocking out of weeks of work to different projects based on the project proposal, without worrying too much about the fine details of the projects.

In order to help make the high level plan as accurate as possible, without any detailed information, the work is split into three streams, based on a stream for each pair of developers, and projects are split into the three primary disciplines; DTT, DSat and Content. So a project which requires work across all three disciplines will use all three streams, and hence the whole team, whereas a project which only requires work in one discipline will only use one stream, and can be planned concurrently with another project.

The high level plan is also a useful place to make a note of any key dates, such a transmission, or test, along with other small pieces of work.

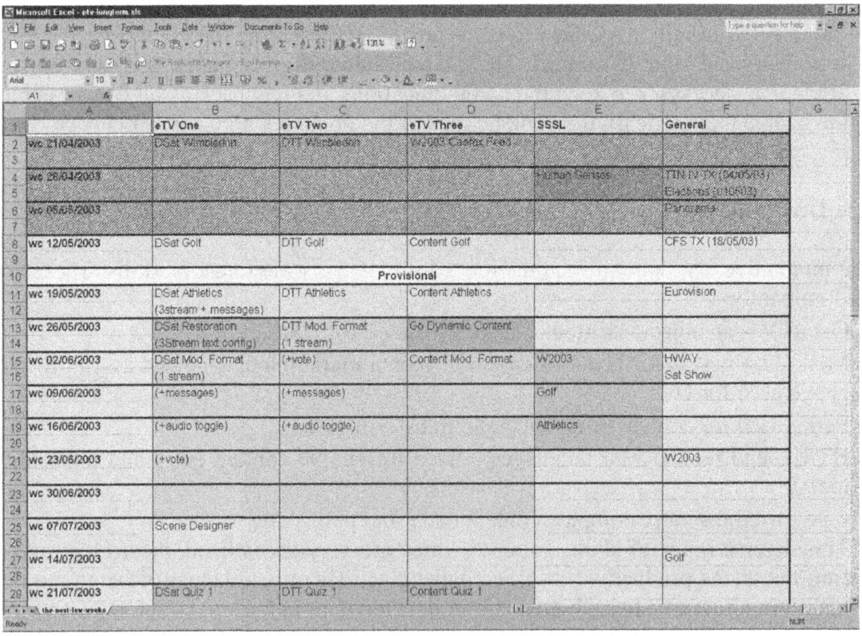

Fig. 1. Example Long Term (Release) Plan

The long term plan is reviewed against the actual progress at the start of weekly iterations, and a project's scope may be adjusted in order to keep it on track, or the time allocated to a project may be adjusted in order to allow the necessary functionality to be completed. In the latter case, it is very easy to see the impact of a project slipping, because subsequent projects must also moved and adjusted in order to ensure all the work still fits in.

3 Iteration Planning

A 'provisional' line on the long term plan marks the point up until which the team has planned projects in more detail. As each project approaches its planned build time, it is broken down into stories, and each story is estimated using a simple scale of 1 to 5, representing its relative size. A 1 point story would be something small, simple and low risk, such as configuration work, and a 5 point story would be something large, difficult and high risk such as a use of complex new technology.

The team has tracked its velocity by recording the total number of points for stories completed during the weekly iterations, and charting in Excel the moving average trend of the average points completed over the last 4 weeks. The velocity trend is used as a guide to how many stories can be planned into the available time.

While some on the XP mailing list [3] have recommended against charting a velocity average, as opposed to a strict use of Yesterday's Weather, the team's experience is that such short iterations lead to an unstable velocity, as shown in Fig. 2. While a review of stories and estimates should lead to an improvement in estimation and minimize this effect, the use of a trend provides the more stable indication of velocity which is essential for accurate future iteration planning, while still allowing the rapid feedback of one week iterations. It can also be seen that the trend line in Fig. 2 still shows a decrease in velocity, highlighting a possible problem with the process somewhere.

4 Tracking

Once projects have been broken down into user stories, estimated by the technical team, and prioritized into iterations with the producers, their progress is tracked using a wiki [4]. A simple hierarchical structure is used, with an overall projects page, which links to page for each project, each of which links to a page for each discipline (DSat, DTT or Content), which finally link to a page for each story. Where stories are duplicated across the different disciplines, a common page is shared.

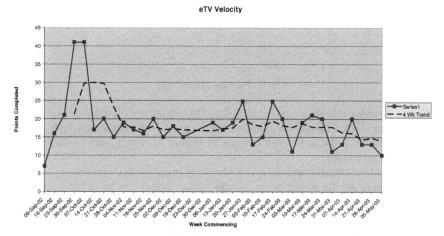

Fig. 2. Velocity Chart

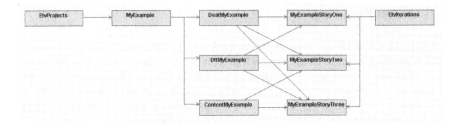

Fig. 3. Wiki structure

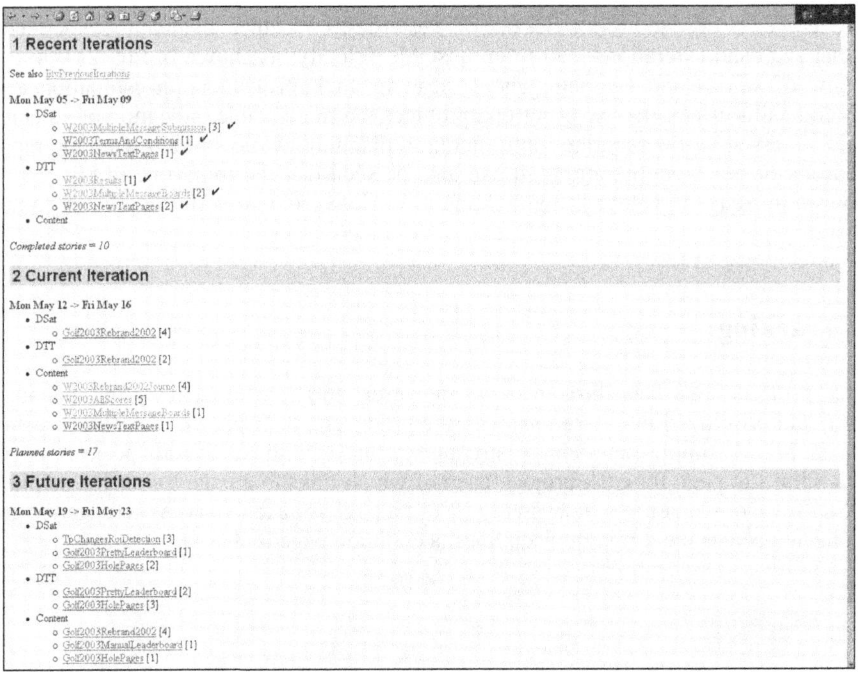

Fig. 4. Wiki Iterations Page

Figure 3 shows this structure for a project "My Example". It also includes a separate page that is used for the iteration plan. This page, an example of which is in figure 4, groups the links to the story pages according to which weekly iteration they have been planned into.

The wiki allows details and decisions about the projects and their stories to be easily documented. As the weeks progress, the various pages can be quickly updated to reflect current status, and they are easily available for viewing by the whole team.

Each week, that iteration's story cards are also put up on the wall to highlight the current work, and to provide a focus for regular stand-up meetings. These are not always every day, in the same location, (and chairs are allowed), and are therefore not as strict as Scrum [5] advocates. However, they facilitate the necessary level of communication to track progress on a daily basis.

5 Example

A recent project had been allocated two of the three streams for five weeks in the long term plan. The team's velocity at the time was 17.5, so to simplify the numbers it was rounded up to 18. This meant that within a weekly iteration, each of the three streams could represent six points of work. Therefore, two streams over five weeks represented 60 (2 x 5 x 6) points. Over the course of a few days the editorial proposition was discussed with the producer, and stories were written and then estimated. When the actual planning began, the total number of stories was 114, adding up to 228 points, which was significantly over budget!

The first task was to cut down the proposition to include only those stories that were absolutely essential. In other words, if they weren't included, the service would not be worth launching. This reduced the points total to around 120 – still double what we had time for.

The next step was to discuss the possibility of having extra time with the creative director. He identified two small projects which were very low priority, and could be dropped completely, freeing up a further stream for two weeks i.e. 12 (1 x 2 x 6) points. This increased the budget to 72 – still lower than required.

At this point the situation seemed pretty hopeless, and it was obvious that something drastic was going to have to be done. After a short break for lunch, the producer was able to come up with a simplified proposition, for which new stories were quickly written and estimated. This resulted in a new total of 31 stories, totaling 63 points, giving some room to play with as the project progressed. It was decided that this was enough to begin development with, and progress would be monitored before deciding on possible extra stories.

Over the course of the project a number of further new stories came out, as functionality was completed and the producer reviewed and tested the developing service. Some of these were prioritized and implemented, while others could not be completed. Some of the original stories were also reprioritized and implemented. The final delivery consisted of 45 stories, totaling 84 points.

Table 1. Summary of project stories

	Implemented	Not Implemented
Original	35 (72 points)	79 (156 points)
New	10 (12 points)	5 (10 points)

While these numbers are inherently crude due to granularity of the story points, they give a good indication of by how much the final project was reduced from the original aspiration. Within a very short space of time, the group was able to negotiate a plan that was satisfactory to everyone. It was realistic and achievable by the technical team, and met the editorial needs of the producer. In fact, the final service contained more functionality than originally planned, and the producer was extremely happy with the service. In an email to the team, the creative director said, "It's the best. It's absolutely fantastic!"

The planning process was not easy, (it was very intense), but the unanimous consensus was that it was better to go through the pain at the start of the project when it could be controlled and minimized rather than the end.

6 Conclusion

The team is able to manage the various complexities of multiple customers, projects and disciplines by working in a way which allows them to treat the work as if there were only a single customer, project and discipline. Thus they work on a single pool of stories which are shared by all the different customers, projects and disciplines.

The practices allow the editorial team to juggle all the projects, prioritizing and balancing the scope of each to maximize value for the business. At the same time, individual producers are allowed the freedom to fine-tune their propositions, either because of resource or time constraints or because they have changed their mind.

In general, the process is "barely sufficient" [6], and the plans are seen as "hypotheses to be tested rather than predictions to be realized" [7] so they are constantly adjusted to reflect reality.

Acknowledgements. Thanks to everyone involved in the eTV team at the BBC for being willing to adopt agile practices. Thanks also to Humphrey Lau and everyone else who has reviewed this paper.

Biography

Karl has been developing Interactive TV services for the BBC since October 1999, and has led the eTV technical team since May 2002. He has been promoting agile methods since discovered XP in late 2000.

References

1. Beck, K.: Extreme Programming Explained. Addison-Wesley, 2000.
2. Jeffries, R.: Petition the King, http://www.xprogramming.com/xpmag/PetitionTheKing.htm
3. Extreme Programming Yahoo Group. http://groups.yahoo.com/group/extremeprogramming/
4. Leuf, B. and Cunningham, W.: The Wiki Way. Addison-Wesley, 2001.
5. Beedle, M. and Schwaber, K.: Agile Software Development with Scrum. Prentice Hall, 2001.
6. Cockburn, A.: Agile Software Development: Software Through People. Addison-Wesley, 2002.
7. Highsmith, J.: Agile Software Development Ecosystems. Addison-Wesley, 2002.

A Tail of Two Projects: How 'Agile' Methods Succeeded after 'Traditional' Methods Had Failed in a Critical System-Development Project

Robert Bedoll

The Boeing Company, Renton, Washington
robert.f.bedoll@boeing.com

Abstract. This paper will contrast two software development projects – both addressing exactly the same problem – in the Boeing Commercial Airplane Company Electrical design organization. The first project used a traditional 'heavy-weight' software development methodology, invested 60 man-years, and failed. The second project used a agile development approach, invested four man-years, and continues to be dramatically successful. Both projects addressed a paradigm-shift in the business process used to design and integrate electrical wiring in Boeing airplanes. This paper presents a recipe for success for an agile project in a non-agile world. It covers specific real-world lessons learned, and discusses the circumstances under which agile methods can be exceptionally effective and successful. It also points out where agile is not effective, or where the agile advantage can become a disadvantage.

1 The Environment

The Boeing Commercial Airplane Company (BCA) is a division of The Boeing Company. BCA produces the Boeing family of airplanes: the narrow body 737 and 757, and the wide body 747, 767, and 777. BCA employs 78,000 people, of whom about 10,000 are engineers. BCA Information Services is a 5,000-employee group within BCA that provides software in support of the engineering and manufacturing of Boeing airplanes. Within that group, my organization develops and supports software specifically for the Electrical Wiring Engineering organizations.

1.1 Software Development within BCA

In the early 1990s, the BCA IS division standardized on a software development methodology called P-Plus, which it purchased from DMR System, Inc. P+ is a 'heavyweight' development methodology; it calls for six development phases (Opportunity Evaluation, Preliminary Analysis, System Analysis, Functional Design, Construction, Implementation) with up to 108 different document deliverables. To support this process, Boeing trained and developed an infrastructure of P+ coaches; major projects were each assigned a P+ coach, whose job was to guide the development team through the P+ process and ensure that the proper deliverables were produced.

F. Maurer and D. Wells (Eds.): XP/Agile Universe 2003, LNCS 2753, pp. 25–34, 2003.
© Springer-Verlag Berlin Heidelberg 2003

1.2   The Engineering Problem – Airplane Wiring

In 1995, a project was begun in BCA to develop a new generation of software to support the design and manufacturing of airplane wiring. Although designing and tracking wiring for an airplane seems on the face of it to be a relatively straightforward process, in reality it can be a task of daunting complexity due to the sheer volume of wiring, the amount of variability between airplanes, and the manufacturing cycle. A small plane like a 757 will have over 50,000 wires, grouped into about 900 wire bundles, connecting about 12,000 pieces of equipment. Because of the number of different options available for an airplane, the different requirements of each airline, and the difficulties in coordinating thousands of different suppliers, each and every airplane has different wiring and connectors – sometimes slightly different, sometimes dramatically different. Hence there is a group of about 1000 engineers whose sole job is to engineer and reengineer the electrical equipment and wiring for each and every airplane – and the build rate can be up to 2 airplanes per day.

Also in 1995, Boeing launched a major computing initiative designed to reinvent the way airplanes were specified and manufactured. The program was named DCAC, for Define and Control Airplane Configuration. Its central tenant was that an airplane could be designed and configured using 'options', much like a car, where air-conditioning and four-wheel drive are options that, once specified, automatically pull in a pre-designed set of parts and wiring. (Of course, a car might have two dozen options, where an airplane has two thousand options).

2   The 'Heavy-Weight Development' Story

In 1996, my organization launched a project to design and develop a software system that would bring the notion of option driven design to Electrical Wiring and Equipment. The basic concept was simple and straightforward – every wire on an airplane model would be assigned an option expression (such as 'Option A and Option B and not Option C). When an airline ordered an airplane, a list of several hundred options would be assembled and fed into the program. The option expression for each wire would be evaluated against the customer option list, and the program would determine what wires were required, group them into bundles, and upload the whole collection to the existing IMS-based WIRS system, which tracks airplane wiring for engineering and manufacturing.

2.1   The Project

Although no business process yet existed to support this, a full-scale development project was started, with a staff of 20 (architects, programmers, DBAs, designers). A standard three-tier architecture was chosen: an Oracle database backend (running on Sequents), application server code written in C++ and Motif (running on HP servers), and the desktops running X-windows. The traditional P+ methodology was followed. Dozens of documents, and thousands of pages, were produced, reviewed, and approved by the customer. User Interface designs were captured in documents that often ran into a hundred pages for one screen.

The development cycle went something like this:

Requirements definition (1 month) -> Design (3 months) -> Coding (4 months) -> Functional testing (2 months) -> Start over with the next release.

By the time the release got through functional testing, it had been ten months since the original requirements definition started; by that time the users had changed their mind about what they wanted the system to do, and so the process started over again, without even getting into real end-user testing.

After persisting in this cycle for three years (about 8 releases, with overlap between releases), the customer finally deemed that there was enough functionality to begin end-user testing. User testing went on for 2 months, at the end of which the users declared that both the software system and the business process were unusable. At that point, after investing sixty man-years, the project was essentially scrapped.

The project life cycle looked like this:

Start -> Develop for 3 years -> Test by end-users for 2 months -> Scrap it.

2.2 Lessons Learned

There are a number of lessons that are learned from such an activity. Although they appear somewhat obvious, they bear repeating:

- **Unproven Business Process:**
  Massive development efforts based on an unproven business process are a waste of time, effort, and money.

- **One-Year Development Cycles:**
  A process that requires close to a year between the start of the requirements definition and the emergence of finished code is almost certain to be 'overtaken by events'. No matter how carefully the original analysis is done, or how detailed the requirements documents are, or how many approval signatures are obtained, it is still the case that after a year has passed, many of the assumptions on which the original analysis were based have changed, or the user champions or management has moved on, or something else has changed to significantly alter the original requirements.

- **Paper Documents:**
  Paper documents are a terrible way to get customer buy-off on complex GUI designs. If the documents are not detailed, the user gets insufficient feel for how the application will work. If the documents sufficiently detailed, the customers will not make it past the first few pages before their eyes glaze over. Getting customer 'approval' will give you 'contractual' protection – you can always tell the user that you built what they approved – but it will not force them to accept a system that they think is unusable.

- **Traditional Development Tools:**
  C++ and Motif, even with GUI-design toolkits, are too complex and cumbersome to provide rapid customer feedback on new designs. Once a paper design was finished, approved, and turned over to a programmer, it would often take them one to two months to produce a working version of that design. Only then could a customer representative actually play with the design and determine if it was

workable (and this was often six months after the requirements activity started). Naturally, this led to a lot of design rework and revision, and caused the development and testing cycle to draw out even more.

- **Delayed End-User Testing:**
  Our customers did not want to let the end users test the software until at least 80% of the final required functionality was there. Because of this, we did six major releases, almost three years of work, before end-users were allowed to sit-down with the software and test it against business processes. It wasn't until that time that the end-users declared that the system, and the processes, were unworkable.

3 The Next Attempt

Two years later, in early 2000, the 757 airplane model decided to take another try at doing 'design-by-option'. This time, the approach was slightly different. The goal was to take as much of the wiring in the airplane as possible, and make it 'standard', which meant it would be on every 757, regardless of the customer. The reduction in variability would save a tremendous amount of engineering and manufacturing time. Wiring that couldn't be declared standard would be assigned to an option or option expression. Wiring would then be moved between wire bundles to create as many standard, non-changing wire bundles as possible, and to isolate all changes to a small number of highly variable bundles. The involved organizations were 757 Wire Design and 757 Wire Install, together about 60 engineers. The challenges to achieving this were significant:

- **Engineering Challenge:**
  Wire Design and Wire Install had to evaluate 50,000 wires, determine which were stable and which varied (and why), and assign these wires to 800 new wire bundles. At the same time, they were modifying the wiring so that most of it could be used on either the short or the long versions of the 757.

- **Schedule Challenge:**
  Because of delivery commitments to customers, 757 was given a schedule of only about 5 months, significantly less time than would normally be required.

- **Business Process Challenge**:
  Since this activity had never been done before, the engineering business process was uncertain, fluid, and untried.

3.1 The IS Challenge

The legacy IMS-based system that supported the engineering and manufacturing of wiring could not be modified to accommodate the additional information required, so our organization was asked to come up with a tool to support this effort. IS faced challenges similar to Wire Design and Wire Install:

- Schedule:
  A computing tool had to be ready for 757 to begin using within two months.

- **Budget**:
  Budget was only available for 2 – 3 persons.

- **Process and Tool Evolution**:
  Because the business process was uncertain, the tool had to be able to evolve to match the evolving process.

- **Production Use:**
  The 757 engineers would be using the tool for actual production airplane design work from day 1 – there would be no 2-month 'system test'.

3.2   The IS Requirements

The tool requirements looked something like this:

- A database-driven tool that would allow 757 to view, analyze, classify, and modify all 50,000 wires and 15,000 equipments on a 757.
- Accessible to sixty engineers in multiple organizations, in multiple geographic locations, on multiple platforms (PCs and Unix workstations).
- A modern GUI.
- Sophisticated features for
  - Managing wiring content by option expressions (e.g. option A or B and not C)
  - Splitting wiring bundles into multiple bundles
  - Making mass changes and alterations
  - Support for internal 'releases' to indicate that a design was 'complete'.
  - Reports comparable to those generated by the current legacy IMS system (about 20 reports)
  - Ability to initialize the tool from data in the legacy system
  - Ability to upload finished data back into the legacy system

4   Our Agile Approach

Based on the failure of the traditional approach with the previous project, it was obvious that the same approach would not work for this problem. The same customer problems existed that had led to previous failure, most notably a fluid and evolving business process (uncertain requirements). Furthermore, neither the schedule nor the budget would support a traditional approach. Therefore, we decided to try an 'experimental' agile approach to determine its viability for a real production problem. We adopted the following principles:

- Rapid prototyping of designs, with immediate customer feedback
- Continuous involvement of the customer

- Weekly production releases: Follow our standard development cycle (requirements – design – code – test – release) but compress it from formal releases every three months to formal releases every week.
- Start simple and keep it simple
- Evolve the tool to follow the evolving business process
- Provide a one to three week cycle time for new feature introduction
- Maintain a small development team
- Produce abbreviated versions of our standard design documents. Let the prototyping drive the design documentation.
- Retain our SEI (Software Engineering Institute) Level 2 rating.

4.1 Implementation

We implemented those principles as follows:

Rapid Prototyping: After spending several months using Microsoft Access and Visual Basic to do prototypes, we chose them as our prototyping and development tool. Even though we were primarily an Oracle, Java, and C++ shop, we found that new features could be prototyped in Access in less than a day, and we could get user feedback on actual working code within 2 – 3 days, dramatically faster than using any other language or tool.

Continuous Customer Involvement: We had a full-time customer liaison, who spend half his time with the end users and half with the development team. We did weekly user training and weekly user and management reviews. This was helped by the fact that the customer really needed the tool – there was no way for them to do the job they were being asked to do, in the timeframe they were given, without a computing tool.

Weekly Formal Releases: Because we are an SEI Level 2 organization, we needed to continue to follow our formal, documented processes. We did this by compressing and overlapping all steps in the process, with minimal emphasis on formal approval signatures. We documented this compressed process in a separate development process document for this project. Each release was limited to a small, incremental increase in functionality. We tried to stay one step ahead of the business process, and implement features just as they were needed. (Typical features would be specific reports, the addition of new database attributes, or advanced capabilities for changing an attribute like wire gauge across a group of wires). This lead to 'just-in-time' training, and 'just-in-time' feature introduction. Complex features were introduced incrementally.

Start Simple. Keep it Simple: We started with only a simple data structure (less than two dozen data tables) and less than 1000 lines of VB. We quickly – and relentlessly – evolved the application, but never made it more complex than it needed to be to support the current business process.

Evolve the Tool to Follow the Business Process: Each week we added functionality to support the evolving process. When the process changed, we changed the tool.

Because we took small steps, the amount of rework (throw-away and redo) was limited.

Small Development Team: We limited the team to three developers and one half-time tester. This reduced the documentation requirement and allowed us to be nimble.

Prototype Drives the Design Documentation: Rather than do elaborate written GUI designs, which take weeks or months, we did one or two-day prototypes, reviewed them with the customer, and let them dictate the finished design.

4.2 The Customer Results

Our development activity began in earnest in August of 2000 (when funding was finally approved). End users began using the tool in mid-September, after only about 6 week. Usage grew to about sixty users (24 simultaneous users) by February 2001.

While the tool evolved and grew, the users were using it to redesign the wiring on the 757. They did all their redesign using the tool, making about 80% of the airplane wiring standard on every airplane, and determining what airplane minor-model or customer option controlled the rest of the wiring. They then used the tool to configure the wiring for a new airplane, and uploaded the wiring of the entire airplane to the legacy IMS-based WIRS system, which feeds the data to manufacturing. Since then, the customer has used the tool to design and release wiring for several new minor model designs and four new customers.

In the 18 months of use, we have had no unplanned downtime, outages, or database failures.

Because we were able to work closely with the customer and respond rapidly to their changing requirements, and because the tool proved to be so stable, the customer confidence and satisfaction remained high. Customer management says they could not have succeeded without the tool.

We are now expanding usage of the tool to other Boeing airplane models (the 767, 777, and 767 Tanker).

4.3 The Tool Results

The Tool Evolution:
- The Tool began production on a shared file server in September 2000, with about six users. Written entirely in Microsoft ACCESS, it had only about 24 tables and 1000 lines of Visual Basic, but it was enough to get the users started.
- The tool steadily grew to sixty tables and 45,000 lines of Visual Basic over the course of a year. It had about sixty different users, with a peak user load of about 24.
- After a year, in September 2001, the ACCESS database was moved from a file server to an SQL Server backend. This was done to improve performance under heavy user load. The tool itself – the font-end – remained in ACCESS and VB. Currently the tool consists of 88 tables and 60,000 lines of VB.

- The tool was interfaced to the legacy IMS-based systems for wiring configuration control, and for sending data to manufacturing. (The interface consists of database feeds and 3270 emulation).
- The Development team has remained at two to three developers and a half-time tester.
- By 2003 the tool had grown to over 100,000 lines of VB, with a VISIO graphics engine. The tool is in use by 5 different wire design organizations within Boeing.
- The amazing thing is that we have yet to encounter a significant Access, VB, or SQL Server problem. (Though using an SQL Server backend does slow development of new features, and adds some unpleasant challenges).

5   Ingredients for Success

Evolving a tool while the customer is using it for production work, and releasing new features on a weekly basis, is a lot like building a car while driving it down the road at 60 mph. And yet, the whole process was highly successful – this goes dramatically against the established doctrine that development projects for critical production systems requires years of careful planning, meticulous design documentation and review, and many months of rigorous user testing. (Having been in this business for over thirty years, had I not been there myself I would have said it could not be done!) So a good question is, why can we do this now when we couldn't do it in the past?

5.1 Key Factors

Complete, Dedicated and Willing Involvement of the 'Customer' and End Users. Our customer liaison spent half his time with us, and half with the end users. This kept the development team and the customers completely in sync. It also maintained customer confidence on those occasions when we missed feature delivery dates.

Users Were Eager for Tools. Given the engineering tasks and schedule, and the existing legacy systems, the users needed the tools, so there was very strong customer 'pull'. This also meant that the users would temporarily put up with features that were not completely polished and 'complete'.

Robust and Solid Development and Prototyping Tools. ACCESS proved extremely fast for prototyping and debugging, and amazingly solid for production use (much to our surprise). For experienced and productive programmers, ACCESS/VB development proved almost 10 times faster than C++/Motif, and twice as fast as Java.

Rapid Cycle Time, Small Weekly Steps, and Immediate Feedback. ACCESS and VB allowed us to do things extremely quickly. For example, new reports and screens were prototyped, demonstrated, reviewed, revised and released within 1-2 weeks.

Simplicity. A small development team allowed us to focus on the customer, and kept process and communication concerns to a minimum. A small user community let us interact directly and constantly with the end users, and prevented us from being pulled in too many different directions. It also allowed us to release features which where not completely polished – the users would accept interim capabilities. A single airplane model focus removed worries about having to deal with huge amounts of data, and kept the problem within the technical capabilities of ACCESS. (As opposed to our production Oracle database, which mirrors much of the data on the legacy IMS WIRS system, and contains over 100 million rows of data).

5.2 The Limitations

There are limitations to what a project like this can achieve, and a 'rapid' development project can quickly turn into a 'retarded' development project if all the right conditions do not remain.

Customer Involvement – As soon as customer involvement drops off (or our customer liaison becomes too busy with other assignments), then rework increases significantly because the development team goes down a wrong path for too long before it gets a course correction.

Customer Need – As soon as the customer is not completely dependent on the tool, then their threshold for tolerating incomplete features decreases dramatically.

Scalability – Once the user community outgrows the technical capability of the tool, then significant rework is necessary to more to a more capable environment. We were fortunately able to move the database backend to SQL Server, which provided a much more scalable environment than ACCESS alone, and allowed us to preserve most of the rapid development features of ACCESS as a front end. However, it took us several months to move to SQL Server, and development and debugging is neither as easy nor as fast as an all-ACCESS environment.

Complexity – Some features just cannot be done simply, and some require changes throughout the application. (For example, when we added 'configuration control and management' to wiring, the development cycle was four months, including a one-month production freeze while we merged the constantly-changing production code with the long-term development code).

5.3 Some Interesting Social-Political Issues

A successful agile project uncovers some very interesting 'people' issues.

ACCESS and VB as Toys. ACCESS and VB are seen by our C++ and Java programmers as toys – not worthy of professional programmers. Several of our Java programmers refused an assignment on this project, even though it had great customer support, because they saw VB programming as being sent back to the minor leagues. The reality is that it often is much easier to do things in VB and ACCESS, and for an experienced programmer this translates directly into greatly increased productivity.

Customer Expectations. Since ACCESS and VB allowed us to give the users significant features with a very rapid cycle time, their expectations have been raised, and they now expect all features to be delivered immediately – and cheaply. Of course, this is not always possible.

Customer View of IS. Many of our engineering organizations like to avoid dealing with IS because of our formal and protracted development cycles. By being able to respond to problems as quickly as engineering users, while at the same time applying traditional professional programming processes – like configuration control and formal testing and release cycles – we are moving this tool in areas that have shunned our tools in the past.

6 Summary – Real–World Success vs. Real-World Failure

Contrasting the two development activities gives this brief summary of the differences between success and failure.

Business Process:

Success: The tool evolves incrementally, along with the business process.

Failure: The process is build after the tool is done, or the tool is created to an imagined business process.

Customer Involvement:

Success: Daily contact and hands-on evaluation of new-feature code by the end users within days of requirements definition.

Failure: Monthly paper-design reviews, and hands-on feature evaluation by the end users nine months after requirements.

Simplicity and Focus:

Success: A single group of sixty users; a single airplane program with a small set of airplanes.

Failure: 2000 users, all five airplane programs with all airplanes past, present, and future (several thousand planes).

Development Tools and Processes:

Success: ACCESS, Visual Basic, lean development processes (but still a formal testing and release process)

Failure: C++, Motif, heavy-weight, paper-intensive development processes.

The Rules of the Game

Ken Auer[1], Erik Meade[2], and Gareth Reeves[3]

[1] RoleModel Software, Inc.
5004 Rossmore Dr.
Fuquay-Varina, NC 27526 USA
+1 919 557 6352
`ken.auer@rolemodelsoftware.com`
[2] Object Mentor, Inc.
565 Lakeview Parkway, Suite 135.
Vernon Hills, IL 60061-5757 USA
+1 847 573 1565
`emeade@objectmentor.com`
[3] CSS LCC
175 West Jackson, Suite 400
Chicago, IL 60604, USA
+1 312 542 8520
`reevesg@pobox.com`

Abstract. This paper examines using rules to define Extreme Programming (XP) as its values do not differentiate it from other Agile processes, and its practices are the path to XP.

1 Introduction

We will boldly assert the following truths:
- XP's values make it Agile.
- XP's practices do not define XP.

So, if it's not the practices, what defines Extreme Programming (XP)?

We will briefly support these two assertions and then present a further assertion: XP is defined by it's rules. Finally, we present and discuss those rules.

2 XP & Values

We can say XP is an agile process because it shares the values defined in the Agile Manifesto (http://www.agilealliance.org):
- Communication - Individuals and interactions over processes and tools
- Simplicity - Working software over comprehensive documentation
- Feedback - Customer collaboration over contract negotiation
- Courage - Responding to change over following a plan

F. Maurer and D. Wells (Eds.): XP/Agile Universe 2003, LNCS 2753, pp. 35–42, 2003.

XP's values are the Agile Alliance values. SCRUM's values are Agile Alliance values. XP and SCRUM share the same values, but what makes them different?

3 Defining XP

Defining XP by the practices has at least two problems.

Some practices are fuzzy in definition. For example, one team's definition of having a 'Customer on site' can be vastly different from another's. To complicate matters even further, we have seen that it is possible for a team to be doing all of the XP practices and yet still not be *extreme*. They can check off all of the practices, but they miss the point of why they are doing them and have had no real social change in their environment. (We'll elaborate more on this in our example at the end of section 6, "Bending the Rules").

Another problem with this approach is it's commonly understood you can be doing XP without doing all of the practices. This was reinforced at XP Universe 2001 when Kent Beck drew the analogy that practices are etudes. For those who are not familiar with etude:

é·tude
a short musical composition for a solo instrument intended to develop a point of technique or to display the performer's skill, but often played for its artistic merit

In this paradigm, the etudes (or practices) become the path to XP, they are not what defines XP.

Many have suggested some practices are more important than others. Others have proposed additional practices. If XP were defined by it's practices it is not clear when something is or is not XP. If the list of official practices change, does something go from being XP to not XP?

4 What about Rules?

What makes Baseball, Baseball (and not Basketball)?

It's not the values that make it baseball. You can have different values that motivate you to play baseball. Ken values the intricacies of the game that can be leveraged by an otherwise inferior athlete to beat his opponent. Ken's 5-year old son, Caleb, values the fun of running around the bases. Their values are different. It's still baseball.

You can execute the practices almost perfectly like major-leaguers or poorly like Caleb, who is still working on hitting the ball and knowing where/when to run. The execution of practices can be vastly different. It's still baseball.

What is it that defines baseball? The rules.

Sometimes, rules clearly suggest a practice. A rule such as "You must arrive safely at first base before being put out" would imply the practice of running to first base after hitting the ball. Some rules offer wider constraints and suggest a variety of strategies and/or practices for "playing better".

We tend to think of Software Development as comparable to a game, as per Alistair Cockburn's premise[1]. So, the argument being put forth is that we should not define XP merely by its values or its practices. We should define XP by its rules. Once the rules are defined many of the practices used on XP projects would be suggested, while still leaving room for a variety of strategies or practices that help us "play better".

5   The Rules of XP

So what are the Rules of XP? One of the main reasons the three authors have come together from different organization is to validate that the rules apply across a variety of organizations. Each of our organizations has different ways in which we apply these rules. Each of us has been involved in multiple XP projects whose implementations of XP have varied. Lastly, each of us has seen projects which attempted to do XP but fell short in one way or another.

We've chosen to categorize the rules of XP in two parts: The *Rules of Engagement* and the *Rules of Play*.

In baseball, the Rules of Engagement could be thought of as those that define the size of the field, the size of each team, an inning, the number of innings, etc. The game can't begin without the Rules of Engagement. These rules are prominent when a contest is arranged and begun, but they are also present throughout the contest. However, due to the intensity of the Rules of Play during the playing of the game the Rules of Engagement become less prominent. Without them, you don't have an identifiable game. But they don't really define the minute-by-minute activities, only a framework under which those activities take place.

The Rules of Play happen within the Rules of Engagement. Together, they define the minute-by-minute activities. During a game, the Rules of Engagement can often seem a distant thought. The Rules of Play in baseball include "pitcher pitches a ball toward home plate while batter is in the batter's box...", and all the other rules determine what legally happens once the pitch is set in motion, a runner is on base, etc. When a batter is having a ball coming at him at 90+ miles per hour, he is not giving much thought to the number of innings in a game or what inning he is currently in. If the pitch goes by him, he takes a step back and ponders those things the Rules of Engagement define. He steps back into the batter's box and a subset of the Rules of Play take over his mind.

So, in XP, we have the following Rules of Engagement:

E1. An XP team consists of a group of people dedicated to the production of a software product. This product may or may not be a piece of a larger product. There can be many roles on this team, but there must be at least a customer and a developer role.

E2. The customer must set and continuously adjusts the objectives and priorities based on estimates and other information provided by the developers or other members of the team. Objectives are defined in terms of *what* not *how*.

E3. The customer is always available and supplies information on demand to assist developers in forming estimates or supplying desired deliverables. The customer is an integral part of the team.

E4. At any point, any member of the team must be able to measure the team's progress towards the customer's objectives.

E5. The team must act as an Effective Social Network, this means:

1. Honest communication leading to continuous learning[2].

2. Minimal degrees of separation from what is needed by the team to make progress and the people/resources that can meet those needs.

3. Alignment of authority and responsibility.

E6. Timeboxing is used to identify segments of development effort and each segment is no more than one month in duration.

As we've developed these rules and have become familiar with other Agile processes, it seems that these rules may be very similar to those of other Agile processes. We certainly do not believe we can assert this with authority, but we suspect they are at least similar. However, whatever similarities they might possess in their Rules of Engagement, XP seems to differentiate itself from other Agile processes in its Rules of Play. The Rules of Play are simple, they happen within the Rules of Engagement:

P1. Work produced must be continuously validated through testing.

P2. Write unit tests first (before coding), Program in pairs (if there is more than one developer on the team), and refactor code to meet Coding Rules (P3) while working on current customer priorities.

P3. All code written for potential use in the software product must:

1. Pass all the unit tests (or not make any unit tests fail)

2. Clearly express every concept

3. Contains no duplication

4. Contains no superfluous parts

P4. Collective Ownership. Everybody has the authority and at least two people have the understanding necessary to do any task.

It is these Rules of Play, which make XP fundamentally different than other Agile processes. In fact, if we could name the whole process over, we would call it "Extreme Software Development" and following the Rules of Play would be called "Extreme Programming". (Then the development team could be *Extreme Programming* even if the Rules of Engagement were not followed... which evidently appears to happen often in the industry. *Extreme Software Development* would not occur until both sets of Rules were followed).

6 Bending the Rules

The rules listed above are the summarized version of the complete rules of XP. The details of each of the rules are left out because this paper is meant to make a point about the necessity of rules in general, and these rules in particular, not to be an exhaustive rulebook.

That said, some rules have more flexibility than others.

In baseball, you can bend the rules a little, and still arguably be playing baseball. When Ken plays with his kids there are less than the regulation number of players and he only gets one out per half-inning and they get three. It's not "official" baseball. It is actually a better game given the context. Get rid of the baseball, the bat, or the bases, and it's NOT baseball at all... not even "unofficial" baseball. The points at which it goes from "official" baseball to "unofficial" baseball to "not" baseball is somewhat fuzzy and could certainly be argued. However, it should be clear that when the context of the game permits all the rules to be used, they should be. And when they can't be, it is certainly not "official" and something is lost.

By bending the rules, something can also be gained. In the context of Ken playing with his kids, trying to play by all the rules would make the game uninteresting to the kids. By bending the rules, they are engaged. As they grow, the real rules can be given to them and they can grow in appreciation of them.

Given some context, some form of "unofficial XP" might be the right thing to do. Often, however, adjustments can be made within the rules that may be "unorthodox" while still "official XP". In baseball, you can legally play with five infielders and two outfielders or, you might temporarily have a pitcher switch to the outfield.

We've tried to define the rules in a manner that identifies which rules are the most flexible. For example:

Timeboxing (E6)
Timeboxing is important for providing feedback and also for forcing key decisions. One, two, and three weeks have been vehemently argued by experienced XPers as the ideal size of an iteration. Often these arguments are strongest given the constraints of the environment in which one is working. There have been known cases where developers used short (e.g. one or two week) "internal iterations" and longer (e.g. four weeks or three months) "external iterations" to publish results to an audience wider than the team. However, we find it hard to imagine a situation where it was not vital to have internal iterations of a month or less. Go over that, and you may still be doing "unofficial" XP. Get rid of the idea of iterations altogether, and you're doing something else.

Continuous Validation through Testing (P1)
The best way to do this is certainly to have automated tests and keep them in a state such that they can be run very quickly. This is a practice that eXPerts do very well most of the time. However, there might be environments and teams where, for at least a period of time, it is difficult to achieve this level of excellence. "Automated Tests" is a practice that is a "fundamental strategy" to XP. Without it, you probably won't execute XP as well. This is somewhat analogous to the strategies and practices that ex-

perienced baseball players treat as second nature such as where they are positioned in the field to maximize their potential to limit progress by their opponents. An inexperienced ballplayer might miss these things or at least execute them poorly in spite of having a good coach, but would still be playing the game of baseball. Even the most experienced ballplayer might occasionally come up against a situation he's never seen before and won't know "the best thing to do".

Measuring Progress toward Objectives (E4)

Again, the best way to do this is to have the customer write acceptance tests that can be run automatically regularly (e.g. nightly) and whenever desired. Early in a project, it is often difficult to do, and there may be certain types of requirements or contexts in which it makes sense to do some of this measurement manually or less often. But, if the customer can't identify what's done and what's not, you're not even doing "unofficial" XP.

Other rules, worded in order to keep them succinct, might need their points of flexibility made more explicit. For example:

Customer Sets and Adjust Priority (E2)

In reality it is not always possible and sometimes not even logical to have a single customer set the priorities and define the objective of the system in detail. Usually this takes a team of people. At times, there may be people who have to wear both a "customer" hat due to their subject matter expertise as well as a "developer" hat. As long as the "hats" are made explicit, this would be an acceptable bending of the rule. If a manager who "knows the business" sets and adjusts priorities, you may be doing "unofficial XP". If the developers do it, you are doing something else.

Test-First Programming in Pairs (P2)

We've yet to hear of a great answer as to how to do test-first for certain types of user interface development. If no one on the team can figure out a useful test for some subset of the code, you can probably identify it as an exception. If you program in pairs but have a bunch of exceptions that encourage code to be written by individuals at times, you have stepped over the line to "unofficial XP". If not writing the test first becomes the rule rather than exception, you are playing a different game!

Other rules, though a bit vague, just don't have much room to bend. For example, the team MUST act as an Effective Social Network (E5). RoleModel recently had a client that was doing virtually all of the practices of XP (they weren't doing all of them well, but they were doing them). We would assert that they were not doing XP, but not because of their sometimes poor execution of the practices. The fundamental issue was that they were not acting as an Effective Social Network:

1. They did not have open, honest communication between management, the customer(s), and the development team or even within the development team.

2. There were often dictates made by management that got in the way of progress (e.g. you must use Lotus Notes for project tracking even though "off the shelf" Notes didn't provide the capabilities needed. Of course, you cannot use Notes until you've attended an official training class on it. There was a long waiting list for the class and it might take months until one could actually at-

tend. And contractors were not going to be given such a class. No Notes Programmer was made available to the team at first and, when they eventually were, they had limited availability and had to clear everything they were asked to do through some third party).

3. Some people, namely "contractors", were second-class citizens. If "employees" didn't like something the contractors suggested, they would make decisions without them and then dictate the way things were going to be done. The fact that the *coach* was a contractor made it very difficult for him to actually coach.

4. Meetings with people from the customer team had to be scheduled. A lot of time was spent by the developers talking about how to spin the discussion with the customer to make the developers look like they've thought it all through. Often this discussion included debate whether they should even expose any uncertainty to the customer.

7 Conclusions

There have been many discussions over what exactly defines XP over the past several years. There have been presentations and articles written about experiences with XP that have gotten XPers in a huff because the authors/presenters "clearly didn't understand what XP was". Most published attempts at defining XP have discussed its values and practices and often include a disclaimer that you can do XP without doing all of the practices. Since its listed values read somewhat like "motherhood and apple pie", they have fallen far short of defining XP. Its changing list of practices as well as the statements about moving beyond the practices and discussion of "less essential" practices has made it difficult to identify what XP really is. This has left a real void because shared definitions are important in order to have effective communication be it critical or instructional.

Once a game is defined by its rules, the rules seldom change significantly. However, players learn effective strategies and constantly refine their execution of those strategies. New strategies are often being explored. The most effective ones eventually become commonplace... until a better strategy is discovered.

Ken possesses a copy of a small book entitled "Official Baseball Rules"[3]. It exhaustively defines the game of Baseball. Until this paper was written, there has been no real source for the equivalent definition of XP. When we look at the Rules of XP, it is much easier to identify what XP is than trying to define it by the 12, 13, or 19 practices (+/- 2 that are "less essential").

However, the Rules only tell you enough to play the game - not enough to play it effectively.

Ken also possesses a copy of "The Complete Book of Baseball Strategy"[4]. It provides a list of 169 "Stratagems" (practices?) many of which are generally applicable as well as some that are specific to people in different roles (First Baseman, Pitcher,

Coach, etc.). It also provides a series of drills (the equivalent of etudes?) that "drill" the stratagems into players. Of course, even though the title includes the word "Complete", there are certainly useful stratagems that can be found (either explicitly or by reading between the lines of the experiences of others) in other books and resources. We would suggest that the majority of the XP literature to date has provided the moral equivalent of basic (the practices) and situational stratagems to help their readers execute better. There are more stratagems to be explored.

Now that we've got that cleared up, let's play ball!

Acknowledgements. This paper was inspired by a rash of e-mail discussions among several others including Kent Beck, Alistair Cockburn, Ward Cunningham, Jim Highsmith, Ron Jeffries, "Pragmatic" Dave Thomas, and Don Wells to whom credit is due for both their contributions of ideas and getting Ken's thoughts out of his head and into writing. Thanks are also due to the other participants at the OOPSLA 2001 Workshop "Refining the Practices of eXtreme Programming" who provided much input based on discussions of Ken's original position paper to this workshop.

References

1. Alistair Cockburn, *Agile Software Development.* Addison-Wesley Pub Co, 2001
2. Joshua Kerievsky, *Continuous Learning.* On-line at
   http://www.industriallogic.com/xp/ContinuousLearning.pdf
3. *Official Baseball Rules.* The Sporting News, 1986
4. Hal Wolf, *The Complete Book of Baseball Strategy.* Exposition Press, 1974

Achieving ISO 9001 Certification for an XP Company

Graham Wright

Development Team Coach
Workshare
20 Fashion Street
London, E1 6PX
(44) 020 7539 1361
graham.wright@workshare.com

Abstract. It is generally assumed that certification such as ISO 9001 is incompatible with Agile Development Methods, particularly eXtreme Programming. However it is possible to achieve certification in a manner that is compatible with XP and does not reduce agility. The key to this is making the documentation, process monitoring and audit trail required for certification a natural output of the development process rather than an artificial product created purely to satisfy those requirements. This paper describes the successful certification of an XP company.

1 Introduction

The company described in this paper, Workshare [1], adopted XP in February 2001. The company produces document content management and collaboration software. Currently five products have been released, built around a common code base. The development environment differs from that of many XP shops in a number of ways including a reliance on C++ and COM, a high GUI content within its products and a large development team. During the past two years the XP process has been tailored to manage this large team. This has resulted in the concept of the "virtual white board" which in turn became central to achieving ISO 9001:2000 TickIT [2, 3] certification. For brevity this is subsequently referred to as ISO 9001

The company began preparing for certification in March 2002 and was recommended for certification following a successful audit in February 2003. This recommendation was confirmed during April 2003. A key feature of achieving this was that the documentation, process monitoring and audit trail required for certification was already place within the company as a result of the earlier efforts required to manage a large engineering team producing multiple products.

We believe that we are amongst the first, if not the first, company using XP for all its development to gain ISO 9001 certification.

2 ISO 9001 Requirements

ISO 9001 requires companies to set up quality management systems to "monitor, measure and continually improve their business processes" [3]. Guidance for applying ISO 9001 requirements to the software industry are contained the TickIT guide [3].

F. Maurer and D. Wells (Eds.): XP/Agile Universe 2003, LNCS 2753, pp. 43–50, 2003.

TickIT arose from the recognition that the process for software development and maintenance is different than that of most other industrial products. The desire to devise an ISO registration scheme for software resulted in TickIT being formulated by IT professionals in the United Kingdom. The objectives of TickIT are as follows:
- To ensure the ISO standard is applied appropriately to software
- To ensure consistency of certification with the IT Industry
- To enable mutual recognition of registration across the IT industry.

The TickIT guide tends to state more of how to implement an ISO 9001 system, while the standard states what must be done.

In practice certification requires a company to formulate a quality policy and manual, institute a quality management system and maintain sufficient records to prove that the processes within the company are quality driven, measured and reviewed, and that there is a continual improvement in those processes.

3 Some Common Misconceptions

There are a number of misconceptions concerning ISO 9001 and the XP process.

Firstly it is commonly assumed that gaining certification is merely a matter of following any documented process; secondly many in the XP community believe the level of documentation required for certification contradicts core XP principles and is inherently non-agile; thirdly it is not understood that certification is for the entire company and not just for the development process within that company.

The first misconception is due to the fact that earlier versions of the ISO standard did emphasise the documentation of procedures over the quality of those procedures. However the current standard is based on quality within a process: "ISO 9001:2000 is intensively process-orientated and requires an organisation to identify, manage and continually improve all processes" [3, page F1].

This emphasis on process leads to the second misconception that certification standards such as ISO are incompatible with Agile Methods such as XP, either because the standard specifies a process that can not be followed using XP or because proving that the process is being monitored and improved places such an overhead on that process that it ceases to be agile.

Although ISO 9001 "does not define a particular life cycle model" [3, page F2] it does reference the model described in ISO/IEC 12207 [4], which is essentially a high level description of the old waterfall process in its V-model form. However other methodologies can map their processes to this reference model. This has already been done for DSDM, the most process heavy of the Agile methodologies [5]. The key factor is not the process but the ability to demonstrate that this process can meet the ISO 9001 objectives of managing and improving quality. There is nothing explicit or implicit in XP that precludes this. Indeed it can be agued that the change in emphasis within the ISO standard from documentation to process favours those methods such as XP that have a clear set of practices. However in order to maintain agility it is essential that demonstrating quality and improvement in the process relies on natural outputs from XP rather than on artefacts created purely for the certification audit.

Finally although this paper describes ISO certification as it relates to XP it is important to realise that certification applies to the entire company and is based on all the procedures within that company not just to the software development process. So for instance XP starts with a customer story but certification would also depend on the quality of processes leading to the inception of that story, not solely on the quality of the implementation of that story. For Workshare, being a commercial software house, this involves all the processes involved in managing external customer issues and feature requests as well as the formulation of high-level business strategy.

4   Managing a Large Team

Since Workshare adopted XP we have attempted to do things "by the book" and not deviate from any of the core practices. However because of the size of the team (30 programmers, 11 customers / product managers, 11 QA in our London office with a smaller team in South Africa) and the multiple products we have expanded our integration, testing and management procedures.

As in a standard XP shop developers run all the unit tests on their machine before copying changed files to an integration machine. The tests are run again before checking into the source repository, the results of which are also recorded in a central database. The files changed for each story are recorded, initially manually on integration sheets but now also in a central database. Builds are produced twice a day on separate machines and a second set of tests is run on the output. These functional tests consist of tests that take too long to run during integration or that involve gross or round trip behaviour. QA run their own sets of tests; acceptance tests are run when the story is first integrated, acceptance and regression tests are run on the output of the build machines.

We found a collection of story cards did not give sufficient information to manage the engineering process. Our solution was Bluesky, a browser based application acting as a virtual white board containing story cards. This is an electronic copy of all the information contained in the story cards together with additional information such as;

How far each story and task has progressed,
Initial and subsequent estimates for the story and tasks,
The product and build containing the integrated story,
Confirmation that the customer has seen the completed story,
Results from QA, both of the initial integration and from the final build.
The data contained in the Bluesky and auxiliary databases, together with the integration sheets, provided the information required by the ISO 9001 auditor to verify our compliance with the processes detailed in the engineering quality manual.

5   Bluesky – A Virtual White Board

	Story		Developer	Customer
	63.3 ST6333 - Toggle UI pane when redline on open should close redline		Chris Stevenson	Catherine Smith

IEst	E	D	A	R	CS	Build(s)	Status
0.50	0.50	0.50	0.00	0.00	Yes	4387	

Fig. 1. Bluesky, Top-level view summarising progress of each story

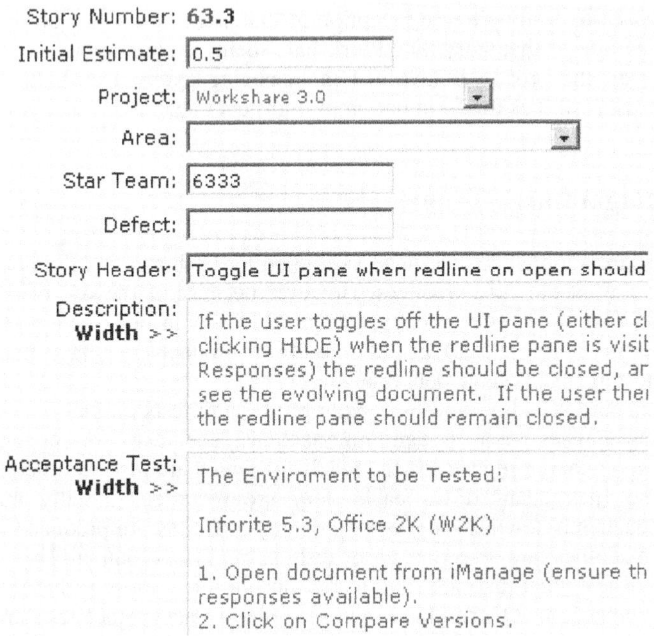

Story Number: **63.3**

Initial Estimate: 0.5

Project: Workshare 3.0

Area:

Star Team: 6333

Defect:

Story Header: Toggle UI pane when redline on open should

Description:
Width >> If the user toggles off the UI pane (either cl clicking HIDE) when the redline pane is visit Responses) the redline should be closed, ar see the evolving document. If the user thei the redline pane should remain closed.

Acceptance Test:
Width >> The Enviroment to be Tested:

Inforite 5.3, Office 2K (W2K)

1. Open document from iManage (ensure th responses available).
2. Click on Compare Versions.

Fig. 2. Bluesky, Individual story card including acceptance tests

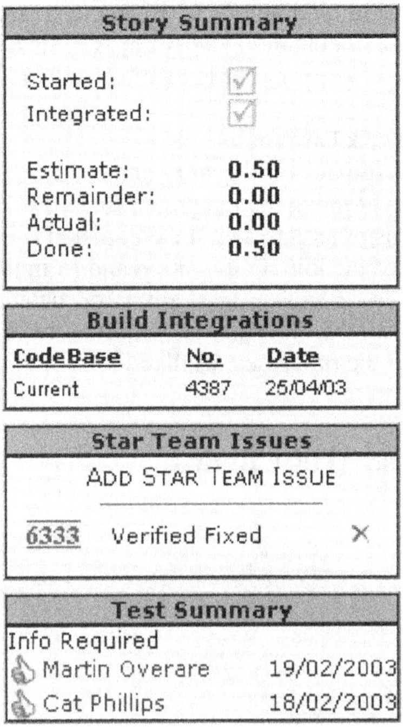

Story Summary

Started: ☑
Integrated: ☑

Estimate: **0.50**
Remainder: **0.00**
Actual: **0.00**
Done: **0.50**

Build Integrations

CodeBase	No.	Date
Current	4387	25/04/03

Star Team Issues

ADD STAR TEAM ISSUE

6333   Verified Fixed   ✕

Test Summary

Info Required
🖊 Martin Overare   19/02/2003
🖊 Cat Phillips   18/02/2003

Fig. 3. Bluesky, QA test results are included with story card

Description	Agent	Est	Act	Int
Add icons into starteams current view	Adam Creeger	0.10	0.10	✓
Add new link with description	Adam Creeger	0.10	0.10	✓
Add new icon	Adam Creeger	0.10	0.10	✓

Fig. 4. Bluesky, Task list is contained at the end of story card

6 Achieving ISO 9001 Certification

Workshare began preparing for ISO 9001 in March 2002 and was recommended for certification in February 2003. The company was required to appoint a process compliance manager and produce a company wide quality manual together with individual quality manuals for each department within the company. The company's quality policy explicitly stated our "commitment to developing high quality software applications is demonstrated by our adoption of innovative, agile methodologies".

In achieving certification no changes were made to our existing XP practices.

We documented our existing processes in the engineering departments quality manual and collected existing data from the databases described above to provide both key performance indicators and the basis for measuring improvements to those processes. The effort required for certification was that of preparing this documentation, a task undertaken by the our company's management, and had minimal impact on the day-to-day activities of the XP team.

Our existing data enabled the process to be tracked from initial presentation of a story, through the implementation of that story, to the verification that the implementation met customer requirements and resulted in no regression within the system as a whole. This fulfils the ISO 9001 requirement of monitoring and measuring the process. The same data also provides a target for enhancing quality, for instance by increasing the number of new tests associated with each task, improving the accuracy of story and task estimates or reducing the number of failures detected in QA. This fulfils the ISO 9001 requirement of continual improvement in the process.

Although for smaller XP teams the process at Workshare may appear overly formalised there are no reasons why less formal processes preclude certification. All XP development is story based and the sum of these stories forms the requirements specification for the system. All XP teams are test driven, auditors love tests and the recording of those tests provides the basis for verification that customer requirements have been met. All XP teams are based on pair programming which enhances quality through continuous code review. Continuous integration reduces the possibility of regression in a system. Any XP team is maximising the quality provided to its customers. All certification requires is the auditing of the benefits XP brings to software development.

7 Mapping XP to ISO 9001:2000

As described above achieving certification requires all the process in the company to comply with the standard. The development process itself must comply with section 7.3 of the ISO 9001:2000 standard [2], "Design and development". This ISO standard is terse and the good practice that meets this standard is detailed in the TickIT guide [3] of which Part F, Section 5 "Software quality management system requirements – primary life cycle processes" impacts directly on the day-to-day practice of XP.

Although the standard does not explicitly define a particular life cycle most compliance auditors will think in terms of, and the TickIT guide is implicitly structured in the form of the, waterfall model. However the guide also contains best practice for prototyping and iterative development, which provides a starting point for mapping XP practices to the standard.

Table 1. Examples of the mapping of ISO 90001 requirements to XP practices

ISO 9001	XP
7.3.2 Design and development inputs Inputs relating to product requirements shall be determined and records maintained. These inputs shall include functional and performance requirements …	Requirements are specified in customer stories and acceptance tests.
7.3.3 Design and development outputs The outputs of design and development shall be provided in a form that enables verification against design and development input and shall be approved prior to release.	Test first design both specifies design and verifies the implementation of that design. Tests are preserved forever and their results recorded. Release is dependent upon all the tests in the system running successfully.
7.3.4 Design and development review At suitable stages, systematic reviews of design and development shall be performed in accordance with planned arrangements.	Pair programming is continuous code review. Short iterations enable the customer to continual review functionality as it is developed.
7.3.5 Design and development verification Verification shall be performed in accordance with planned arrangements to ensure that the design and development outputs have met the design and development input requirements. Records of the results any necessary actions shall be maintained.	Acceptance tests detail customer requirements. "Acceptance tests allow the customer to know when the system works and tell the programmers what needs to be done" [6]. The success or failure of these tests is recorded. The verification by the customer that the story meets their requirements is recorded ("customer seen").
7.3.7 Control of design and development changes Design and development changes shall be identified and records maintained.	XP expects requirements and therefore design and implementation to change throughout a project. These changes are recorded in the stories contained in each iteration.

However it must be emphasised that mapping the XP, or any other Agile, process to more commonly understood lifecycles is not the prime requirement for gaining certification. Rather it is necessary to prove that the process is monitored, measured and continually improved. The examples below are provided to show that nothing explicit or implicit in the XP practices are incompatible with the ISO 9001 view of the software lifecycle.

Table 2. Examples of the mapping of TickIT primary life cycle process to XP practices

TickIT	XP
5.2 Supply Good practice is evident if records show that customer requirements are reviewed prior to commitment.	The fact that the customer has seen and approved the story prior to integration is recorded. The customer is in the same room as the developers and always available to discuss requirements.
Good practice involves agreeing customer expectations and involvement in the project.	The planning game ensures that the agreed functionality is delivered to customer at the end of the iteration.
5.3 Development Good practice involves having a clearly defined and documented life cycle.	XP clearly defines a set of practices that covers design, implementation and testing.
Good practice is evident if the eventual product is not rejected because some requirements were not identified.	Iteration planning ensures requirements are added incrementally and as agreed between customer and developers.
Good practice is evident if there is an agreed and controlled software requirements document, model, prototype or database.	Customer stories and acceptance tests fully define the software requirements.
Good practice involves defining applicable standards and conventions for software coding, documentation and testing.	A core XP practice is the coding standard. Test first design makes testing central to XP. Unit tests document the behaviour of the system.
Good practice involves preparing test plans and developing appropriate test data for each software component and combination.	Test first design means the tests always precede the implementation of any software.
Good practice involves having procedures and guidelines for system integration and testing.	Continuous integration with all test running on the integration machine avoids integration failures.
6.4 Verification Good practice involves ensuring code is testable, understandable and maintainable and conforms to relevant programming standards.	Pair programming is a continuous code review. Refactoring continuously improves maintainability. By definition test first design means code is testable.

8   Fulfilling More Stringent Certification Requirements

For certain sectors software, and the companies producing that software, must meet more stringent requirements than those of ISO 9001. For instance the pharmaceutical industry requires GAMP4 guidelines [7] to be followed. These differ from ISO 9001, amongst other factors, in requiring a more rigorous audit trail from customer requirements to changes in the code base. Again this is nothing inherent in XP that prevents such traceability. GAMP4 has stricter requirements regarding specification documentation and standard operating procedures but concedes that "there are acceptable methods other than those described in this guide that are capable of achieving the objective of adequately validated automated systems" [7, page 14]. To this end Workshare works with each client on a case-to-case basis to demonstrate that XP can be such a method when combined with ISO 9001 certification.

9   Conclusions

Formal certification is a requirement for certain types of software or for sales into areas such as the pharmaceutical industry. There is nothing inherent in XP that prevents companies from meeting certification standards such as ISO 9001. There is nothing inherent in the audit requirements of such standards that reduce the agility of those companies. The key factor in successful certification without a negative impact on agility is to base quality management on the natural outputs of the development process rather than on artefacts produced solely for audit purposes. The additional overhead for certification was that of producing the various quality manuals detailing our existing process. This was a management task and had little impact on the day-to-day work of the development team.

References

1. Workshare, http://www.workshare.com.
2. ANSI/ISO/ASQ Q9001–2000, American Society for Quality, Milwaukee (2000).
3. The TickIT Guide, British Standards Institute, London (2001).
4. IEEE/EIA 12270, Institute of Electrical and Electronic Engineers, New York (1998).
5. DSDM and TickIT, British Standards Institute and the DSDM Consortium, London (2001).
6. Jeffries, R., Anderson, A. and Hendrickson, C.: Extreme Programming Installed, Addison Wesley, Boston (2001) 31.
7. The Good Automated Manufacturing Practice (GAMP) Guide for Validation of Automated Systems in Pharmaceutical Manufacture, ISPE, Tampa (2001).

The Reflective Practitioner Perspective in eXtreme Programming

Orit Hazzan[1] and Jim Tomayko[2]

[1] Department of Education in Technology and Science, Technion – IIT
Haifa 32000, Israel
oritha@tx.technion.ac.il
[2] School of Computer Science, Carnegie Mellon University
Pittsburgh, PA, U.S.A.
jet@cs.cmu.edu

Abstract. This paper examines ways by which a reflective mode of thinking may improve eXtreme Programming (XP) practices. It describes the reflective practitioner perspective and suggests specific ways in which such an approach may be interwoven into XP practices. Specifically, the focus is placed on the construction of ladders of reflection. These ladders illustrate how one may increase the level of abstraction of his/her thinking when reflection is interwoven in the process of software development, and how such an experience may promote one's comprehension of the relevant development process.

Keywords: reflection, extreme programming, reflective practice, software engineering.

1 Introduction

This essay suggests adding a reflective practice (RP) perspective to eXtreme Programming (XP). Based on Donald Schön's work with educating professionals, it is suggested that as a reflective practitioner one may improve the performance of the XP practices. Generally speaking, the RP perspective, first introduced by Donald Schön [11, 12], guides professional practitioners (such as architects, managers, musicians and others) towards examining and rethinking their professional creations during and after the accomplishment of the process of creation. The working assumption is that such a reflection improves both proficiency and performance within such professions. Analysis of the field of Software Engineering (SE) and the kind of work that software engineers usually accomplish in general [10], and the XP practices in particular, support the adoption of the RP perspective to SE in general and to XP in particular. Specifically, it is suggested that a reflective mode of thinking may improve the application of some of the XP practices. This paper examines this possible contribution.

We present the main ideas behind the RP perspective, discuss the potential contribution of the RP perspective to XP, and, based on this analysis, suggest directions for future research.

F. Maurer and D. Wells (Eds.): XP/Agile Universe 2003, LNCS 2753, pp. 51–61, 2003.

2   Reflective Practice[1]

The two main books which present the Reflective Practice (RP) perspective are *The Reflective Practitioner* [11] and *Educating the Reflective Practitioner* [12]. While the first book presents professions for which reflective thinking is (or should be) inherent in, such as architecture and management, the second book focuses on how *to educate* students of such professions to be reflective practitioners. In this section we establish the rational for implementing the RP perspective to SE in general and to XP in particular.

In the two books mentioned above, Schön analyses the added advantages one may obtain from continuously examining one's practice and one's thinking about his/her practice. With respect to science and engineering, Schön says that "[b]etween 1963 and 1982 ... [i]ncreasingly we have become aware of the importance to actual practice of phenomena – complexity, uncertainty, instability, uniqueness, and value-conflict". ([11], p. 39). At that time, the Computer Science community observed a similar phenomenon with respect to developing software systems (Cf. the "Software Crisis" terminology introduced in 1968 at the NATO Conference in Garmish, Germany). Many at the conference recognized that software development should be guided by a professional-systematic approach. The mental complexity involved in developing software projects was acknowledged, and, as a result, there was tremendous awareness of the impossibility of managing software systems without systematic (engineering oriented) methods. However, though the complex nature of the profession of software development was known at the time when Schön wrote his books, he did not discuss the application of the RP perspective with respect to SE. Yet, the relevance of RP to SE in general and to XP in particular, is illustrated by the following three quotes taken from Schön's work.

The Subjects of Reflection:

> *When a practitioner reflects in and on his practice, the possible objects of his reflection are as varied as the kinds of phenomena before him and the systems of knowing-in-practice which he brings to them. He may reflect on the tacit norms and appreciations which underlie a judgment, or on the strategies and theories implicit in a pattern of behavior. He may reflect on the feeling for a situation which has led him to adopt a particular course of action, on the way in which he has framed the problem he is trying to solve, or on the role he has constructed for himself within a larger institutional context.* ([11], p. 62)

Laying out the topics which are possible subjects for reflection in SE, we may start with the actual creations (the software systems), going through a reflection on the way algorithms are developed and used in software systems, and moving on to skill-related topics such as development approaches, topics related to human-computer interaction, aspects of software development methodologies, ways of thinking, etc. In fact, it seems that we might end up with a rich object collection that can be subjects of thought. It might be the result of the fact that "[m]any of the things we make with software today are more complex than most buildings and, as in building design,

---

[1] This section is largely based on Hazzan ([5]).

software design embraces many aspects: function, safety, human interface, ergonomics, graphics, algorithms, data structure, program structure, protocol, and application interface, among others." [14]. If we limit the discussion to XP practices, we may suggest the following objects for reflection: the way unit-tests are developed, how a specific simple design was determined, how a specific path of refactoring emerged, etc.

Listening to the Code:

> *In the designer's conversation with the material of his design, he can never make a move which has only the effects intended for it. His materials are continually talking back to him, causing him to apprehend unanticipated problems and potentials. As he appreciates such new and unexpected phenomena, he also evaluates the moves that have created them.* ([11], p. 100-101)

The analogy to SE with respect to this topic seems to be trivial [10]. When one develops a software system, one actually is in an ongoing conversation with the creation. In fact, several aspects of software systems are shaped in an ongoing interaction with the computer as a mediator that reflects to the software developer how far away s/he is from what s/he wants to achieve. In other words, the computer is the medium through which a software constructor talks to his/her creation – the software system. Within the XP framework, this kind of interaction with the material is especially dominant in the process of unit-testing and in refactoring processes that interweave on-going testing.

The Ladder of Reflection:

> *We can [...] introduce another dimension of analysis* [for the chain of reciprocal actions and reflections that make up the dialogue of student and coach in the architecture studio]. *We can begin with a straightforward map of interventions and responses, a vertical dimension according to which higher levels of activity are "meta" to those below. To move "up", in this sense, is to move from an activity to reflection on that activity; to move "down" is to move from reflection to an action that enacts reflection. The levels of action and reflection on action can be seen as the rungs of a ladder. Climbing up the ladder, one makes what has happened at the rung below an object of reflection.* ([12], p.114)

The ladder of reflection described in this quote refers to student-tutor dialogue in the architecture studio. Hazzan ([5]) expands the ladder of reflection presented by Schön to a student-coach dialogue in a software studio and with respect to an individual work. The idea in both cases is to illustrate how one may increase the level of abstraction of one's thinking when reflection is interwoven in software development. In the continuation of this paper a ladder of reflection is presented with respect to a pair programming session, a planning game session and a refactoring process. These cases illustrate how a ladder of reflection may promote one's comprehension of the relevant development process and may lead to insights that eventually may save time and money.

3   Reflective Practice in eXtreme Programming Practices Card

This section illustrates how a RP perspective may support and improve the application of the XP practices. First we explain the fitness of RP to XP. Then, the potential contribution of the RP perspective to each of the XP practices is examined.

It seems that a RP approach fits very well to XP, since XP emphasizes learning through reflection processes. For example, the estimation of the team's velocity is improved from project to project based on a reflective process; when a pair is engaged in a pair programming session, the navigator reflects on the drivers' coding. Thus, it seems that one of the implicit XP guidelines is reflection. Still, as far as we know, it is not outlined inherently in the practices themselves. Similarly to some of the XP practices, RP is not explicitly directed to code production but in the long term it may improve code production and quality. As XP incorporates activities that are not directly oriented to code production, yet may improve code development processes, we suggest that the RP perspective may be integrated naturally in XP.

This work follows other publications that emphasize the importance of reflection and retrospective in the context of software development in general and with respect to agile methods in particular (such as [6] and [2] respectively). We propose that our contribution is in the introduction of a reflective perspective into each of the XP practices by the construction of ladders of reflection that guide software developers to think on higher levels of abstraction.

In the discussion that follows, the XP practices are gathered in three groups, according to the subject they focus on: the team, the customer and the code. We do not claim that each practice focuses only on one of these three subjects. However, it seems that each of the XP practices influences significantly one subject out of these three.

Team	Customer	Code
Pair programming *	Customer on-site	Testing
40-hour week	Planning game *	Continuous integration
Collective ownership	Small releases	Coding standards
Metaphor		Refactoring *
		Simple design

The role of the RP perspective is discussed in depth only with respect to one practice in each group (marked with *). That is, the focus is placed on pair programming, planning game, and refactoring. Specifically, in order to illustrate the potential contribution of a RP approach to software development that is guided by XP, we demonstrate a ladder of reflection for these three practices. We hope that, where possible, this illustration clarifies how the RP perspective may benefit the other practices in each category.

In the description that follows, it is assumed that readers are familiar with the XP practices [1].

3.1   Team

It seems that the RP perspective fits well to parts of this group of practices. The rationale behind this assumption is that a reflective mode of thinking improves the comprehension of one's own thinking as well as of others' ways of thinking. As software development in general, and software development guided by XP in particular, are based on team interaction, it is reasonable to assume that the more one is aware of mental processes and ways of thinking (of oneself or of the others), the more the teamwork is improved. In what follows the focus is placed on pair programming. The contribution of the RP perspective to the other XP practices that focus on the team is described briefly.

Pair Programming: This practice is one of the more discussed XP practices (cf. [15]). This practice should be applied firmly. In other words, "[a]ll production code is written with two programmers at one machine". [1]. Benefits of this practice are presented in many research reports (cf. [9, 13]).

This practice specifies that any piece of code should be written by two developers, each of whom has a different role: the one with the keyboard and the mouse thinks about the best way to implement a specific task; the other partner thinks more strategically. As the two individuals in the pair think at different levels of abstraction, the same task is thought about at two different levels of abstraction *at the same time*.

In what follows we illustrates how a reflective mode of thinking may be introduced into the practice of pair programming. The illustration is based on the construction of a ladder of reflection during a pair programming session (see Table 1). The idea is to illustrate how a pair of programmers may increase the abstraction level of its thinking when reflection is interwoven within the process of software development.

Table 1. A ladder of reflection: The case of pair programming

Ladder rungs	Pair dialogue
Designing *[a process of reflection-in-action]*	A: Did we consider all the exceptions?
Description of designing *[it takes the form of description with: appreciations, advice, criticism, etc.]*	B: Good question. Let's think about the best way to search for exceptions. I'm trying to understand what to think about when I'm looking for potential exceptions.
Reflection on description of designing *[reflection on the meaning the other has constructed for a description he or she has given]*	A: I think that this is not such a simple task. I have never thought about such systematic ways to look for exceptions. OK. Let's give it some thought. *[Working on formulating a systematic way for finding exceptions]*
Reflection on reflection on description of designing *[the parties to the dialogue reflect on the dialogue itself]*	B: Now that we have developed a systematic way for finding exceptions, I think we must analyze these strategies and reflect on the path that led us to finding these guidelines. A: Yes, this may improve our ability to solve problems of a similar nature in the future.

Looking at the various rows of Table 1, one may find that the subjects of reflection on each rung are objects of different levels of abstraction: While detailed elements are the focus on the first rung, ways of thinking are at the center of attention on the fourth rung.

Sustainable Pace: A reflective mode of thinking can be interwoven even in this simple-for-implementation XP practice. The working framework that this practice establishes enables one to detach oneself from the details involved in software development and, if one wishes, to reflect on what had happened during the day, without being swamped with details for long hours every day.

Collective Ownership: As the code is accessible to more minds, programmers must examine code that is written by others. Thus, they have to reflect and consider what reasons lead to specific decisions that their friends took while programming. In addition, when reviewing code that others wrote, developers may improve their understanding of their own code and its interface to the rest of the code.

Metaphor: The common use of metaphors is to bridge between a known domain and an unfamiliar domain. While thinking about an appropriate metaphor, developers must expand their perspective and analysis of the developed application. It is suggested that a RP perspective may improve developers' performance in looking for an appropriate metaphor.

3.2 Customer

The literature is full of evidence of crises in software development processes. In many cases these crises result from some misunderstanding or other between clients and software developers. In other words, the client's needs and requirements are misunderstood, and as a result, the software system does not satisfy customer's needs. The following data illustrate this phenomenon: "Three quarters of all large software products delivered to the customer are failures that are either not used at all, or do not meet the customer's requirements." [8]. Thus, addressing customers' ways of thinking is fundamental from the SE point of view. We suggest that a reflective mode of thinking like the one suggested by the RP perspective, may improve one's ability to understand the conceptions held by others in general and customer's needs in particular. The idea is that two processes occur simultaneously: A person improves his/her thinking about his/her mental processes; as the latter takes place, the person's understanding of his/her interaction with the environment is improved.

On-Site Customer: In the case of software development that is guided by XP, the customer is part of the development environment. As the customer is on-site for answering questions, it is suggested that when both customer and developers are guided by a reflective mode of thinking, developers, as well as customers, may improve their understanding of the developed application. This can happen, for example, when after some issue is clarified, the customer and the developers will reflect on their current understanding of the application vs. the one that preceded it.

Planning Game: One of the significant advantages of the planning game is that both the customer and the entire team participate in it, and thus all know the development process. Furthermore, guidelines that lead to decisions with respect to a specific release or iteration are clear to all. We take advantage of this fact and show how the fact that the customer and team define together the next release/iteration makes it possible to introduce a reflective mode of thinking. Table 2 presents a ladder of reflection which illustrates how this might happen.

As can be observed, the customer improves her understanding throughout the planning game scenario described in Table 2. In fact, she got her insight only when she was asked to reflect about similar situations in the past in which she needed similar features. It is not argued that hadn't she asked to reflect on past experiences she would not have recalled such cases. However, it is plausible to assume that this insight would have arrived later (maybe only after an inappropriate feature would have been developed). As can be observed, the team also improved its communal understanding with respect to decision-making processes and guidance of customers in describing their needs. The contribution of such lessons to software development processes is clear.

Small Releases: Beck [1] tells us to "[p]ut a simple system into production quickly, then release new versions on a very short cycle." Such an experiment invites a reflective mode of thinking very naturally. In fact, the small releases are introduced to let developers re-examine their progress in small cycles. We suggest that the use of a RP perspective on those small releases may even strengthen the risk management that results from keeping the releases small. Specifically, we suggest that the question to be answered usually - "Does this release carry us toward the eventual goals of the project?" - can be answered more easily by a RP approach.

3.3   Code

Based on arguments that address architectural creations, it is suggested that the reflective perspective may improve the application of those XP practices that concern with the code: testing, refactoring, simple design, continuous integration and coding standards. In this argument the code is viewed as the analogical object to the architectural creation, for which the RP perspective has been developed originally. Thus, as a RP perspective may improve the creation of the architectural creations, it is suggested that the application of a RP perspective in those XP practices that deal with the code, may improve the code. Specifically, if a reflective mode of thinking is interwoven into each of these practices, the team may improve the code it produces and the result would be a code that is more correct, more readable and easier for future maintenance.

Refactoring: In our opinion, as this practice is so similar to process of re-design in the case of architectural creation, it may be largely benefited from the RP perspective. Table 3 illustrates a ladder of reflection in the case of refactoring. The dialogue here is conducted during a refactoring session in which a pair of programmers changes a procedural design to an object oriented design (cf. [3]).

We expand the discussion of the application of a RP in refactoring by quoting Kent (in [3]): "[Refactoring] is like a new kind of relationship with your program. When

Table 2. A ladder of reflection: A planning game session

Ladder rungs	A conversation during a planning game session
Designing *[a process of reflection-in-action]*	Customer: In fact, I want this feature to behave this way *[moves her hands to illustrate]*. Developer 1: Can you think about a similar feature you needed before?
Description of designing *[it takes the form of description with: appreciations, advice, criticism, etc.]*	Customer: What do you mean? Would you like me to think about a similar case in the past in which I wanted a similar feature? Interesting. I have never been asked to do something like this before. But yes, I can think about a situation in the past when we needed a new system for our inventory management. I wanted the application to have this feature and only when we received the system I realized that, in fact, what we need is something else, more ... *[illustrates with her hands]*. Let's call it B. Wow! Does that mean that we should not have at all the feature I described before?
Reflection on description of designing *[reflection on the meaning the other has constructed for a description he or she has given]*	Developer 2: We do not know. We can check the two options. But, can you please recall, what, in the case you just mentioned, led you at the end to realize that what you need is B, and why you didn't (or couldn't) realize this before, I mean, before you got the system and started working with it. Customer: Truly, the problem was that we did not consider the full setting in which the system would work. I think that we should consider the same issue now, before I make the final decision. *[The customer and the developers think about the way the application will be used, focusing on the specific considerations that were neglected in the customer's previous experience. At the end they decided about a third option that should be applied for these specific circumstances.]*
Reflection on reflection on description of designing *[the parties to the dialogue reflect on the dialogue itself]*	Customer: It's amazing. I must trace with you the full path we went through together. *[The customer and developers dedicate the next 15 minutes for this purpose].* Customer: I do not want even to think about the catastrophe that could have happened if you develop one of the first two options we talked about. I must learn the lesson. First of all, I'd like to apologize for my resistance to take part in the planning game. I must confess that only now I understand how I should manage the all business with the new application. Tracker: I think we also learnt something from this experience. First, we should not be afraid to ask our customers difficult questions and to insist on getting answers. Second, the specific circumstances you introduced us to may be useful in our future projects. Finally, we should remember that before making final decisions and moving on, sometimes it is worth checking whether we consider all options. I believe that eventually, even if we stay with the first option, this would not be considered a waste of time.

Table 3. A ladder of reflection: A refactoring session

Ladder rungs	A dialogue during a refactoring session
Designing *[a process of reflection-in-action]*	Developers 1: We were told that the system was originally developed by a procedural approach. Right? Developer 2: Yes. Developer 1: And we should change it to OO. Developer 2: Ya. Developer 1: I heard about Fowler's book that explains very precisely how to do it. *[Worked according to Fowler's book ([3]) and changed the design. All the tests passed.]*
Description of designing *[it takes the form of description with: appreciations, advice, criticism, etc.]*	Developer 2: Let's think what we have done. Developer 1: Why? We already did it and all the tests passed. Developer 2: Yes, but we should get something out of all this work, beyond the code. Some wisdom that will help us in future development. I'm sure that there is some wisdom in such processes that is beyond the actual change of the code. Developer 1: OK. Let's try to identify the moment when each of us realized what we are doing; I mean, when we really understand what the purpose of all this change is.
Reflection on description of designing *[reflection on the meaning the other has constructed for a description he or she has given]*	Developer 1: If I have to indicate the moment I understood why all this work is worth something, I would say that it was the moment I realized that there are methods different than set or get methods. When we started typing `public Boolean isFull` I got it. Developer 2: So, can we decide that in the future, before we start working on a task of this kind, we will check first whether there are methods different than set and get? You know what, let's try it for what Joe just asked me to check. *[Checked and realized that in this case it would not be worth to dedicate the 5 hours needed for such a change. Moved to their next task].*
Reflection on reflection on description of designing *[the parties to the dialogue reflect on the dialogue itself]*	Developer 1: Let's adopt it as our habit-of-mind when such tasks come up. I think that if we had known this lesson before we started all this stuff, we could improve our work and make it more productive, not to mention all the hours that we could save.

you really understand refactoring, the design of the system is as fluid and plastic and moldable to you as the individual characters in a source code file. You can feel the whole design at once. You can see how it might flex and change – a little this way and this is possible, a little that way and that is possible." (p. 410). This quote is chosen as its spirit is similar to the way artists talk about their creation process. Possible conclusion would be that if refactoring is similar to one aspect of artistic creation processes, and if the later find the RP approach helpful, software developers may introduce a RP perspective into development processes in general and into refactoring sessions in particular. Needless to say that many computer scientists view software development like art. From reasons of space limitation we quote here only Knuth who says, with respect to the artistic nature of programming, that "[t]he process of preparing programs for a digital computer is especially attractive because it not only *can be economically and scientifically rewarding, it can also be an aesthetic experience much like composing poetry or music.* ([7], p. V).

Testing: Beck defines the practice of testing as follows: "Programmers continually write unit tests, which must run flawlessly for development to continue. Customers write tests demonstrating that features are finished." We add and say: "Reflect on how you test and on what you learn from it and improve your understanding of testing processes".

Simple Design: Rasmusson ([9]) says that "[i]f simplicity is the destination, refactoring is the vehicle for getting us there." Based on the above illustration, it is clear how a RP approach may support this practice. In fact, the source of RP is in examining design processes. Specifically, a reflective mode of thinking may improve developers' understanding of what simple design consists of.

Continuous Integration: If one reflects of the integration process, his or her understanding of the code may be improved. Again, similarly to the case of Small Releases, a reflection on the continuing goals of the project helps determine how close integration is to the completion of the software.

Coding Standards: The RP perspective in this case may be expressed by the way a team chooses/develops its coding standard. After all, according to the XP's attitude of "they're just rules", "[t]hey are the rules that the team embraces" (look at Jeffries's essays *"They're just rules!"*, http://www.xprogramming.com/Practices/justrule.htm). The coding standards can be formulated based on a reflective process in which the team establishes the standards that fit its own communication style. After these conventions are set, a reflection may be helpful in cases where a particular convention seems not to achieve its targets: a reflective mode of thinking may help in understanding the source of this mismatch.

4   Conclusion

In this article we suggest to add the practice of reflection to XP practices. It is argued that a reflective mode of thinking may improve software developers' understanding of their own (and their teammates) ways of thinking and, as a result, they may improve both the way they develop software and their understanding of the development environment. In our opinion, a reflective mode of thinking is especially suited to the community of XP since XP encourages collective knowledge which, in one way or another, forces software developers to understand the other person's ways of thinking. Such a reflective mode of thinking may also solve such problems as the following, suggested by Glass ([4]) in the context of the industry/academia communication chasm: "Industrial people tend to reinvent the same ad hoc wheel they invented last year, and not even remove any of the flat spots". (p. 13). It is suggested that practitioners' reflection on the way they solve problems (when conducted on a regular basis) may help in real-life situations.

The focus in this paper is placed of constructing ladders of reflection and on how they may improve software development processes. Our suggestion is to explore specific ways (or maybe even, procedure) for making reflection an integral part of XP both in the industry and in the academia. In the academia a reflective practice perspective can be integrated naturally into software engineering programs which include students' software projects that are developed by XP. It is suggested to add activities which induce students to reflect on the way they develop software systems. Within the scope of students' projects, such tasks can be offered to students in different activities such as design, coding, and testing.

References

1. Beck, K. (2000). Extreme Programming Explained: Embrace Change. Addison-Wesley.
2. Cockburn, A. (2001). Agile Software Development, Addison-Wesley.
3. Fowler, M., Beck, B. (Contributor), Brant, J. (Contributor), Opdyke, W. and Roberts, D. (2002). Refactoring: Improving the Design of Existing Code, Addison-Wesley.
4. Glass, R. L. (1997). Revisiting the industry/academe communication chasm, Communication of the ACM 40(7), pp. 11–13.
5. Hazzan, O. (2002). The reflective practitioner perspective in software engineering education, The Journal of Systems and Software, 63(3), pp. 161–171.
6. Kerth, N. L. (2001). Project Retrospectives: A Handbook for Team Reviews, Dorset House.
7. Knuth, D. E. (1969, 2nd Printing). The Art of Computer Programming. Addison-Wesley.
8. Mullet, D. (July, 1999). The Software Crisis, Benchmarks Online - a monthly publication of Academic Computing Services, a division of the University of North Texas Computing Center 2(7), http://www.unt.edu/benchmarks/archives/1999/july99/crisis.htm.
9. Rasmusson, J. (2002). Strategies for introducing XP to new client sites, Proceedings of the XP/Agile Universe 2002, LNCS 2418, pp. 45–51.
10. Schön, D. A. interviewed by John Bennent (1996). Reflective conversation with materials. Terry Winograd, Bringing Design to Software, Addison-Wesley, pp. 171–184.
11. Schön, D. A. (1983). The Reflective Practitioner, BasicBooks.
12. Schön, D. (1987). Educating the Reflective Practitioner: Towards a New Design for Teaching and Learning in The Profession, San Francisco: Jossey-Bass.
13. Shukla, A. and Williams, L. (2002). Adapting Extreme Programming for a core software engineering course, Proceedings of Conference of Software Engineering Education and Training - CSEE&T 2002, pp. 184–191.
14. Singer, A. (1994). Towards a definition of software design, Design+Software - The ASD Newsletter, http://www-pcd.stanford.edu/asd/info/articles/definition.html.
15. Williams, L. A., Kessler, R. R. (2000). All I really need to know about pair programming I learned in the kindergarten. Communications of the ACM 43 (5), pp. 108–114.

Graph Theoretical Indicators and Refactoring

J Adrian Zimmer

`azimmer@ossm.edu`

Abstract. Metrics of software quality grow stale after a while and there is always a need for new ones. Graph theory can be a fruitful source. We discuss how. Before that we discuss what metrics do and we suggest the word "indicator" better describes that function than the word "metric".

Keywords: software metrics, indicators, graph theory, circuits, XP, extreme programming, refactoring, restructuring, quality assurance, object-oriented design, ood, coupling, cohesion, management, software engineering, software maintenance, software quality, UML

1 Introduction

Kent Beck calls metrics "the basic XP management tool" [4]. Managers want metrics so they can make objective assessments of software quality or programmer performance. Programmers are not fond of them because they never measure quality or work done with much precision. Both managers and programmers know that the more a manager uses a metric, the more the desire for good numbers will distort the outcome. As Beck says, "Metrics tend to go stale over time." [5]. A stale metric should be retired for a while in favor of a fresh one. This implies a continuing need for new metrics.

This paper concerns metrics of software quality created with graph theoretical models. Graph theoretical models have long been a source of quality metrics. See, for example, [17]. Four models are described here. Each of them is capable of providing multiple metrics but only in the case of the most familiar model is that done here.

It cannot be overemphasized that we are not searching for silver bullets. The very word "metric" implies something that is probably beyond our reach. "Indicator" is a better word. Indicators can point to places where there may be potential problems; they cannot be relied on to measure the extent to which a problem exists. When an indicator shows a better value for software artifact A than it does for software artifact B, there is reason to look at B to see if it is deficient but there is not reason to conclude that A's quality has been proven to be better.

Some purposes to which indicators have been put are:

- To find places in a software system that *may* benefit from refactoring.
- To encourage programmers to watch out for *certain kinds* of complexity.
- To *help* determine whether a software system is of sufficient quality to be considered "finished".

This list is not meant to be exhaustive. It *is* meant to be limited to usages in which an indicator points to a potential problem as opposed to usages in which an indicator is supposed to identify a real problem.

F. Maurer and D. Wells (Eds.): XP/Agile Universe 2003, LNCS 2753, pp. 62–72, 2003.

Although indicators (hyped as metrics) have been available for decades, our understanding of them is pretty much in its infancy. One influential paper of the 90's [6], for example, offers some empirical justification that is little more than showing the indicators can be calculated on real software and, then, speculating on what the results might mean. Since the speculation is done in terms of the viewpoints supporting the indicators, not much is added by doing it.

With or without empirical justification, we need plenty of indicators so that managers who are using indicators now can switch indicators when their staffs become too good at playing the numbers game with the current indicators. This paper suggests some plausible new indicators and explains the use of graph theory for the nonspecialist. As compared with the indicators in [6], the rationales for these indicators are oriented less towards existing and potential reuse and more towards readability, complexity, and cohesiveness.

I am *not* advocating that empirical research on indicators be dropped. There have been research designs in the past that seem to provide real information about what works. For example, one can say "My indicator says version A has better quality than version B of this program. I will test this by setting programmers to simple maintenance tasks on both versions and see how they do." This approach raises its own experimental design issues as well as some issues of how well we can measure maintenance productivity. However, even if these issues are not completely solved, this approach provides better evidence of the effectiveness of an indicator (or at least of a suite of indicators) than simply discussing what the indicator has said in terms of prior expectations for its use.

Today, some protection against the inaccuracy of indicators may be had by employing a suite of indicators in the hope that they will tend to cancel out each other's errors. For now, our best defense against the misuse of indicators seems to be to educate practitioners in the thinking behind them.

1.1 A Subjective Note on Refactoring

My first reaction to a seemingly intractable bug has always been "this code is too complicated". Since I am not particularly good at debugging, I have spent more time refactoring than most. For me, rewriting code to achieve simplicity removes bugs.

I tend to be concerned with one rather ambiguous kind of simplicity: the number of different concepts I have to juggle at once. When I have to juggle too many concepts it raises a *too many eggs* warning for me.

This too many eggs warning is related to a concept described in the fifties by a psychologist, G. A. Miller in a paper titled "The Magic Number Seven Plus or Minus Two" [18]. Miller made a strong case that the human mind has difficulty keeping track of over approximately seven qualitatively different things at one time. Papers on classical software engineering picked this idea up as evidence of what we all know: the more concepts a programmer has to juggle at once, the more something is likely to fall and make a mess.

Deciding that there are too many eggs to juggle at once is quite subjective. What counts as an egg? What does "at once" mean when applied to an activity that takes hours or sometimes much longer? I do not always know the answers to these questions but, even so. the too many eggs concept helps me to refactor in a positive direction.

When not concerned with juggling eggs, I tend to be concerned with classes (or before that with modules). Following Constantine, Stevens, and Myers [7], I want classes to have tight cohesion and loose coupling.

In "Restructuring for Style" [21], I replaced the concepts of cohesion and coupling with a less subjective concept of data cobweb. That notion is revisited below in the section titled "Data Cobweb Graph".

A data cobweb was said to exist between any two objects that were referenced in the same statement. To achieve a refactoring of an example program, I searched for sets of objects that could be organized into a single instance class, which I called an "object-module". I started with a kind of protoclass whose state had lots of data cobwebs within it and few data cobwebs connecting it the rest of the program state.

Another way I tried to ensure cohesiveness was to guide my refactoring not only by data cobwebs but also by my ability to write simple invariants for the protoclass's state. This goal has worked very well for me from time to time. It is not discussed further in this paper. The techniques of this paper are not suitable for working with invariants.

"Restructuring for Style" showed, by example, how data cobwebs and clean invariants could be used to refactor a program by creating a protoclass and then a single instance class. The example program had been analyzed previously in the literature [3] with a proof of correctness. As evidence that the refactored program was easier to understand than the original, I pointed out a small bug that the proof of correctness had missed.

1.2 Fowler's Guidelines for Refactoring

In his book *Refactoring, Improving the Design of Code* [10], Martin Fowler lists lots of refactoring techniques. To help readers know when to refactor, one chapter, cowritten with Kent Beck, lists some warnings of code problems called *bad smells* [11]. A couple of these smells are mentioned here because they help explain some of this paper's indicators.

One smell comes from class data members that are insufficiently related to each other. Fowler and Beck say that data comes in clumps and that insufficiently clumped data members are a warning that a class is not sufficiently cohesive. Clumping can be detected [12] by "deleting one of the data values" and asking whether "the others make any sense?" If the remaining data values still make sense, the data is not clumped.

Data clumping, like data cobwebs, is a concept to help discover cohesiveness. Data clumping looks at the semantics of a program and data cobwebs look at the structure of a program.

A second smell is that of feature envy [13]. Feature envy exists when there is "a method that seems more interested in a class other than the one it actually is in." He suggests that such a method is envious of the features in another class. This envy is evidenced structurally when the envious method call a lot of methods of the class it is envious of. The method call graph, defined below, can help discover some cases of feature envy.

A final smell of interest here is what Fowler and Beck call a data class [14]. "Such classes are dumb data holders and are almost certainly being manipulated in far too much detail by other classes." The manipulating classes, of course, show feature envy. Another function of the data cobwebs graph will be seen to help discover data classes and thus some more cases of feature envy.

2   Some Graph Theoretical Models and Quality Indicators

Four graph theoretical models of source code are presented here. The first is over a quarter of a century old. The second is just a UML diagram that shows a dependency relationship between classes. Graphical models three and four seem to be new.

2.1   Control Flow Graph

In the oldest of these graphical models, nodes are program statements and a node v is joined to a node u by an edge incase it is possible for control to flow from v to u. This graph is directed. Call it a *control flow graph.* Declarative statements are not nodes.
   As an example, here is some code in which the statements have been given labels.

```
A for I in range(0,len(V)-1):
B IMAX = 0
C for J in range(I+1,len(V)):
D if V[IMAX] < V[J]:
E IMAX = J
F swap(V,I,IMAX)
```

and here is its control flow graph.

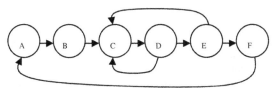

Forgetting the directions on the edges of a control flow graph permits something called the *cyclomatic number* to be calculated. The cyclomatic number is the number of nodes minus the number of edges plus the number of connected components. In a program with just one entry point and no dead code there will be just one connected component. The cyclomatic number in the above example is 3. Roughly speaking, the cyclomatic number counts the number of loops and conditional statements you have in your code.[1]
   The cyclomatic number is a traditional measure of complexity. Smaller values indicate a less complicated control flow. If you can accomplish a task with less complexity, your code is assumed to have higher quality.

---

[1] There is a bit more: cyclomatic numbers are the size of a basis of a vector space whose minimally dependent sets are isomorphic to circuits in the graph. This vector space interpretation seems to imply that the cyclomatic number helps describe the complexity of loops in a program's control flow. This conclusion is not particularly true because to get to the vector space the control flow graph had to have the directions on its edges forgotten.

2.2 Class Uses Graph

Our second graphical model is the *class uses graph*. The class uses graph arises directly from UML's dependency relationship [15]. Nodes are classes. An edge joins a node v to a node u in case v depends on u. "Depends" is defined as "changes to one element [class] may cause changes to the other". The uses graph is directed.

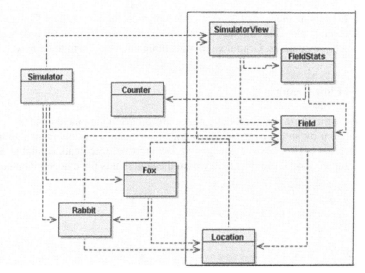

The example shown above is a UML class dependency graph taken from the BlueJ IDE which was loaded with a teaching example that comes with the book *Objects First with Java* [2] by the creators of BlueJ. To create an example of a directed circuit in a class uses graph, an arrow has been added from Location to SimulatorView. This arrow made the design look less clean. That was intentional.

The design does not use inheritance because it is the first of two examples showing the advantage of abstract superclasses. In the second example, an abstract Animal class is created and made the superclass of Fox and Rabbit. See the section on "Inheritance" below for a discussion on what effect the inclusion of an Animal class could have on the class uses graph.

You can imagine for yourself what the class uses graph for this example looks like. Simply replace the class boxes with node circles and fill in the dotted lines to become graph edges.

A programmer who is working on a class C must keep in mind all the classes on which depends. This number is C's out-degree in the class uses graph. When this out-degree gets too large, we have a warning of too many eggs to juggle while thinking about C.

The *class context* indicator is the largest out-degree in the class uses graph. For this example, it is 4 because the Simulator class has out-degree 4 and no other class has a larger out-degree.

Software systems are easier to understand and describe when they can be partitioned into layers. Done right, layering helps to limit the number of eggs one must juggle at one time. It also enables some parts of systems to be built before others.

The virtues of layering hold not only for software systems but also for the class hierarchies of software systems. If a class depends on another, which itself depends on another, and so on and if the original class is reached again in this dependency chairn, then the classes involved cannot go into different layers.

Such circular dependencies are called directed circuits. In object-oriented designs, directed circuits seem inevitable. Too many, however, is not a good thing. Graph theory has a concept for a set of nodes such that any two of them can be found in a circuit. The nodes make up a *strongly connected component*.

In the example above, the part of the graph inside the box on the right is the largest strongly connected component of the graph. Each node not in the box is a strongly connected component of its own.

The *entanglement indicator* is the maximum number of classes in a strongly connected component of the class uses graph. Large values of the entanglement indicator indicate too many classes are entangled.

The entanglement indicator for the Fox and Rabbit example is 4. Before I changed the class structure, there were no directed circuits and so each strongly connected component had size 1. A class uses graph with an entanglement indictor of 1 is a tree which is the best possible structure as far as this indicator is concerned.

Although the class uses graph is nothing new, the entanglement indicator seems to be. One of the points of this paper is that any investment in a tool to create a graphical model can be amortized over multiple indicators.

2.3 Data Cobweb Graph

The data cobweb graph was mentioned above. In this paper, its nodes are data fields in a single class. Two nodes are joined by an edge if a method of the class references of both of them. The resulting graph is undirected.

Consider the following code:

```
class DataClass {
  private int a;
  private int b;
  public int getA() { return a; }
  public int getB() { return b; }
  public int setA(x) { a = x; }
  public int setB(x) { b = x; }
}
```

Since no method references both a and b, the data cobweb graph looks like this:

Given any class C, the shortest path between data fields u and v in the data cobweb graph of C represents the least number of methods of C which must be invoked before a change can propagate from one of u and v to the other. [2]

---

[2] Well, at least, the least number of methods within that class. If a smaller number of methods is possible outside the class, we may still question the cohesiveness of the class itself.

The *cobweb length* indicator is the length of the longest shortest path in the data cobweb graph. The higher the cobweb length indicator is, the more you have two data fields that are not clumped together. For the example shown above, the cobweb length is infinity which is as bad as it gets. This happens for what Fowler and Beck call the data class smell.

2.4 Method Call Graph

A fourth graph theoretical model is the *method call graph*. Its nodes are methods. The methods are partitioned by the classes they belong to. An edge joins a method u to a method v incase u and v are not in the same class and u calls v. The resulting graph is directed.

Consider this code:

```
class Student {
 public void f() {}
 public void g() {}
 public void h() {}
}

class History {
 public void act(Student s) { s.f(); s.g(); s.h(); }
}

class English {
 public void act(Student s) { s.h(); }
}
```

The method call graph for this code is:

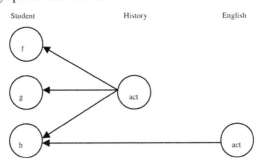

The method call graph has enough information to help ferret out some cases of feature envy. Making use of this information provides an example of how indicators are constrained by the fact that graphical models only view structural information.

Notice that the method History.act() calls a lot of methods from a different class Student. That might be due to feature envy and it might be because Student was designed to have its methods called a lot. The class DataClass above was designed to have its methods called a lot and that was a bad thing. It is not always a bad thing. A vector class, for example, is designed to have its methods called a lot and that is a good thing.

Thus the simple application of the method call graph can be expected to cry "feature envy" too often. We can fix this by considering more structure but at the expense of letting some instances of feature envy escape our scrutiny.

The additional structure we want to look at is the way other methods use the class whose features might be the subject of envy: instead of merely looking at the fact that History.act() calls lots of methods of Student, we will also consider the fact that no other class calls all those methods. This means History.act() is delving into what every other class considers to be Student's business. The reason is likely to be feature envy.

More precisely, the feature envy indicator of a software system is the highest feature envy *number* for any method u and class D where u does not belong to D. The *feature envy number* for u and D is found by looking at all the edges from u to methods of D and counting those which are incident only to u.

In the example system, the highest feature number of 2 is found for the method History.act() and the class Student. To see why this feature number is 2 notice that methods Student.f() and Student.g() are called only by History.act().

3 Making It Work

The indicators given in the previous section can all be calculated from their various graphs. The graphs themselves, however, can only be created under certain assumptions.

Necessary assumptions include things like no function creating functions, no pointers, nothing like Java's reflection, etc. Static type checking for everything except subtypes seems to be necessary as well. However that may be, parsing code and creating graphical models is beyond the scope of this paper. One source of information is [16] which describes the Borland tool set. The indicators which that tool set will calculate are based largely on the indicators described in [6] but they do include the cyclomatic number as well.

As for calculating the indicators of this paper from their various graphical models, it is easy to count nodes, edges, and out-degrees. Two of the indicators involve more. The entanglement indicator requires that a strongly connected component be found. See [1] for a method to do that. The cobweb length indicator requires that all the shortest paths of the cobweb graph be found. See [8] for a method to do that.

3.1 Inheritance

Indicators concerning the quality of the inheritance hierarchy were not considered for this paper. The reason for discussing inheritance is merely to improve the usefulness of the class uses graph and the method call graph.

Consider again the Fox and Rabbit example given with the class uses graph above. If an abstract Animal class is introduced in such a way that the Fox and Rabbit classes are derived from it, I suggest that the nodes for Fox and Rabbit should disappear and a node for Animal be put in their place. My reasoning is that the Animal base class is an abstract paradigm that is implemented by derived classes. The base class could be considered the end and the derived classes the means. The class uses graph does not need to represent the means.

Any hierarchy that exists for subtyping could be treated the same way. Structurally, such a hierarchy might defined as a flat single-inheritance hierarchy having an abstract base class and having no new public methods added in any of the derived classes. When found, such a hierarchy would be replaced by its base class.

In another situation, the roles are reversed. Consider a base class that exists solely so that some code can be reused. In this case, it is the derived class that is the end and the base class that is the means. Such a hierarchy exists for reuse and could be defined structurally as a flat single-inheritance hierarchy having a concrete base class and at least one new public method in each derived class.

For reuse hierarchies, I suggest the base class be omitted from the class uses graph and the derived classes kept. Again, what is being kept represents the end purpose of the inheritance hierarchy.

For hierarchies that follow neither pattern, all classes would appear in the class uses graph. Since the class uses graph only has one kind of edge, there would be no special edges for inheritance, instead an ordinary edge would be drawn from each derived class to any of its base classes.

The same approach could be used for the method call graph but in that case the purpose is just to remove some classes from the node set. No new edges would added.

3.2   The Human Factor

Here is an example that shows the kinds of things that can go awry when relying solely on structural considerations:

```
class Buttn extends JButton {
 public Buttn( String Label ) {
 super(Label);
 addActionListener( new ButtnAction() );
 }
}
class ButtnAction implements ActionListener {
 public void actionPerformed ( ActionEvent E ){
 // code here unlikely to involve Buttn
 }
}
```

JButton and ActionListener belong to the Swing library and so would not appear in our class uses diagram. Are there in-house classes that should be treated like library classes? Which ones today? Which ones tomorrow? A human has to be around to decide.

There is a UML dependency relationship from the Buttn class to the ButtnAction class. This seems backwards. Buttn doesn't really need ButtnAction; it performs a service for ButtnAction.

Twenty years ago, D.L. Parnas defined a "uses" relationship between two software entities u and v by saying v uses u in case v needs a correct execution of u to complete the task described in its specification [19]. Parnas's uses relationship would have the arrow going in the right direction.

But Parnas's uses relationship has to be determined by a human, a computer is unlikely to get it right.

The distinction between subtype and reuse class hierarchies made in the previous section has a neat structural characterization. But, again, that characterization is unlikely to always work. A human could do better.

There will always be subtleties that cannot be caught with by considering program structure. Some of them could be handled rather easily with a little human input—probably in a class's documentation.

By planning for such input, we can start adding nonstructural considerations to our indicators. If we are careful about how we permit human input, we ought to gain in accuracy what we loose in objectivity. Human inaccuracy can be partially corrected for in the usual way through automated sanity checks.

4 Conclusion

The main points of this paper are that graph theory can be used to create indicators of software quality, that the method emphasizes structure and cannot cover everything associated with quality, and that humans need to be involved with the interpretation of these indicators and, possibly, also with the creation of particular graphical models.

Four kinds of graphical model have been described: the control flow graph, the class uses graph, the data cobweb graph, and the method call graph. The latter two are new. The indicators derived from these models have had as their rationale the discovery of complexity, as in the cyclomatic number, the class context indicator, and the entanglement indicator, or in class cohesiveness, as in the cobweb length indicator and the feature envy indicator. The entanglement, cobweb length, and feature envy indicators are new and have not yet been used to help evaluate any software.

An educational analogy provides a more positive ending. Our educational system relies on tests in spite of evidence that tests do not measure what we want them to measure. Tests are used because we need to measure educational progress and tests are our only tools for doing so. Software quality indicators can be viewed in much the same way. If you do look at them that way, you will always be looking for new ones. You will also will never use them to drive your refactoring efforts. That would be like teaching to a particular test. You can get good scores that way but you do not get good results.

Afterword

Coupling is an important topic that is largely ignored in this paper. Mostly that is due to space and time considerations. Note that there is a wealth of information about coupling in the class uses and method call graphs. One might, for example, count all the edges going one direction between two partitions of a method call graph. This count would give the cardinality of a set M of all methods belonging to one class and called by another. A large number would bear looking into. So would a large number of data types appearing as parameters or return values of the methods in M.

Biography

Trained as a Ph.D. graph theorist, the author has worked, taught, and published in the areas of computer science, software development, and software maintenance for over a quarter century. For all of the nineties, he was a member of the editorial board of Wiley's *Journal of Software Maintenance: Research and Practice.* Currently he teaches college-level computer science to gifted high school students at a boarding school in Oklahoma. He loves it.

Dr. Zimmer can be found at www.ossm.edu/~azimmer and at the Oklahoma School of Science and Mathematics, 1141 N. Lincoln Blvd., Oklahoma City, OK 73104

References

1. Baase, Sara, *Computer Algorithms*, Addison-Wesley (1988) ISBN 0-201-06035-3 pp 184–190
2. Barnes, D. J. and Kølling, M., *Objects First with Java*, Prentice Hall (2003) pp 256–270 (See also www.BlueJ.org .)
3. Basili, V. and Mills, H., "Understanding and documenting programs", IEEE Trans. On Soft. Eng., Vol. SE-8, IEEE Computer Society (1982) pp 270–83
4. Beck, Kent, *Extreme Programming, Embrace Change*, Addison-Wesley, ISBN 0–201–61641–6, p 72
5. ibid, p 73
6. Chidamber, S. R. and Kemerer, C. F., "A Metrics Suite for Object Oriented Design", IEEE Trans. on Soft. Eng., Vol. 20, IEEE Computer Society (1994) pp 476–493
7. Constantine, L. Stevens, W. and Myers, G., "Structured Design" IBM Systems Journal Vol 13 (1974) 115–139
8. Cormen, T., Leiserson, C., and Rivest, R., *Introduction to Algorithms*, 2nd ed, (2001) MIT Press/McGraw Hill ISBN 0–262–03293–7 pp 629–640
9. ibid, pp 488–493
10. Fowler, Martin, *Refactoring, Improving the Design of Code*, Addison-Wesley (2000), ISBN 0-201–48567–2
11. ibid, pp 75–78
12. ibid, p 81
13. ibid, p 80
14. ibid, p 86
15. Fowler, M. and Scott, K., UML Distilled, Addison-Wesley (1999) p 108
16. Gronback, R.C., "Software Remodeling: Improving Design and Implementation Quality", Borland White Paper, www.borland.com/products/white_papers/pdf/tgr_softwareremodeling.pdf
17. McCabe, T.J., "A Complexity Masure", IEEE Transactions on Software Engineering, Vol 2. (1976) pp 308–320.
18. Miller, G. A., "The Magic Number Seven, Plus or Minus Two: Some Limits on Our Capacity for Processing Information", The Psychological Review, Vol 63 (1956) pp 81–97
19. Parnas, D. L., "Designing Software for the Ease of Extension and Contraction", IEEE Transactions on Software Engineering Vol 5, (1979) pp 270–283.
20. Woodfield, S.N., Dunsmore, H.E., and Shan, V.V., "The Effect of Modularization and Comments on Program Comprehension" , *Proc. of 5th Conf. on Soft. Eng*, IEEE Comp. Soc. 1981, pp 215–223
21. Zimmer, J Adrian, "Restructuring for Style", Software Practice and Experience, Vol 20, Wiley (1990) pp 365–389

The Test Automation Manifesto

Gerard Meszaros[1], Shaun M. Smith[2], and Jennitta Andrea[1]

[1] ClearStream Consulting Inc., 3710 250 5th Avenue SW,
Calgary, Alberta, Canada T2P 3H7
gerard.meszaros@acm.org,
jennitta@clrstream.com
http://www.clrstream.com
[2] Sandbox Systems Inc., 1550 770 8th Avenue SW,
Calgary, Alberta, Canada T2P 3R5
shaun@agilecanada.com
http://www.sandboxsystems.com

Abstract. Two key aspects of eXtreme Programming are automated testing and frequent refactoring. But is refactoring the best way to arrive at a set of tests that are both sufficient and maintainable? This paper builds on previously cataloged test smells, classifies these smells into two broad categories and introduces principles (or goals) for test automation. It also provides the start of a generative pattern language that helps guide the construction of automated tests that should not require extensive refactoring.

1 Introduction

Much has been written about the need for automated unit and acceptance tests as part of agile software development. But writing good test code is hard and maintaining obtuse test code is even harder. Since test code is optional (not shipped to customers), there is a strong temptation to give up testing when the tests becomes difficult or expensive to maintain. Once you have given up on the principle of "keep the bar green to keep the code clean", much of the value of the automated tests is lost.

Over a series of projects we have faced a number of challenges to automated testing. The cost of writing and maintaining test suites has been a particular challenge, especially on projects with hundreds of tests. Fortunately, necessity is the mother of invention and we, and others, have developed a number of solutions to address these challenges. We have also gone on to introspect about these solutions to ask ourselves why they are good solutions and what is the underlying test automation principle that they uphold? We called these collected principles The Test Automation Manifesto. We believe that adherence to the principles of the Manifesto will result in automated tests that are easier to write, read, and maintain.

F. Maurer and D. Wells (Eds.): XP/Agile Universe 2003, LNCS 2753, pp. 73–81, 2003.

1.1 History

On our first test-first project, we encountered a number of problems: the cost of updating existing tests was beginning to become a major component of the overall cost to implement a new feature, the cost of writing automated tests for new features was increasing, and the effort required to run the test suite was growing. Changes to the software under test's (SUT) API would impact dozens of tests. For example, adding a parameter to a class constructor would mean revisiting every test that created an instance of that class. We found that as tests were developed for more complex requirements, the effort to setup and teardown test fixtures was becoming greater than the effort to exercise and verify the new behavior. And we found that we could no longer just press the "run" button to run the test suite; we would have to truncate all the tables in the database before we could run a test suite because a previous run had not cleaned up after itself. Test automation, which had seemed so simple at the beginning, was becoming a burden. We still enjoyed the benefits of automated testing, but the investment cost was increasing. We had to find ways to reduce the cost while producing the valuable return we wanted.

1.2 Economics of Test Automation

Of course there will always be a cost to building and maintaining an automated test suite. Ardent test automation advocates will argue that it is worth spending more to have the ability to change the software later. This "pay me now so you don't have to pay me later argument" doesn't go very far in a tough economic climate. And the argument that the quality improvement is worth the extra cost doesn't go very far in these days of "just good enough" software quality.

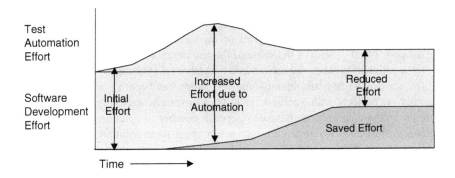

Fig. 1. The Effect of Test Automation on Software Development

The goal should be to make the decision to do test automation a "no-brainer" by ensuring that it does not increase the cost of software development. This means that the additional cost of building and maintaining automated tests *must* be offset by savings through reduced manual unit testing and debugging/troubleshooting as well as the remediation cost of the defects that would have gone undetected.

2 Bad Smells in Test Code

At XP2001, van Deursen et al [8] introduced a number of "bad smells" that occur specifically in test code. They recommend a set of refactorings that can be applied to the tests to remove them. Many of our initial problems with test automation involved those smells as well a number of others that we identified and developed solutions for. We have also discovered that there are at least two different kinds of test automation smells: "code smells" that must be recognized when looking at code, and "behavior smells" that manifest themselves when you least expect. The latter are much harder to ignore because tests are usually failing as you try to integrate your code and you must unearth the problems before you can "make the bar green".

2.1 Bad Smells – Code

Code smells are the "classic" bad smells as first described by Fowler in [3]. These smells need to be recognized by the test automater as they maintain the test code. Most of the smells introduced by Fowler are code smells. Code smells typically affect maintenance cost of tests but they may also be early warnings signs of behavior smells to follow.

Hard Coded Test Data – Lots of "Magic Numbers" or Strings used when creating objects which is likely to result in an *Unrepeatable Test.*

Test Code Duplication [8] – The same code sequences appear many times in many tests. More code to modify when something changes (causes *Fragile Tests*)

Mystery Guest [8] – When a test uses external resources such as a file containing test data, it becomes hard to tell what the test is really verifying. These tests often have a "lopsided" feel to them (either setup or verification of outcome is external to test).

Complex Test Code – Too much test code or *Conditional Test Logic.* Hard to verify correctness; more likely to have bugs in the tests

Can't See the Forest for the Trees – So much test code that it obscures what the test is verifying. The tests do not act as a specification because they take too long to understand.

Conditional Test Logic – Tests containing conditional logic (IF statements or loops). How do you verify that the conditional logic is correct? Does it always test the same thing? Do you have "untested" test code?

Complex Undo Logic – Complex fixture teardown code increases the likelihood of leaving the test environment corrupted by not cleaning up correctly. This results in "data leaks" that may later cause this or other tests to fail for no apparent reason.

2.2 Bad Smells – Behavior

Behavior smells are smells you encounter while running tests.

Fragile Tests – Every time you change the SUT, tests won't compile or they fail. You need to modify lots of tests to get things "green" again. This greatly increases the cost of maintaining the system. Contributing code smells include *Test Code Duplication* and *Hard Coded Test Data*.

Fragile Fixture – Tests start failing when a shared fixture is modified (e.g., new records are put into the database). This is because the tests are making assumptions about the contents of the shared fixture. A contributing code smell is *Mystery Guest*.

Interdependent Tests – When one test fails, a number of other tests fail for no apparent reason because they depend on a previously run test's side effects. Tests cannot be run alone and are hard to maintain.

Unrepeatable Tests – Tests can't be run repeatedly without manual intervention. This is caused by tests not cleaning up after themselves and preventing themselves or other tests from running again. The root cause is typically *Hard-coded Test Data*.

Test Run War [8] – Seemingly random, transient test failures. Only occurs when several people are testing simultaneously. This is caused by parallel test runs (executing the same tests) interacting with each other through a shared test fixture. A common root cause is *Hard-coded Test Data*.

2.3   The Trouble with Refactoring of Tests

In [8], the authors provided suggested refactorings for each of the bad smells. When we refactor production code, we rely on our automated tests to discover any problems introduced by the refactorings. But when we refactor our tests, what will alert us to broken tests? If a test fails when it used to pass, we can be certain that we have broken the test, but is "no news, good news"? Unfortunately not!

Tests are themselves inherently hard to test in an automated way. The only feasible way to test the tests is to see them fail when the SUT is known to contain defects that should cause the test failure. This can be accomplished manually either by writing the tests before the code they test (and they should fail) or by introducing defects into the SUT after the tests are written. While this may be a reasonable expense when first writing tests, to do so every time we refactor tests would be prohibitively expensive and would act as a significant barrier to refactoring of tests. Tools such as Jester [6] may help in this process but the output requires manual inspection and interpretation.

2.4   Beyond the Refactoring of Smells

We believe there is an alternative to all this test refactoring. Many of the smells can be detected very early in test automation or avoided entirely. Rather than asking what refactoring you should apply to remove a smell, we prefer to ask what principle is being violated when the smell is present and what can we do to prevent such violations.

Note that we are not advocating "big up-front design" of the tests. As consultants, we have seen many examples of testing frameworks built in anticipation of testing needs – needs that may or may not be real. These frameworks usually end up causing more problems than they solve. What we *are* advocating is thoughtful application of test automation patterns that we have found help us *avoid* the smells. The patterns all support a small set of test automation principles that are being violated when the various smells are present. We propose these principles and patterns as a "Test Automation Manifesto".

3 The Test Automation Manifesto

Based on many years of experience building and maintaining automated unit and acceptance tests, we propose the following "Test Automation Manifesto".

Automated tests should be:

Concise – As simple as possible and no simpler.
Self Checking – Test reports its own results; needs no human interpretation.
Repeatable – Test can be run many times in a row without human intervention.
Robust – Test produces same result now and forever. Tests are not affected by changes in the external environment.
Sufficient – Tests verify all the requirements of the software being tested.
Necessary – Everything in each test contributes to the specification of desired behavior.
Clear – Every statement is easy to understand.
Efficient – Tests run in a reasonable amount of time.
Specific – Each test failure points to a specific piece of broken functionality; unit test failures provide "defect triangulation".
Independent – Each test can be run by itself or in a suite with an arbitrary set of other tests in any order.
Maintainable – Tests should be easy to understand and modify and extend.
Traceable – To and from the code it tests and to and from the requirements.

4 Test Automation Patterns

Refactoring to eliminate smells is a good way to remove a problem once it has been created. "Generative" test automation patterns can be used to guide test automaters in avoiding the problems in the first place. In our experience, the following patterns can help ensure that automated tests comply with the principles espoused in The Test Automation Manifesto.

4.1 Readability Patterns

Readability patterns support the Manifesto principles of Concise, Necessary, Clear, Specific and Maintainable.

Tests as Specification
A test should visibly tie the expected outcome to the conditions that should cause it. It should be obvious in each test exactly what behavior it is specifying.

Single Glance Readable
A quick read of a test should be enough to understand what it tests. The test should fit in a single pane of a window without scrolling.

Intent Revealing Fixture
The part of the test that describes the test fixture (the pre-conditions of the test) should focus on what's relevant to this specific test. Anything irrelevant is hidden (encapsulated). This avoids the introduction of objects and values that have no direct bearing on the condition being tested. Well-named *Finder Methods* or *Anonymous Creation Methods* are an effective ways to do this.

Finder Methods
When reusing objects in a shared fixture use clearly-named *Finder Methods* in your test rather than using hard-coded object keys. This makes it easy to understand why the test is using specific objects and avoids the *Mystery Guest* smell.

Outcome Describing Verification Logic
The verification part of the test should make it very clear what the expect outcome should be. No "reading between the lines" should be required.

Single Condition Test
Tests should verify a single test condition (a single scenario or requirement). This makes them much easier to understand and maintain. They also make it easier to organize the tests in a way that makes it obvious which conditions are covered and which ones remain to be tested. Single condition tests also contribute to *Defect Triangulation.*

Declarative Style
All parts of the test should describe what *is* (fixture) or *should be* (expected results), rather than provide a recipe for how to create/verify it. Use of an *Expected Object* is one way to do this for expected results.

4.2 Robustness Patterns

Robustness patterns support the Manifesto principles of Self Checking, Repeatable, Independent and Maintainable.

Independent Tests

Each test is self-contained and makes no assumptions about which other tests have run before it or will run after it.

Clean Slate Fixture

Each test sets up everything it depends on. This avoids depending on other tests, either on purpose or accidentally, and ensures that all objects are in a well understood state.

Anonymous Creation Methods

Tests use common utility methods to create unique objects for each test and test run. Only the attributes of interest to the test are passed as "constructor" arguments. This ensures tests are repeatable and robust. It also prevents *Test Run Wars* since each instance of this test will create its own, unique objects so it cannot "collide" with itself when run from multiple clients simultaneously. These methods reduce the cost of writing tests by providing reusable building blocks which can be quickly assembled into new tests.

Automated Test Cleanup

Automated Test Cleanup replaces hand-coded teardown methods with the automatic destruction of test fixtures (objects, database data, files, etc.). Using this technique, the authors have not written a teardown method in almost three years. Automated cleanup eliminates complex and un-testable logic in a test's fixture teardown code and avoids test environment corruption by ensuring all fixtures are deleted. *Automated Test Cleanup* also greatly reduces the cost of writing tests by completely eliminating the most error-prone and certainly the most tedious work.

SUT API Encapsulation

Reduces maintenance cost by isolating tests from unimportant changes to SUT API. Helps make test more readable by focusing on what *is* important.

4.3 Reuse Patterns

Reuse patterns support the Manifesto principles of Concise, Clear, and Maintainable.

Reuse through Test Building Blocks

Tests reuse common logic by invoking common building block methods rather than by inheriting and overriding. This facilitates *Single Glance Readable* tests.

Anonymous Creation Method

Reusable and testable fixture setup logic (see Robustness Patterns).

Custom Assertions

Custom assertions are reusable object comparison logic that implements "test-specific equality". These are refactored using *Extract Method* when the same set of assertions appears in two or more tests. It simplifies the tests greatly yet avoids polluting production code with non-production object comparisons, which may need to vary from test to test anyway. Non-trivial custom assertions (e.g., comparing XML documents) can and should be tested with unit tests of their own. This reduces the amount of un-testable code in tests.

Parameterized Test

To apply the same test logic in a number of circumstances, write a test that takes a parameter that is used to determine which pair of inputs/expected-outputs to use. Either write a set of individual tests that just delegate to the *Parameterized Test*, or use a single *Data-driven Test Suite* that contains the values to be tested.

Templated Framework Tests

When testing framework plug-ins where every plug-in needs to be tested the same basic way, create a *Parameterized Test* that implements Template Method [4] that calls plug-in-specific logic to setup the fixture and verify the outcome. Use a *Parameterized Test* to tell the *Framework Test* which plug-in to test.

Data-Driven Test Suite

When you have a large number of tests that require the same logic but different data, consider creating a data-driven test suite that reads the data and calls the appropriate *Parameterized Tests*. This allows tests to be created without programming each individual test case. The FIT framework [2] is a good example of this style of testing.

4.4 Other Patterns

Round-Trip Test

Avoid over-specification (and *Fragile Tests*) by testing inputs and outputs at same "black box" interface.

Pass-Thru Test

Verify the interactions of the SUT with other software when these interactions are part of the design requirements. Use "stubs" or "mock objects" [5] to play the role of the other software so that you can verify the interactions.

Stub Out Slow

Replace any slow component that is depended upon with a test stub. For example, stub out a database to speed up tests by orders of magnitude [7].

Stub Out Dependencies Beyond Control

Anything beyond your direct control should be stubbed out so it doesn't cause unexpected results or delays.

5 Conclusion

Over a series of projects we have learned not only to ruthlessly refactor our production code to keep it clean, but we have also learned to do the same with test code. But the principles of test code refactoring are not the same as those for production code refactoring.

The Test Automation Manifesto defines the principles that underlie highly effective tests. All test code refactoring activities should improve the alignment with these principles. Does a refactoring improve robustness? Does it make it more concise or clear? If not, it is probably the wrong refactoring.

When first writing a test, the Manifesto acts as a checklist of the qualities that lead to tests that are less likely to need refactoring. We have found that applying the generative test automation patterns leads us to produce clear, maintainable, robust automated tests that are much less likely to require refactoring to add these qualities after the fact.

References

1. Appleton, B.: Generative Patterns. Available on-line at
   http://www.cmcrossroads.com/bradapp/docs/patterns-intro.html#GenerativePatterns.
2. Cunningham, W.: FIT: Functional Integrated Test. Available on-line at http://fit.c2.com
3. Fowler, M.: Refactoring: Improving the Design of Existing Code. Addison-Wesley (1999)
4. Gamma, E., Helm, R., Johnson, R., Vlissides, J.: Design Patterns: Elements of Reusable Object-Oriented Software. Addison-Wesley (1995)
5. Mackinnon, T., Freeman, S., Craig, P.: Endo-Testing: Unit Testing with Mock Objects. In: The First International Conference on eXtreme Programming and Agile Processes in Software Engineering (2000), Collected In: Succi, G., Marchesi, M., (eds.): Extreme Programming Examined. Addison-Wesley (2001)
6. Moore, I.: Jester – A JUnit Test Tester. In: The Second International Conference on eXtreme Programming and Agile Processes in Software Engineering (2001)
7. Smith, S.M., Meszaros, G.: Increasing the Effectiveness of Automated Testing. In: The Second International Conference on eXtreme Programming and Agile Processes in Software Engineering (2001), Collected in: Marchesi, M., Succi, G., Wells, D., Williams, L. (eds.): Extreme Programming Perspectives. Addison-Wesley (2002)
8. van Deursen, A., Moonen, L., van den Bergh, A., Kok, G.: Refactoring Test Code. In: The Second International Conference on eXtreme Programming and Agile Processes in Software Engineering (2001)

Test-Driven Database Development: A Practical Guide

Rong Ou

Sabre Airline Solutions
1 East Kirkwood Blvd. MD 7340
Southlake, TX 76092 USA
rong.ou@sabre.com

Abstract. Test-Driven Development (TDD) is one of the core programming practices of XP. However, developing database access code test-driven is often difficult, if not impossible. This paper presents a practical solution to this problem, making use of local development databases for testing and Open Source tools for schema migration and test data management. The examples are outlined in Java, but the basic ideas and principles are widely applicable to different languages and platforms.

1 Introduction

Test-Driven Development (TDD) [1] is one of the core programming practices of XP [2]. However, a large amount of the enterprise software development today centers around relational databases. This presents a challenge for enterprise developers who wish to adopt or are currently practicing XP: database access code is difficult to test in isolation.

Traditionally there are two approaches to this problem:

Don't Test. Or more precisely, don't test too much. Since testing against a shared development database can be slow and error-prone, "the basic rule is to go to the actual database as infrequently as possible, consonant with safety, so that the tests run as rapidly as possible" [3]. This sounds like the Chinese proverb "fasting for fear of choking". If we can make the database tests run as fast as normal tests, as we will demonstrate in this paper, there is no need to abide by this rule.

Mock Objects. With this approach, database access objects (for example, JDBC connections and statements) are replaced "with dummy implementations that both emulate real functionality and enforce assertions about the behavior of our code" [4]. A typical test case looks like this [5]:

```
public class TestMaililingList extends TestCaseMo {
  public void testAddNewMember() throws SQLException {
    mockConnection.setExpectedPrepareStatementString(
        MailingList.INSERTION_SQL);
    mockStatement.addExpectedSetParameters(
```

F. Maurer and D. Wells (Eds.): XP/Agile Universe 2003, LNCS 2753, pp. 82–90, 2003.

```
      new Object[] {EMAIL, NAME});
    mockStatement.setExpectedExecuteCalls(1);
    mockStatement.setExpectedCloseCalls(1);

    mailingList.addMember(mockConnection, EMAIL, NAME);

    mockStatement.verify();
    mockConnection.verify();
  }
  [...]
}
```

It is apparent that we have to know exactly what the production code looks like before we can write the test, which goes against TDD. Perhaps more importantly, we are not even testing the thing that is most likely to break: the SQL strings. This violates the XP rule of testing *"everything that could possibly break"*.

A different approach to this problem is needed.

2   An Example

Before we go into too much theorizing, let us first look at an example.

We are given a project to develop a security module for an application. The data has to reside in the database. The first story is to develop the login function, where we look up a user given a user name. For simplicity's sake, there is no password involved.

During our exploration phase, we have decided to use Hibernate [6] as our Object Relational (O/R) mapping tool. An O/R mapping tool is not absolutely necessary, but we will see in a moment why it saves us a lot of trouble. We have also decided to use the HSQL Database Engine (HSQLDB) [7] as our *local development database* [8], even though our deployment database will be Oracle. In addition, we will use Dbunit [9] to manage test data, XDoclet [10] to generate mapping files, and Apache Ant [11] to manage the build process.

With that out of the way, let us start working on the login story.

1. **Write a test.** We start with a plain old JUnit [12] test case:

```
public class LoginTest extends TestCase {
  public void testLogin() throws Exception {
    User user = Login.login("user");
    assertNotNull(user);
  }
}
```

2. **Make it compile.** To make the test compile, we create two empty classes:

```
public class Login {
  public static User login(String userName) {
    return null;
  }
}


public class User { }
```

3. **Run test. Fail.** Of course, we could return an empty User object to make the test pass. Since we know what we are doing, let's skip that step.
4. **Write mapping class.** We add more code to the User class:

```
/**
 * @hibernate.class table="USER_INFO"
 */
public class User {
  private Long userId;
  private String userName;

  /**
   * @hibernate.id generator-class="hilo" column="USER_ID"
   */
  public Long getUserId() {
    return userId;
  }

  /**
   * @hibernate.property column="USER_NAME"
   */
  public String getUserName() {
    return userName;
  }
}
```

This is saying: we want the User class to be persistent, mapped to a database table USER_INFO. It has an object identifier (OID) which is mapped to a surrogate key USER_ID [13]. The userName attribute is mapped to the USER_NAME column.

5. **Generate mapping file.** We run the hibernate.doclet ant task (see Appendix A) to generate the O/R mapping file User.hbm.xml.
6. **Export schema.** This is the magical ingredient that makes using an O/R mapping tool worthwhile. Simply running an Ant target (export.schema, see Appendix A) generates a new database schema from the mapping files in seconds.
7. **Create test data in XML.** This is the last bit we have to do for the test. Create an UserInfo.xml file:

```
<?xml version="1.0">
<dataset>
  <USER_INFO USER_ID="1" USER_NAME="user"/>
</dataset>
```

and we can change our test case to extend `DatabaseTestCase` from Dbunit:

```
public class LoginTest extends DatabaseTestCase {
  protected IDataSet getDataSet() throws Exception {
    return new FlatXmlDataSet(getClass().
                  getResourceAsStream("UserInfo.xml"));
  }
  [...]
}
```

8. **Implement login function.** We finally get to do the real code:

```
public class Login {
  public static User login(String userName) {
    try {
      // get a session

      Iterator iterator = session.iterate(
        "from user in class " + User.class.getName() +
        " where user.userName = '" + userName + "'");
      if (iterator.hasNext()) {
        return (User) iterator.next();
      }
    } catch (HibernateException e) {
      // handle exception
    }
    return null;
  }
}
```

9. **Run test. Pass.**

This approach is a little bit more involved than vanilla TDD, but not by too much, considering the fact that we created a database from scratch in the process.

3   Lessons Learned

As with any complex subject, a simple example does not do it justice. In our real world project, using a similar approach, we were able to reduce the running time of our test suite (560 tests), from over an hour by hitting a shared Oracle database, to about 70 seconds by hitting a local HSQLDB instance. It takes about 20 seconds to rebuild the local HSQLDB instance from scratch.

To reiterate, the components that made this approach possible:

- **Local development database.** This is a must for two reasons. One is to make tests run faster; the other is to provide the isolation needed so that running tests and test failures are localized. Any database can be used for this, from MySQL to PostgreSQL to Oracle, and it doesn't have to be the same database as the deployment database. HSQLDB is a good choice because it is very lightweight and maintenance free.
- **O/R mapping tool.** A good O/R mapping tool provides a database encapsulation layer to remedy the "Object-Relational Impedance Mismatch", and tool support to automate schema migration. In theory it is not absolutely necessary, but it surely makes our life a lot easier (see Sect. 4 for alternatives).
- **Test data management.** Even though we normally don't need a lot of test data, it's still a pain to manually insert and delete them. By externalizing them into XML files, we gain the capability to reuse the data in other situations (for example, acceptance tests).

From our experience, we also found further optimizations to this approach:

- **Write an `AllTests` suite.** This can be accomplished in a generic manner by searching through a package hierarchy to add any class that ends with `Test`. The reason for this is to avoid unnecessarily invoking the JVM multiple times.
- **Share a database connection for testing.** Even though we are testing against a local database, repeatedly opening and closing database connections can still add as much as 50% overhead. The solution for this is to write a base test case class that returns a `static` connection which can be reused by Dbunit.
- **CleanDbTest.** If we rely solely on Dbunit to load and delete test data, there is no need to worry about leftover data. But we might also need to test data creation and unintentionally leave some data behind. One way to guard against this is to write a `CleanDbTest`, which is both a JUnit `TestDecorator` and `TestListener` that verifies the database is clean after each test is run. We only need to run `CleanDbTest` periodically to verify the integrity of the whole test suite; if the cost is acceptable, the verification can be added to the `tearDown` method in the base test class.

4   Variations

The example given lives in an ideal world: we start from a clean slate, there is no legacy code, no legacy database. The real world is a lot messier. Let us look at some variations to the basic scheme.

4.1   New Projects with Existing Database Schema

For most projects, a legacy database is already in place and cannot be changed (at least not substantially). The techniques outlined in this paper can still be applied. Most O/R mapping tools (Hibernate included) have utilities to reverse engineer an existing database schema into Java classes and mapping files. There are also Open Source tools specialized in this category, for example, Middlegen [14], which has a Graphical User Interface (GUI) to allow easy manipulation of names, data types, relationships, and cardinalities etc.

Working with an existing database schema does have its drawbacks. For example, the tables may not be using surrogate keys. Composite keys with business meanings are harder to handle in O/R mapping tools and not all tools fully support them, so this is a critical factor to consider when selecting a tool.

4.2   Existing Code Base

Even if an existing code base is only doing straight JDBC calls, it might still be worthwhile to go through the exercise of mapping an existing database schema to Java classes. We gain better understanding of the data model, and get the capability to migrate schema to the local development databases for free.

If that is not an option, there are tools out there to do schema migration between databases. HSQLDB has a *Transfer Tool* to transfer data from any JDBC data source to another, but it seems to be more geared towards data management than development. Perhaps an in-house tool can be developed, or a commercial vendor can be considered.

4.3   Acceptance Tests and Integration Tests

This paper mainly deals with developer-written unit tests. Acceptance tests and integration tests are best ran against a shared integration database, to make sure schema changes haven't slipped through, and problems with database idiosyncracies are caught at an early stage.

The test data created for unit testing, in the form of external XML files, can be used for both acceptance testing and integration testing.

5   Limitations

There are certain limitations of this approach that might impact the decision to adopt it.

5.1   Stored Procedures and Triggers

Since we are using a different database from the target deployment database to do unit testing, it is difficult to test stored procedures and triggers, for these are highly vendor specific.

On the other hand, if the goal is to achieve database vendor independence, testing on different databases is a good way to reach that goal.

5.2   Database Idiosyncracies

Even though there are ANSI SQL standards, almost all database vendors either add extensions or only implement a subset of the standards. If we want to make use of a feature that is in the target deployment database but not in our chosen unit testing database, we have to either test that feature against the integration database, or bear the cost of creating and maintaining a private instance of the target database.

In practice we found that using a tool like Hibernate to encapsulate the database access layer makes it much easier to test locally with a low footprint database like HSQLDB, because the tool takes away the job of database abstraction.

6   Conclusion

We have found that testing against local development databases and making good use of existing Open Source tools enables us to develop database access code faster, more naturally, and with more confidence. In the grand scheme of things, it is also an enabling factor to facilitate evolving the database design along with the code [15].

Acknowledgements. I would like to thank the following reviewers and colleagues for their contributions to this paper: Frank Luo, BK Adarsh, Deepa Chopra, Damon Hougland, Zheng Lin, Philipp Meier.

Author Biography

Rong Ou is a Principle Software Architect at Sabre Airline Solutions, where he develops and architects enterprise software solutions for the airline industry. He has been in the software industry for eight years, playing the role of developer, architect, OO mentor and XP coach. Currently he is a member of one of the largest XP teams in the industry, with over 200 people in the development organization. He has a BA in Physics from Peking University and a MS in CS from The University of Texas at Austin.

References

1. Beck, K.: Test-Driven Development: By Example. Addison Wesley Professional (2002).
2. Beck, K.: Extreme Programming Explained: Embrace Change. Addison-Wesley (2000).
3. Jeffries, R., Anderson, A., Hendrickson, C.: Extreme Programming Installed. Addison-Wesley (2001).
4. Mackinnon, T., Freeman, S., Craig, P.: Endo-Testing: Unit Testing with Mock Objects. Extreme Programming Examined. Addison-Wesley (2001) 287–301

5. Freeman, S.: Developing JDBC Applications Test-First. On-line paper available at `http://www.mockobjects.com/papers/jdbc_testfirst.html`.
6. Hibernate. Relational Persistence For Idiomatic Java. Project is available on-line at `http://hibernate.sourceforge.net`.
7. HSQLDB. Lightweight 100% Java SQL Database Engine. Project is available on-line at `http://hsqldb.sourceforge.net`.
8. Dallaway, R.: Unit Testing Database Code. On-line paper and related discussion at `http://www.dallaway.com/acad/dbunit.html`.
9. The Dbunit Database Testing Framework. `http://dbunit.sourceforge.net`.
10. XDoclet: Attribute-Oriented Programming. `http://xdoclet.sourceforge.net`.
11. Apache Ant is a Java-based build tool. `http://ant.apache.org`.
12. JUnit is a regression testing framework. `http://www.junit.org`.
13. Ambler, S.: Mapping Objects To Relational Databases. On-line paper available at `http://www.ambysoft.com/mappingObjects.pdf`.
14. Middlegen. `http://boss.bekk.no/boss/middlegen`.
15. Fowler, M., Sadalage, P.: Evolutionary Database Design. On-line paper available at `http://www.martinfowler.com/articles/evodb.html`.

A   Appendix: Sample Build File

```xml
<project name="tddd" default="main" basedir=".">
  <property name="build.dir" location="${basedir}/build"/>
  <property name="build.classes" location="${build.dir}/classes"/>
  <property name="lib.dir" location="${basedir}/lib"/>
  <property name="src.dir" location="${basedir}/src"/>
  <path id="class.path">
    <pathelement location="${build.classes}"/>
    <fileset dir="${lib.dir}" includes="*.jar"/>
  </path>

  <target name="hibernate.doclet"
      description="Runs XDoclet to generate the mapping files">
    <taskdef name="hibernatedoclet" classpathref="class.path"
      classname="xdoclet.modules.hibernate.HibernateDocletTask"/>
    <hibernatedoclet destdir="${build.classes}">
      <fileset dir="${src.dir}">
        <include name="**/*.java"/>
      </fileset>
      <hibernate/>
    </hibernatedoclet>
  </target>

  <target name="export.schema"
      description="Exports schema to database">
    <taskdef name="schemaexport" classpathref="class.path"
      classname="net.sf.hibernate.tool.hbm2ddl.SchemaExportTask"/>
```

```
<schemaexport
    properties="${build.classes}/hibernate.properties"
    quiet="no" text="no" drop="no"
    output="${build.dir}/schema-export.sql">
  <fileset dir="${build.classes}">
    <include name="**/*.hbm.xml"/>
  </fileset>
</schemaexport>
</target>

[...]

</project>
```

A Testing Checklist for Database Programs: Managing Risk in an Agile Environment

Rolf Nelson

nelson@quoininc.com

Abstract. Quoin Inc. has been using agile testing methodologies, such as continuous integration and unit testing, in its development of SQL-based Java software since 1998. Based on that experience, we present a checklist containing twenty-six database-related items to consider when testing such software. The checklist is annotated with examples of good and bad development and testing practices. While this paper targets projects that use both SQL and Java, most of the checklist items are applicable to any database transactions in any language. Managers and developers can use this checklist as a starting point for discussion of what types of tests to require for their particular project, especially when operating in an agile environment such as XP. Referring to the checklist will enable the project to develop more robust code with less effort.

Keywords: Agile, XP, SQL, Java, testing

1 Introduction

Continuous Integration and Unit Testing are two XP (Extreme Programming) practices. Generic checklists exist as starting points to help managers and developers think about what types of tests are appropriate and necessary for their own particular project. This paper should be used as a supplement to such an existing generic checklist, to add additional items that are common to many projects that manipulate databases. The target audience for this paper is managers and developers on projects that use Java and SQL who would like to produce robust code more efficiently; however, most of the items on the checklist can be applied to any database project.

The checklist is based on Quoin's experience with using agile development practices to develop robust Java code that makes SQL calls against databases, especially large, shared, mission-critical databases. Not all items will apply to all projects.

2 How to Use This Checklist

This checklist contains twenty-five questions to consider asking when planning a test suite for your units. A unit can be as small as a single object method call, or as large as the entire end-to-end program. Agile testing requires acknowledging that no test suite is perfect, and being aware of what is being tested and what is being ignored.

F. Maurer and D. Wells (Eds.): XP/Agile Universe 2003, LNCS 2753, pp. 91–95, 2003.
© Springer-Verlag Berlin Heidelberg 2003

This checklist is not meant to be an authoritative guide for every database project; instead, the checklist is a set of suggestions to bear in mind when discussing what degree of test coverage is optimal for the project at hand.

Ideally, you would want the answer to each question below to be "verified as NO," either because an automated test suite verifies that the answer is no, or because the way the architecture is designed logically implies that the answer is no. However, since 100% test coverage is generally unrealistic, most projects will want to prioritize. For example, many projects will not care whether all SQL statement objects have been properly closed after use. In addition, some questions will be irrelevant to certain projects. For example, if a single-threaded program is going to be the only process accessing the database during its run, there is no need to ensure that the transactional logic correctly prevents race conditions. Some test items, such as testing whether SQL statements are malformed, require access to an actual database; a system such as ObjectMother[1] could be used to set up and tear down such tests. Other test items, such as exception handling and testing whether connections are properly closed, would require use of Mock Objects. [2]

For example, in an agile development environment such as Quoin's, the checklist can be referred to for inspiration periodically throughout the whole iteration lifecycle, starting when unit tests are being written prior to code development, and periodically during the continuous integration and QA that runs parallel to code development. Certainly we have never been in a situation where a client demanded that every item on the list had to be tested. Testing in the real world will always be incomplete; as with other business decisions, the final arbiter is what will bring the most value for the least cost to the project.

Some questions are annotated with an example of a good "best practice" and, for contrast, a bad practice.

3   Normal Test Coverage

This section discusses how well tests cover normal program execution, without necessarily taking into account exceptions or error-handling.

- Are any SQL statements malformed?
- Are any database connections ever left open after unit execution?
- Are any SQL statement objects ever left open after unit execution?

Performance can be affected by many factors, including hardware, database size, DBMS version, and load produced by concurrent processes. Nonetheless, trying to forecast production performance is important in some environments:

- Will the unit be unacceptably slow when run against the production database?
- Will the unit be unacceptably slow when run against the production database in x years, due to projected growth in the size of the production database?

- Does date processing fail on boundary conditions?
  - *Good: programs function normally on every day of the year.*
  - *Bad: program breaks on January 30 because it believes that a month from today is February 30.*

- Does the unit fail if floating-point arithmetic is imprecise?
  - *Good: program takes into account that a floating-point number subtracted from itself may not yield exactly zero.*
  - *Bad: program intermittently fails because of dependency on exact floating-point arithmetic.*

- Is the unit susceptible to race conditions?
  - *Good: although testing for all possible race conditions is impossible, test suite does, through load testing or through the artificial introduction of delays, test that the transaction logic is basically correct in the face of concurrent access.*
  - *Bad: test suite ignores the possibility of race conditions.*

- Do business invariants get violated by unit execution?

When querying for data, does the unit:
- Return one or more rows that should, by the correct business logic, not be returned (false positives)?
- Fail to return one or more rows that should, by the correct business logic, be returned (false negatives)?
- Incorrectly return duplicate data?
- Return data in an incorrect order?

4   Error Handling

This section discusses how gracefully units deal with exceptions and errors. Mock objects are particularly helpful in generating errors that would be hard to consistently reproduce when testing against a real database.

- Do SQL errors inappropriately propagate in raw form to the top level?
  - *Good: SQL exceptions are converted to more user-friendly exceptions that contain or log the original SQL exception trace for the convenience of debuggers.*
  - *Bad: SQL exceptions are displayed verbatim and without context, confusing the user.*

- Does the unit fail to rollback gracefully if the program fails halfway through?
  - *Good: the program rolls back from all failures, even those late in the process*
  - *Bad: on failure, the program leaves half the data tables filled in and the other half empty, in violation of the desired business logic.*

- Does the unit fail gracefully if database schema has been unexpectedly changed?
  - *Good: program produces a user-friendly error message.*
  - *Bad: program assumes missing column is meant to be null, and continues processing.*

- Does the unit fail gracefully if expected data is not present?
  - *Good: program produces a user-friendly error message.*
  - *Bad: program throws a mysterious NullPointerException.*

- Does the unit notice if data is unexpectedly duplicated?
  - *Good: program throws a "business invariant exception" if a query for a single database row unexpectedly returns multiple rows.*
  - *Bad: program merely picks the first row returned and continues processing without any warnings.*

5   Test Hygiene

Obviously writing test suites for your test suites is unnecessary for most projects. It is likely that the testers will answer these questions through inspection and knowledge of their own test suites.

- Is test code too similar to the unit code, so that the test code is likely to fail in exactly the same way as the unit code?
  - *Good: test code follows a different algorithm from the program code.*
  - *Bad: test code tests the program code by using the exact same query as the program code, and then checking for differences.*

If each test suite creates its own database from scratch and populates the data it needs, ignore this section. Otherwise, if the tester must share the test database with other processes:

- Do tests fail to clean up after themselves?

- Do tests rely on test database preconditions that may not necessarily be true in the future?
  - *Good: test suite populates, then cleans up, any data it needs.*
  - *Bad: test suite hardwires in certain values that currently happen to be present in the shared test database.*

- Do any tests have race conditions with themselves?
  - *Good: two testers can run the same test suite simultaneously on a shared test database.*
  - *Bad: test relies on hardwired values that will conflict with other testers simultaneously running the same test.*

- Do any tests have race conditions with other likely tests?
  - *Good: shared set of rules and reservation of id's ensures that independently-developed test suites will not conflict with each other when run on the shared test database.*
  - *Bad: test suite developers have no agreed-upon set of rules, and do not communicate with one another.*

6   Miscellaneous Quality Issues

Portability between DBMS systems is increasingly important. While writing standards-compliant SQL statement does not guarantee that the system will work with every DBMS, it does increase the likelihood that the project is not relying on proprietary vendor-specific extensions.

- Are database operations written in non-standard SQL, and therefore likely to fail when run on other database systems?
- Does the unit fail when deployed with other database systems?
  - *Good: system has been successfully tested with multiple popular DBMS's.*
  - *Bad: system has only been tested with one DBMS.*

All files necessary for the success of the project, from source code files to Ant build files to SQL scripts, should be clear and transparent, both to the current development team and to future maintainers.

- Is the SQL poorly documented or incomprehensible?
  - *Good: developers understand that SQL statements should be commented and understandable, just as source code should be commented and understandable.*
  - *Bad: developers believe that only files ending in *.java need to be maintainable.*

7   Conclusion

Adding SQL or other database functionality is essential to the success of many projects, but adds additional risks that need to be controlled. In addition to the many considerations for a normal project, this paper has presented some additional items to consider for database testing. Remember that the testing process is a probabilistic guess, or a bet, on what types of errors are most likely to undermine the success of the project. Choosing wisely what areas of the project to test, and being aware of what areas were deemed too unimportant to spend limited resources on testing, can allow the project risks to be successfully managed.

Author

Rolf Nelson (SM Harvard, BA Dartmouth) is a Senior Software Engineer for Quoin Inc. In addition to seven years of software development experience, he has worked as a project manager for the World Wide Web Consortium.

References

[1] Schuh, P., Punke, S.: ObjectMother: Easing Test Object Creation in XP. In: XP Universe, 2001. <http://www.xpuniverse.com/2001/pdfs/Testing03.pdf>
[2] Freeman, S. Developing JDBC Applications Test-First. Current February 23, 2003. <http://www.mockobjects.com/papers/jdbc_testfirst.html>

JNI Testing

Robert Wenner

Port25 Solutions,
Rathaus-Allee 10,
53757 St. Augustin, Germany
robert@port25.com

Abstract. Testing Java Native Interface (JNI) code is a complex undertaking with many pitfalls. This paper shows how to test Java code that calls C / C++ code. The design presented uses mock objects on both sides of the JNI layer to achieve a clean, reusable test design. It shows that the benefits of being able to test all JNI code will outweigh the extra effort in defining mock objects on both sides.

1   JNI Testing Basics

Unit testing takes on a new dimension when you have to test two different code environments: Java code and native code called from Java through the JNI. This paper shows the development of an example `Recipient` class (someone that email can be sent to) and how to unit test the corresponding JNI layer. `Recipient` is a Java interface to a native C++ library.

1.1   Brief JNI Basics

JNI development is always split in two parts: the Java part that defines and calls some native methods and the native (that is C or C++) part that implements these methods [1][2]. The `javah` tool is used to generate the native method names from the Java package and class information. The native JNI part will usually map these generated names to the real native methods. Figure 1 shows the general modules overview.

Besides function name mapping, the native JNI code usually translates error codes to exceptions, performs data type conversions, and maps from native structures to Java classes (as required).

1.2   Test Scope

The tasks mentioned in the previous section define the test scope. The JNI test is *not* supposed to test the underlying native code, for example by passing an invalid email address. The native code has its own tests somewhere else. In JNI testing the test scope is the JNI itself: the conversion from and to native code, the error handling, etc. In figure 1 the code under test consists of the two modules in the center, the JNI parts.

F. Maurer and D. Wells (Eds.): XP/Agile Universe 2003, LNCS 2753, pp. 96–110, 2003.

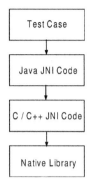

Fig. 1. Modules overview

JNI testing is important because many compile-time checks are transfered to runtime. The C / C++ compiler can not check whether a Java package, class or member exists. It can not perform type checking. Neither can the Java compiler check whether native functions are defined or even called correctly. A problem with any of these will result in an exception or even crash the virtual machine.

A common approach for unit testing is to mock all objects the code under test interacts with [3]. As seen in figure 1 the code under test consists of the Java JNI code (`Recipient.java`) and the native (that is C++) JNI code (`Recipient.cpp`). This leaves the native library to be mocked.

1.3   First Try

Assume `Recipient` takes an email address as an argument to its constructor. The Java code is supposed to pass this argument to the C++ code telling it to create a new native `Recipient`. The Java JNI code calls a native (C++) method which hands the given argument to the native library. The test must then determine whether it was passed correctly. Argument passing is tested by checking whether the native code receives the expected argument value supplied from the Java side. Listing 1.1 shows the JUnit test.

For testing purposes the native library is replaced with a dummy library. The dummy test code checks the arguments passed and if they differ from what was expected, the test fails[1]. The library function for creating a new Recipient (named `makeNewRecipient`) is likely to have a way to indicate an error. In C this is traditionally a return code (and / or possibly setting `errno`). In C++ an exception is thrown. The native JNI part is responsible for mapping the return code to a Java exception. A possible mock library function may look like listing 1.2.

---

[1] To make sure the dummy library is used instead of the real life library the Makefile may set the `$LD_LIBRARY_PATH` on Unix or copy the dummy library to the current directory on Windows.

Listing 1.1. Simple test case

```
public class FirstRecipientTest extends TestCase {
   public FirstRecipientTest(String name) {
      super(name);
   }

   public void testConstructor() {
      // dummy library throws if given address != me@here.com
      Recipient rcpt = new Recipient("me@here.com");
   }
}
```

Listing 1.2. Simple native mock

```
int makeNewRecipient(const char* address) {
   if (strcmp(address, "me@here.com") != 0) {
      return BAD_ARGUMENT;
   }
   return OK;
}
```

2   It's Ugly

The test case is in fact separated into two parts of code: the JUnit test case in Java and the mock code in C++. While writing (or maintaining tests) the programmer has keep Java and C++ synchronized.

2.1   Argument Abuse

To make things more realistic[2] let's look at a more sophisticated test. The native library offers a bunch of possible failures from the constructor call (malformed email address, out of memory, handling Java null argument values, etc.) and the tests should check that each error code gets translated to an appropriate exception. Therefore we need a way to tell the mock library which error it should simulate.

Creating a new mock library for each test case is obviously no option. One choice is to place the hint on what to do, possibly by using some magic number, in one of the arguments passed in (i.e. overload an argument for configuring the mock library). Does this sound ugly? It is ugly. Just imagine the big if or switch block in the mock library that would be necessary to determine the course of action the test should take.

Another drawback the programmer faces writing a new test in this manner is switching between native code and the test case to look for argument values

---

[2] read 'harder'

that don't have a special meaning yet. Finally, the approach completely breaks down for testing methods that don't take arguments.

2.2 Errors, Not Failures

Even if the problems mentioned above could be overcome, there is another flaw with this approach: tests will result in errors, not in failures. One can not have an `assertEquals` in the native code which compares the expected and the supplied address and produce a helpful failure message. If the native code detects (or simulates) an error the test will fail with an error. Neither the Java nor the native JNI code knows about unit testing (nor should they).

Changing the code under test for testing purposes is even uglier. A 'test mode' flag would merge the dummy library with the code under test. It then becomes confusing as to whether this flag is only for testing or for real behavior. Furthermore, future developers are likely to be confused by the test flag and may try to use it inappropriately to work around problems.

2.3 Setters and Getters

Another approach would be to define a `setReturnValue` function in the mock library for each native function the native code under test may call. The test case would call this setter during test setup and hand it a return value which the dummy function would pass to its next caller.

There would also need to be one getter function in the mock library for each argument of each mocked function. It would return the last argument value passed to its corresponding mock library function and make it available to the test case. Right before tear down the test case then would check whether arguments got passed correctly.

The biggest drawback with setters and getters is the difficulty in dealing with complex calls. A complex call is a method call in Java that results in more than one native function call. Complex calls occur in object creation if allocation and initialization are done by different functions. Error handling is a another example: an error code determines the type of exception to be thrown and the detail message is obtained from another function. The test author must be aware of all these details. If any of the functions involved is called more than once the getter is required to keep history values (return value stack and arguments lists) and the code gets even harder to write.

3   Bringing Together What Belongs Together

It would be easier if mock code and the test case were in one place. Since testing is done from Java, the JUnit test case would be the optimal place for the mock code.

3.1 Calling Home

Unfortunately the 'we are in test mode now' information is lost when the Java test code calls the Java JNI code. The mock library needs to communicate with the Java object that made the call (the test case). As described previously, modifying the code under test is a bad idea, however, the mock library can easily be modified—its only purpose is testing, anyway.

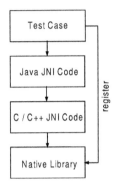

Fig. 2. Modules overview with registering test code

Figure 2 shows the updated modules overview. During test setup the test code calls a native **register** function in the mock library. This function stores a pointer to the Java object and redirects all calls back to the Java object. Redirection is done with usual JNI method calls and the mock library is now a 'redirecting' mock library.

The test code in Java now looks like listing 1.3. The test data (address) is now a constant – one chance less for typos. Notice that the Java test code and the mock code representing the callback routines are located together. This makes the test case easier to understand and maintain.

The mock library now redirects calls back to the test case. It supplies the **register** method and performs the callback to the Java test case (see listing 1.4).

Without going into too many JNI details, here is a brief explanation of how this all works. The **register** method stores a pointer to the native object for which it was called (the test case object). During execution of the call to the constructor, the mock library ensures a Java object is registered before performing the callback. If registration was successful, the mock library looks up the object's **constructor** method and calls it, passing it the address argument. If any of these calls fails the JNI throws an exception in Java and the problem gets reported as an error in JUnit. See [1] or [2] for details.

The mock library uses **NewGlobalRef** for the test case object. This is necessary to tell the garbage collector not to move the test case in memory, since the native code holds a pointer to it. This lock should be released after the test is

Listing 1.3. Test case with mock

```java
public class RecipientTest extends TestCase {
    static {
        System.loadLibrary("DummyLibrary");
    }

    public RecipientTest(String name) {
        super(name);
    }

    private native void register();
    private static final String theAddress = "me@here.com";
    private static int OK = 0;    // see C++ code

    public void testConstructor() {
        register();
        Recipient rcpt = new Recipient(theAddress);
    }

    public int constructor(String address) {
        assertEquals("Wrong address", theAddress, address);
        return OK;
    }
}
```

complete. Therefore, an **unregister** method is defined. It is called during the tear down process of the test (see listing 1.5).

3.2 More Test Cases

The test case presented in listing 1.2 still has a problem. How should different errors that can occur in the constructor be tested? After all, there can be only one method called 'constructor' in the test case. A `switch` statement in the `constructor` method would work, but there is a better solution: a dummy object.

The `constructor` method is in fact a method that simulates native code. Defining a `DummyNativeRecipient` object is straightforward:

The test code now does not define the callback method `constructor` itself but uses an anonymous inner class called `DummyNativeRecipient` as shown in listing 1.7. Figure 3 shows the control flow from Java to C++ and back again.

The `register` and `unregister` calls can be moved to the dummy class or the test `setUp` / `tearDown` methods to make sure they are called. However, using `unregister` in a `finalize` method is not a good idea since the test methods in the test case would be dependant on each other. Imagine this scenario: the first test completes and its mock object should be unregistered in `finalize`. The next test starts and registers with the mock library. Now the garbage collector runs.

Listing 1.4. JNI callback code in C++

```
#include "RecipientTest.h"
#include "Recipient.hpp"

static JNIEnv* environment = 0;
static jobject mockNativeRecipient = 0;

JNIEXPORT void
JNICALL Java_RecipientTest_register
(JNIEnv* env, jobject mockObject) {
    mockNativeRecipient = env->NewGlobalRef(mockObject);
    environment = env;
}

int
makeNewRecipient(const char* address) {
    if (environment == 0 || mockNativeRecipient == 0) {
        return OK;
    }
    jclass mockRecipientClass = environment->GetObjectClass
        (mockNativeRecipient);
    if (mockRecipientClass == 0) {
        return OK;
    }
    char *signature = "(Ljava/lang/String;)I";
    jmethodID methodId = environment->GetMethodID
        (mockRecipientClass, "constructor", signature);
    if (methodId == 0) {
        return OK;
    }
    jstring javaAddress = environment->NewStringUTF(address);
    return environment->CallIntMethod
        (mockNativeRecipient, methodId, javaAddress);
}
```

Listing 1.5. JNI unregister function

```
JNIEXPORT void
JNICALL Java_RecipientTest_unregister(JNIEnv* env, jobject) {
    if (environment != 0 && mockNativeRecipient != 0) {
        environment->DeleteGlobalRef(mockNativeRecipient);
    }
    mockNativeRecipient = 0;
    environment= 0;
}
```

Listing 1.6. Java mock recipient class

```
public class DummyNativeRecipient {
    public native void register();
    public native void unregister();

    public int constructor(String name) {
        return 0;     // ok (taken from C++ code)
    }
}
```

Listing 1.7. Test case with anonymous inner dummy class

```
public class DummyRecipientTest extends TestCase {
  static {
    System.loadLibrary("DummyLibrary");
  }

  public DummyRecipientTest(String name) {
    super(name);
  }

  private static final String theAddress = "me@here.com";

  public void testConstructor() {
    DummyNativeRecipient dummy = new DummyNativeRecipient() {
      public int constructor(String address) {
      assertEquals("Wrong address", theAddress, address);
      return 0; // ok (taken from C++ code)
      }
    };
    dummy.register();
    Recipient rcpt = new Recipient(theAddress);
    dummy.unregister();
  }
}
```

It calls **unregister** for the first test case. **finalize** calls **unregister** and the mock library discards the stored pointers—to the second test case. That second test case mysteriously fails because it doesn't get called from the mock library. Depending on when the garbage collector decides to finish the mock object a test may pass or it may not get called back. This kind of sporadically failing test is very difficult to track down.

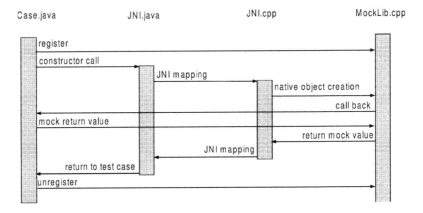

Fig. 3. Call scheme with dummy code

3.3 Mocking Everything

When writing real test cases, it is likely that a test will need more than one dummy method. The MockNativeRecipient can implement all method callbacks and provide default behavior. For example, it would usually signal ok and maybe do some sanity checking. The test cases create their specialized mocks and override the methods they want to test.

One problem still remains with these test cases. We need to make sure the mock code is called. This may not always be obvious, especially when simulating errors. The linker may easily grab the wrong version of the library. For some tests it may be interesting to see how often or in what particular order the mocked methods are called. Fortunately the mock object can track that too (see listing 1.8).

At the end of the test the mock can tell how often the constructor has been called. There can even be an additional check in the **tearDown** method to see if any mock methods have been called. Listing 1.9 shows this for constructor calls and can easily be extended to count whatever is necessary during the test run.

Other mock member variables can track that particular methods have been called. Each method called could append its name to a **String** member or collection. Mock methods could fail upon detecting methods called in the wrong order.

Listing 1.10 shows a complete test class. The native dummy library code and the MockNativeRecipient used are represented in listing 1.4 and 1.8 respectively. The test determines whether the error condition is correctly propagated from C++ to Java. The mock recipient returns an error code. The native JNI code must convert the error code to an **IllegalArgumentException**. If the test case catches that exception in an attempt to create the **Recipient**, the test was successful.

Listing 1.8. Counting method calls

```
public class MockNativeRecipient {
    static {
        System.loadLibrary("DummyLibrary");
    }

    public native void register();
    public native void unregister();

    private final static int OK = 0;

    public int called;

    public MockNativeRecipient() {
        register();
        called = 0;
    }

    public int constructor(String address) {
        called++;
        return OK;
    }
}
```

Listing 1.9. Checking mock calls

```
public void tearDown() {
    if (mock != null) {
        assertTrue("Mock not called", mock.called > 0);
        mock.unregister();
        mock = null;
    }
}
```

4   The Hard Work

Up to now there were simple data types (except for String), a 1:1 relationship between Java methods and C functions, and the need for only one Java object mocked at any given time.

4.1   More than One

The presented mock approach fails if there is more than one Recipient to be mocked at any one time. The mock library can hold only the pointer to one Java Recipient. Registering another one will overwrite and thus lose the first one.

Recall that the scope of these tests is the JNI layer. The Recipient test itself will not need to deal with multiple objects because it is the class being

Listing 1.10. Test case for error handling of a bad email address

```
public class CheckingMockRecipientTest extends TestCase {
    public CheckingMockRecipientTest(String name) {
        super(name);
    }

    private MockNativeRecipient mock = null;

    public void testSimulateMalformedEmailAddress() {
        final int badArgument = 123;
        MockNativeRecipient mock = new MockNativeRecipient() {
            public int constructor(String address) {
                super.constructor(address);
                return badArgument;
            }
        };
        try {
            Recipient rcpt = new Recipient("whatever");
            fail("mock code should have rejected the address");
        }
        catch (IllegalArgumentException expected) {}
    }

    public void tearDown() {
        if (mock != null) {
            assertTrue("Mock not called", mock.called > 0);
            mock.unregister();
            mock = null;
        }
    }
}
```

tested. What about a Message test that deals with multiple recipients? If the test is against an addRecipient method which adds Recipients sequentially, then the test call to the JNI layer only needs to deal with one object at a time. If the method takes a collection of Recipients, the test checks whether the native code extracts the recipients from the collection. It makes no difference how many Recipients are in the collection. (In fact it would be even more interesting to pass an empty collection than one with multiple Recipients.) Testing how the native implementation handles multiple Recipients is outside of the scope of JNI testing.

So, most of the time there is no need for more than one object. If there is truly a need for mocking multiple instances of the same class, a context member can be used. It allows an arbitrary number of mocked objects at any time.

The idea is that each Java object holds a pointer to its native part and the native library has a way to obtain this pointer. Since Java does not have pointer variables a **long** member is used. In the **register** method the native code creates a struct (or class) with whatever it needs to associate with the Java object. Usually this is the **JNIEnv*** and the **jobject** itself, but the mock code may decide to look up often needed methods and cache their method ids, too. Since this new allocated pointer would be lost after returning from **register** the pointer is stored in Java (in the long member). Each time the native code is passed a Java object it retrieves the **long** value from Java, interprets it as a **void*** and gets what it stored on registration.

This approach is not only useful in testing but whenever Java and C++ objects correspond and the C++ part keeps state information. Since the JNI is a C interface there is no information for which C++ object the call was made. Storing a pointer to the C++ object is a way to keep the connection between Java and the C++ object. When testing such code the **MockNativeXyz** base class' methods can make sure the passed pointer is correct.

To use the context member, Java code and native code must exchange the **long** / pointer member somehow. There are two approaches:

1. Passing the pointer in each call as first argument. To hide this implementation detail all native methods are private and have a public wrapper method (**passPointerToNativePart** in listing 1.11). Since the calls pass through the library under test (which does not know about the mocking) this approach is not usable in JNI testing.
2. Making the native code grab the pointer. This incurs the overhead of three additional JNI calls to find the member variable in Java and retrieve its value (see listing 1.12).

The first approach (passing the pointer) needs no further JNI call in C to obtain the passed value. The second approach (the native code retrieving the pointer) needs three JNI calls (lookup the class id of the Java object, lookup the member, and finally access it). The pointer retrieving approach also leads to a higher coupling between Java and the native part. The native part relies on the pointer member being named 'pointerToNativePart' and being of type **long**. Unfortunately these assumptions can not be checked at compile-time. A typo here results in a **NoSuchFieldError** thrown upon execution of the code. That said, and given the fact that JNI calls are somewhat slow, the first approach is highly recommended for "real" native code.

As with listing 1.12 the context member is initialized by the native code when the native object is allocated, for example an **init** method returns the long value to store. The native code may as well access the member directly, the idea is the same as with retrieving the pointer.

As mentioned above the JNI part isn't aware of the mock library and thus the pointer can not be passed through it. Therefore in JNI testing the mock library must retrieve the pointer from the native object it has registered with.

Listing 1.11. Pointer passing

```
public class SomeJniClass {
   static {
       System.loadLibrary("DummyLibrary");
   }

   private transient long pointerToNativePart;

   public SomeJniClass() {
       pointerToNativePart = 0;
   }

   public long passPointerToNativePart() {
       return passPointerToNativePart(pointerToNativePart);
   }

   private native long passPointerToNativePart(long pointer);
   public native long grabPointer();
}
```

Listing 1.12. Retrieving the pointer

```
void*
retrievePointer(JNIEnv* environment, jobject javaObject) {
  jclass javaClass = environment->GetObjectClass(javaObject);
  if (javaClass == 0) {
     return 0;
  }
  jfieldID fieldId = environment->GetFieldID
     (javaClass, "pointerToNativePart", "J");
  if (fieldId == 0) {
     return 0;
  }
  return (void*) environment->
                          GetLongField(javaObject, fieldId);
}
```

4.2 Native Cleanup

Sometimes one needs to test whether native resources are freed correctly (e.g. for file handles or connections held by native code). A destructor would take care of that in C++ but Java only has a finalize method. A test like listing 1.13 tries to make sure the native resources are freed.

  This test is somewhat fragile, however. It relies on the garbage collector finishing its work within the sleep interval. It works on my machine and with my Java VM, but on other platforms the sleep interval may have to be longer or the code may not even work at all. It may be necessary to call the garbage

Listing 1.13. Test freeing native resources

```
public void testFreesNativeResources()
throws InterruptedException {
    MockNativeRecipient mock = new MockNativeRecipient() {
        public void freeResources(long nativeObject) {
            called ++;
        }
    };
    mock.register();
    Recipient rcpt = new Recipient(theAddress);
    rcpt = null;
    System.gc();
    Thread.sleep(200);
    assertTrue("Mock not called", mock.called > 0);
}
```

collector in the beginning of this test as well to make sure no mock object from a previous test interferes with the current test.

Note that the corresponding mock code must not access the registered mock object's JNIEnv (i.e. the pointer to the JNI environment / virtual machine). The JNI doesn't allow exchanging it between threads, and the garbage collector runs in its own thread. The details of obtaining a pointer to the correct VM are beyond the scope of this paper.

4.3   Troubleshooting

JNI testing is cumbersome because many compile-time checks (like checking method calls, arguments, and return values) are postponed until run time. The JNI code will produce a linker error or an exception at runtime. This section provides some tips for avoiding common problems due to these facts.

Fortunately, JDK 1.4 has a -XcheckJni switch to java. If a JNI problem is encountered the VM will print a meaningful warning and exit gracefully instead of core-dumping.

If the native code cannot call the mock code, the JNI layer will throw a ClassNotFoundException or a NoSuchMethodError and the test will fail with that error.

What if the native code does not call the mock code? To have the compiler catch typos add a call to the overridden method in the mock class, for example call super.init() in the anonymous inner MockNativeRecipient's overridden init method. If a method still isn't called compare native mock library and the javah generated header files. Make sure the argument types and return values are correct. Also ensure the native mock call back to Java uses the proper corresponding callXyzMethod function? If init returns boolean and the native mock library attempts to call it using anything different from callBooleanMethod, it will fail silently.

Also make sure all non-void native methods do return a value. Methods are found by the linker (as usual in C) only by name, not by arguments or return value. If the return statement is missing the Java code gets something strange. A Perl script that does a comparison of generated header and implemented functions comes in handy here.

If exceptions are used in the mock code the native code must be able to handle them. If the mock code has thrown (e.g. an `assert...` failed)

If an exception is pending (e.g. an `assert...` failed), the native JNI code must return immediately to Java without doing anything else [2]. During testing, the native code could recognize the situation as an error signaled by the mock library (due to the exception it did not get the expected return value). Thus it may decide to pass the error code to Java and throw, too. This will crash the VM with a segmentation violation. Therefore always check whether an exception is pending before throwing in native code—even if the real native library can never throw an exception in Java.

5   Summary

JNI code is not easy to write or test. It has almost no compile-time checks, and problems with argument conversions, method calls, or member access are likely to crash an application. In the author's opinion no JNI layer is thin enough to go untested.

This article has shown how to keep test code and mock code in one place (in Java), making it understandable and maintainable. The presented native mock keeps tests flexible and straight-forward. There is no need to change the production code for testing.

The overhead of creating the mock library and the Java mock classes is easily outweighed by the benefits of having comprehensive tests across the JNI layer.

References

1. Gordon, R., McClellan, A: Essential JNI: Java Native Interface. Prentice-Hall, 1998
2. Liang, S.: Java Native Interface: Programmer's Guide and Specification. Addison-Wesley, 1999
3. Mackinnon, T., Freeman, S., Craig, P.: EndoTesting: Unit Testing with Mock Objects. eXtreme Programming and Flexible Processes in Software Engineering - XP2000, May 2000

Agile Regression Testing Using Record and Playback

Gerard Meszaros, Ralph Bohnet, and Jennitta Andrea

ClearStream Consulting
Suite 3710, 205 Fifth Ave SW
Calgary, AB
T2P 2V7 Canada
gerard.meszaros@acm.org
{ralph,jennitta}@clrstream.com

Abstract. There are times when it is not practical to hand-script automated tests for an existing system before one starts to modify it. In these circumstances, the use of "record & playback" testing may be a viable alternative to hand-writing all the tests. This paper describes experiences using this approach and summarizes key learnings applicable to other projects.

1 Introduction

Scripting tests by hand as required by JUnit [1] or it's XUnit [2] siblings is hard work and requires special skills to write tests. Writing functional (or acceptance) tests using JUnit is particularly hard because of all the data requirements. One possible alternative is the FIT frameworks [3] but these still require someone to develop utility code to act as "glue" between the testing framework and the system under test (SUT). Each of these approaches requires that the system provide an interface by which the tests can be conducted.

1.1 Catch-22 of XUnit-Based Testing

On several recent agile projects, we found ourselves needing to modify an existing system that had no automated tests. In one case, the manual retest effort was expected to involve several person-years of effort and many months of elapsed time. Hand-scripting JUnit (or equivalent) tests was considered too difficult because the systems were not designed for testability. (e.g. business logic embedded in the UI; no access to an application API; no means of controlling all the test setup (such as "stubbing")). Refactoring the system for testability so that tests could be written was considered too risky without having automated regression testing to verify that the refactoring had not introduced problems. And even if we had done it, we were concerned that we could not hand-script all the necessary tests, complete with their expected outcomes, in the time and resource budget available to us.

F. Maurer and D. Wells (Eds.): XP/Agile Universe 2003, LNCS 2753, pp. 111–119, 2003.
© Springer-Verlag Berlin Heidelberg 2003

1.2 Looking for Alternatives to XUnit

This led us to investigate all possible alternatives to XUnit style testing. Most of this effort focused on "record & playback" (R&PB) styles of test creation, an approach that involved recording functional tests on the system before we made the changes and regression testing the refactored system by playing back these tests. The tests verified the overall functionality of the system and, in particular, much of the business logic it contained. Once the tests were recorded and verified (successfully played back on the original system), we could then start refactoring the system to improve its design. We felt that this would allow us to quickly record a number of tests that we could play back at will. Since we had an existing version of the system to use as a "gold standard", we could leave the effort of defining the expected outcomes to the record and playback framework.

This paper describes the options we considered, their advantages and disadvantages and how we ended up regression testing the system. The work also lead to an understanding of where R&PB can be used in a more general context than the specific projects with which we were dealing.

2   Issues with R&PB Test Automation

R&PB style testing predates XUnit-style testing by many decades. Test automation folklore is rich with horror stories of failed attempts to automate testing. This paper describes critical success factors for making this style of testing work, what to avoid, and best practices in R&PB test automation.

The "robot user" approach to test automation had received enough bad publicity in past attempts at test automation that we found it to be a hard "sell". We had to convince our sponsors that "this time it would be different" because we understood the limitations of the approach and that we had a way to avoid the pitfalls.

2.1 The "Fragile Test" Problem

Test automation using commercial R&PB or "robot user" tools has a bad reputation amongst early users of these tools. Tests automated using this approach often fail for seemingly trivial reasons. It is important to understand the limitations of this approach to testing to avoid falling victim to the common pitfalls. These include *Behavior Sensitivity, Interface Sensitivity, Data Sensitivity* and *Context Sensitivity.*

Behavior Sensitivity
If the behavior of the system is changed (e.g. the requirements are changed and the system is modified to meet the new requirements), any tests that exercise the modified functionality will most likely fail when replayed. This is a basic reality of testing regardless of the test automation approach used.

Interface Sensitivity
Commercial R&PB ("robot user") test tools [4] typically interact with the system via the user interface. Even minor changes to the interface can cause tests to fail even though a human user would say the test should still pass. This is partly what gave test automation tools a bad name in the past decade.

Data Sensitivity

All tests assume some starting point; these are often called the "pre-conditions" or "before picture" of the test. Most commonly, this is defined in terms of data that is already in the system. If the data changes, the tests may fail unless great effort has been expended to make the tests insensitive to the data being used. More recent versions of the test automation tools provide mechanisms that can be used to make tests less sensitive. This has added a lot of complexity to these tools and, as a result, they often fail to live up to their promises. This has likely contributed to the bad reputation they have received.

Context Sensitivity

The behavior of the system may be affected by the state of things outside the system. This could include the states of devices (e.g. printers, servers) other applications, or even the system clock. E.g. the time and/or date of test.

2.2 Agile Project Issues

There are other issues with R&PB testing that are specific to an agile project environment (especially eXtreme Programming.)

Not Test-First

Many agilists (especially advocates of eXtreme Programming) would argue that R&PB test automation completely undermines the notion of automating acceptance tests before the functionality is built because it requires the SUT to exist before the tests can be recorded.

3 Understanding Test Automation Choices

As part of our analysis of the choices available to us, we came up with a way of classifying the approaches to test automation. This helped us better understand why certain approaches worked better in some circumstances than others.

3.1 Approaches to Test Automation

Classifying Approaches to Test Automation

There is more than one way to automate tests. The approaches can be classified using a 3 dimensional grid. The three dimensions are:

- Granularity of SUT. The SUT can be a single unit (module, class or even method), a component, or the entire system.
- Test Creation Approach. The two main options are "Record & Playback" (R&PB) and hand-scripted tests. [1]
- Test Interface. The two main options are testing via the user interface or testing via an internal software interface or API.

---

[1] There is a third approach: the generation of tests from semi-formal requirements specification. However, the authors do not feel qualified to comment on the relative merits of this approach. A sample paper can be seen in [5]

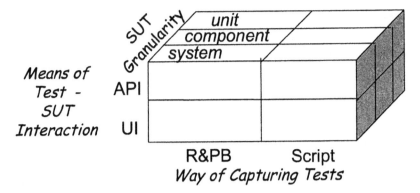

Fig. 1. The three dimensions of test automation

3.2 Common Combinations

While there are 2x2x3 possible combinations, it is possible to understand the primary differences between the approaches by looking at the front face of the cube. Some of the 2x2 combinations are applicable to all levels of granularity while others are primarily used for system testing.

Hand-Scripted Quadrants
The upper right quadrant of the front face of the cube is "modern XUnit". It involves hand-scripting tests that exercise the system at all 3 levels of granularity (system, component or unit) via internal interfaces. A good example of this is unit tests automated using JUnit.

A variation on "modern XUnit" is "Scripted UI Tests" with the most common examples being the use of JfcUnit [6], HttpUnit [7] or similar tools to hand-script tests using the user interface. (It is also possible to hand-script tests using commercial "Robot User" tools.) These would fit into the bottom right quadrant. Where the entire system is being tested, this would be at the system test level of granularity. They could also be used to test just the user interface component of the system (or possibly even some UI units such as custom widgets) but this would require stubbing out the actual system behind the UI.

Record & Playback Quadrants
The bottom left quadrant is "Robot User" This involves recording tests that interact with the system via the User Interface and is the approach employed by most commercial test automation tools. It applies primarily to System testing. This approach is primarily focused on testing the entire system, but like "scripted UI Tests", could be applied to the UI components or units if the rest of the system can be stubbed out.

The top left quadrant is not well populated with commercial tools but is a feasible option when building R&PB into the application itself. It involves creating a record & playback API somewhere behind the user interface. This is then used to record everything that affects the system state into a file that can later be used for input.

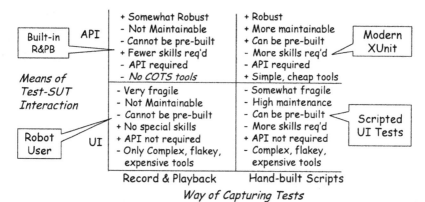

Fig. 2. The four test automation quadrants

4 Implementing R&PB Test Automation

Record and Playback test automation can be implemented using either commercial tools or by building a record and playback capability into the application.

4.1 Using Commercial R&PB Tools

Commercial R&PB testing tools can be used in several ways. Most commonly, they are used to test an entire system including the business logic and the presentation logic.

Testing User Interface Behavior

Testing of user interfaces is one area in which commercial "robot user" tools can be used to good effect. The key is to make the system deterministic enough from a business logic perspective so that the UI tests can focus on verifying UI behavior without having to deal with variations in behavior caused by differences in the context (data, time/date, etc.)

This can be done in two ways:

1. Define a set of test data that can be frozen for the life of the tests. You may need to stub out any interfaces to other systems (or components such as the system clock) to ensure complete determinism.
2. Configure the user interface component to use a dummy version of the business logic component of the application . This "mock application" can be programmed (hard-coded or data driven) to return canned answers to requests. This ensures complete determinism of the "business logic" and allows the tests to focus on changes in UI behavior in response to the canned responses that are returned.

Testing Business Logic

This is probably the weakest usage of R&PB test automation even though many improvements have been made in the way commercial R&PB tools record tests. Either the "hand-scripted via API" or FIT approach would likely be a better long-term option.

If you do choose to use "robot users" to test the business logic, make sure you freeze the test data to eliminate a very common source of false test failures. Also, ensure that the application user interface is stable and that the functionality is not going to change between when you record the tests and when you plan to re-run them.

4.2 Building R&PB into an Application

Commercial "robot user" tools are not the only way to do R&PB style test automation. Depending on the architecture of the system under test, there are several ways to build R&PB right into the application. This is the way we chose to automate the functional tests on several recent projects.

The main advantage of this approach is that it can be applied to any system regardless of the technology of the user interface. It is also more robust than most commercial robot user tools because one source of potential failures – loss of synchronization between the test tool process and the SUT process – is eliminated by virtue of R&PB being built into the application. In effect, it moves the test automation approach from the lower left quadrant ("robot user") to the upper left quadrant ("R&PB via API").

R&PB Decorator between UI and Service Facade

Where the system consists of a cleanly separated UI component and a business logic component accessed via a service façade, the system can be configured to place a Recording Decorator between the two components. It records each request passed into the service component and the response that came back. A leading candidate file format for recording the interactions is XML.

Playback is accomplished by building a test driver that calls the service facade with the recorded requests and compares the actual responses with the previously recorded responses. It is quite simple to build a test driver that reads the XML containing the sets of <request> and <expectedresponse> elements. The user interface component is often omitted during test playback but in some cases it may be present so that test progress can be monitored.

A component container (such as an EJB application server) is well positioned to provide the capability to record the requests being passed to the managed component. Too bad that most do not yet provide this capability.

Building R&PB into the UI of the Application

If the application is not cleanly separated into a User Interface component and a service façade component, it may be possible to build the R&PB capability right into the User Interface. (See Figure 4) This is most cost-effective when it can done by building R&PB into a generic driver so that one doesn't need to sprinkle R&PB hooks throughout the system.

Example 1: A servlet-based application
We used a Transform View [8] architecture in which a servlet calls business methods on a service façade and then invokes an XLS transform on the returned XML. We placed recording hooks into the servlet to record the user's request (URL plus parameters), resulting XML and the resulting HTML after XLST transformation. A test menu was added to the UI to allow recording to be turned on and off.

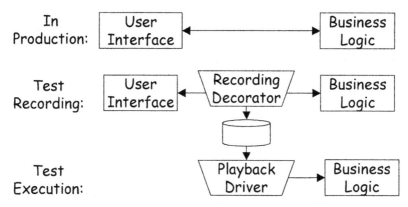

Fig. 3. Record and Playback using a Recording Decorator

Test execution (playback) was done by building a very simple JUnit test that submitted the recorded URLs using HttpUnit and compared the returned HTML with the recorded HTML. To avoid the messiness of manually locating differences between the two HTML strings, we wrote a *custom assertion* (a special version of AssertEquals) that would diagnose the problem and report the location where the two strings differed.

We were also able to easily build unit tests for our XSL transforms by passing the recorded XML and the XSL to the transforming and comparing the resulting HTML with the previously recorded HTML.

Example 2: A project re-engineering a "safety-involved" system
The system contains complex business rules that were not fully understood by the business. We needed to verify that the re-engineered system implemented the rules correctly. Unfortunately, the user interface was tightly coupled to the rules logic so it was not possible to use scripted tests via an API. We placed R&PB hooks into the generic screen I/O utilities whenever possible but we also needed to place hooks in a number of other places in the UI code. By recording on the old system and playing back on the new, we were able to quickly identify any differences in system behavior.

4.3 Test-First Development with R&PB

While at first glance, the title of this section may appear to be an oxymoron, it *is possible* to build playback tests before the system is built. As long as the form of the recorded interaction is human readable, it can also be human writable. (This is one of the key advantages of using XML for recording the interactions.)

Many of the commercial "robot user" tools do record the interactions in a human readable form. Some generate completely proprietary test scripting languages while others record tests in "standard" scripting languages such as VbScript or JavaScript. You can record a few tests using the tool of choice to see how certain types of interactions are done. Then you can start scripting tests based on what you have learned. One key advantage of doing this is that you can make sure the tests are less sensitive by using the "right" approach (e.g. using the *title* of a dialog box rather than the *ID*.)

The FIT approach to testing is an example of how a test might be "pre-recorded". The FIT framework could be modified to generate scripts that are runnable in your *robot user* tool, thus moving the effort of understanding how to interact with the system into test code generation framework.

When recording tests as XML, consider creating XSL style sheets that can transform the XML into HTML FIT tables. This would make the tests easier to read (no XML) and allow users to run the tests easily from a website.

4.4   Critical Success Factors

So, assuming you have decided to give *robot user* testing tools a second chance, what features do you need to look for in the testing tool? And what techniques do you need to apply to system development and test automation to be successful?

Designing the System for Context Independence
You must be able to configure the system with a known starting point consisting of both data and the system date.

Tool Provides Means to Initialize System
Tests must be able start up the system with the known starting point.

Functionality Stability
R&PB testing can only be used to good effect when a significant portion of the applications functionality is expected to be unaffected by the next release. Any tests that encounter modified functionality must be rerecorded as the functionality is verified manually.

User Interface Insensitivity
It must be possible to record tests in a way that changes to the UI that do not affect the business logic do not cause tests to fail. (There may be other tests recorded that verify that the UI behavior has not changed and these will need to be sensitive to this kind of change.)

Separation of Tests for UI and Business Logic
All tests that verify business logic should be recorded in a UI insensitive way. A separate set of tests (either manual or automated) should be used to verify the UI has not changed. It can be useful to have different sets of tests with different sensitivity as these can be used to do "defect triangulation" (narrowing down where the defect is located.)

Limited Lifetime
Recognize that *robot user* tests will have a limited lifetime. They will not survive certain kinds of changes to the user interface or the business logic inside the system. Have a strategy for managing the tests that allows you to identify the those tests that will be impacted and which would need to be either discarded, rerecorded or superceded by newly scripted tests. One good way of doing this is to cross-reference the tests with the requirements by using a test management tool such as Test Director.

5 Applicability

Record and Playback testing should be considered when:
- You need to refactor a legacy system to make it amenable to XUnit-style hand-scripted tests and you feel it is to risky to do so without having regression tests.
- You cannot afford the time or cost of hand-scripting tests
- You do not have the programming skills required to hand-script the tests.

Record and Playback testing should be avoided when:
- You cannot fix the behavior of the system by freezing/snapshot the data on which the system will operate.
- The behavior of the system is expected to change significantly between when the tests can be recorded and when they will be played back.
- If you want to use the automated tests as a specification and there is no existing system that can be used for recording the tests.

6 Conclusion

Sometimes, R&PB testing is your only viable option given various project constraints. E.g. When dealing with legacy systems that do not have automated tests, Record & Playback style testing is a cost effective way to create regression tests that can be used to verify that design changes to the system do not introduce defects.

R&PB testing tools and techniques have matured significantly over the years and can now avoid many of the potential pitfalls when used properly.

When commercial R&PB test automation tools are unavailable, too costly, or too undependable, it is feasible to build the R&PB capability right into the system under test.

Acknowledgements. We would like to thank the many clients who gave us the opportunities to gain the experiences described in this paper.

References

1. *JUnit testing framework*: http://JUnit.org
2. *XUnit family of testing frameworks*: http://www.xprogramming.com/software.htm
3. Cunningham, Ward. *FIT: Functional Integrated Test*. http://fit.c2.com.
4. *Mercury Interactive's WinRunner functional testing tool*:
   http://www-svca.mercuryinteractive.com/products
5. Ammann, Paul, Paul E. Black, *Model Checkers in Software Testing*
   http://xsun.sdct.itl.nist.gov/~black/Papers/ir6777.pdf
6. JfcUnit, *A testing framework for Java Swing user interface*: http://JUnit.org
7. HttpUnit, *A testing frameworks for HTML user interfaces*: http://JUnit.org
8. Fowler, Martin. *Patterns of Enterprise Application Architectures*, Addison-Wesley (2002)

Make Haste, Not Waste: Automated System Testing

Carl Erickson[1,3], Ralph Palmer[2], David Crosby[1],
Michael Marsiglia[1], and Micah Alles[1]

[1] Atomic Object LLC, 419 Norwood Ave SE Suite 190, Grand Rapids MI 49506
{carl,david,mike,micah}@atomicobject.com
http://atomicobject.com/
[2] Burke Porter Machinery, 730 Plymouth NE, Grand Rapids MI 49505
Ralph.Palmer@bepco.com
http://www.bepco.com/
[3] Department of Information Technology, Uppsala University, Uppsala, Sweden
carle@docs.uu.se

Abstract. Haste (High-level Automated System Test Environment) represents
an approach to system testing that is philosophically consistent with standard
XP unit testing practices. Test code runs in the same address space as the
application under test, allowing for ready examination of application state. The
fundamental Haste abstractions of Story, Step, and StoryBook provide a
framework to implement system tests. Utility classes simplify test development.
In addition to acting as XP acceptance tests, Haste tests aid source maintenance
and extension, and can play an important role in a release process. This paper
describes the elements of Haste, our experience with using it to test a complex
Java Swing application, and the perspective of the client for whom the
application was developed. Haste is available under an open source license.

Keywords: System, acceptance, automation, GUI, testing, Haste.

1 System Testing

System tests validate the soundness and behavior of the application from the user's
perspective [1]. In an XP project, system tests serve as acceptance tests. In this role
they measure progress on a project, and provide a form of customer acceptance of the
delivered application [10]. Ideally, they are written by the customers themselves. In
practice, system tests must often be translated by a programmer from an elaborated
customer story into testing code. A lightweight automation framework for system
tests can extend the benefits of XP unit testing to a higher level, supporting test first
development for system tests, and decreasing the difficulty of writing system tests.

There appears to be an emerging consensus on the use of system testing in XP
projects [9]. Consistent with this view, we use system tests for four purposes:

- regression testing for code development and maintenance
- customer communication and specification
- customer project progress gauge and buyoff
- quality control element of the release process

F. Maurer and D. Wells (Eds.): XP/Agile Universe 2003, LNCS 2753, pp. 120–128, 2003.
© Springer-Verlag Berlin Heidelberg 2003

System testing requires exercising an application via its user interface. Without automation, system tests cannot play the same role in XP development that unit and integration tests play, and the four uses identified above for system tests would not be practical. System tests are distinct from unit and integration tests in that they validate the functionality of the application as a whole, rather than a single method, object or component. Test assertions need to be made about the state of the application as a whole, which in turn may be represented by the state of many unrelated objects. Passing a system test means every step in a potentially lengthy process was executed correctly.

Several toolkits have been created for automating system tests of web applications. Examples include HttpUnit [2], Avignon [3], Canoo WebTest [12], and jWebUnit [4]. To our knowledge, no general purpose application system testing framework, analogous to JUnit for unit testing, exists. While it is in fact built on JUnit, Haste was designed for general purpose system testing and reflects the distinct needs of system testing. Haste has been used for system testing web applications and Java Swing applications.

1.1   Automated GUI Testing

Creating automated system tests for applications with graphical user interfaces can be difficult. The rising popularity of automated unit testing seems to have inspired the creation of several GUI test toolkit projects. JFCUnit [5] has a tool class called JFCTestHelper for examining the state of the graphical environment, as well as massaging the event stream to programmatically manipulate components. Tests are coordinated with JUnit. Jemmy [6] is a library for automating Java GUI applications. It has an advanced abstraction tree for finding, examining and manipulating specific graphical components.

Abbot [7] is a very well developed extension to `java.awt.Robot`. An operator class is used to manipulate particular types of components via native events generated with Robot. For system testing, scenarios are recorded, assertions added, and scripts executed to create a test. Marathon [8] lets the tester record, edit and execute GUI tests via an embedded Python interface. The resulting Python code is very easy to understand and hence readable by the customer. Abbot and Marathon have as a goal the automation of system tests, and not simply the automation of GUI component tests. The difference between them and Haste is that they use the script recording approach to organizing system tests, where as Haste offers a programmatic framework for testing.

In our experience, the best toolkit to use for programmatically manipulating Java GUI components depends on the component. Haste lets the tester mix and match GUI component manipulation objects by hiding this implementation detail behind a common interface. Haste also includes a rudimentary toolkit for GUI component manipulation.

2   The Haste Environment

We call Haste an environment because it is less than a standalone tool and more than a testing approach. Haste consists of a framework for system testing, analogous to

JUnit, useful design patterns, a toolkit for GUI automation, and utility classes to support automated system tests in an XP environment. The concepts in Haste are language independent; the first implementation of Haste is in Java.

Haste was created to extend our test-first development environment and testing style into the realm of system tests. The goal was to have a continuum of test suites from unit tests through system tests. Consistency across testing levels encourages the practice of programmers and testers working closely together, or in the case of small scale teams, having programmers do test-first development.

The most important design decision we made for Haste was to execute test code in the same address space as the application under test. This allowed for an internal, programmatic form of testing, rather than an external, scripted approach. This approach saves time and avoids the difficulty of exposing an application's state via an external interface [9]. System testing with Haste is philosophically similar to unit and integration testing, and hence in keeping with standard XP testing practice.

Haste has three main elements. The testing framework element consists of three key abstractions and several utility classes. The second element is a pattern for exposing the internal state of objects for making test assertions. We call this a Narcitecture. The Haste framework and Narcitecture are used for testing all types of applications. Testing applications with graphical user interfaces is possible with the third element of Haste: Pilots and Droid. Pilot interfaces simplify and standardize access to complex GUI components. A Pilot hides the actual GUI manipulation object used. The Droid class allows programmatic execution of an application via the generation of native input events. Droid is not required for Haste tests, and it may be replaced by other utilities for programmatically manipulating graphical components.

2.1   Haste Abstractions

The key abstractions of the Haste testing framework are the Story, Step, and StoryBook. The class relationships for these abstractions are illustrated in Figure 1.

Story. A Story corresponds to a test of a user story. Each Story consists of a set of ordered steps. Steps make JUnit assertions, and the failure of any assertion causes the execution of the Story to stop and be reported as a failure. Story differs from the JUnit TestCase upon which it is built in two important ways. First, the individual test steps are executed in a well-defined and intentional order, unlike test methods in a TestCase. Second, failure of any step causes failure of the Story. A Story stops executing at the first failure of a Step. The interface for Story is shown below:

```
public abstract class Story extends junit.framework.TestCase{
    protected abstract List steps();
    protected abstract boolean storySetUp() throws Throwable;
    protected abstract void storyTearDown() throws Throwable;
}
```

Step. A Step is a relatively small, independent action within a Story. Steps are implemented as classes. This allows for easy sharing of common test steps between user stories. A Step consists of Java statements and JUnit assertions that exercise and validate some aspect of the application under test. For graphical applications, Pilots allow the code for Steps to be easily read and to correlate clearly with a user story elaboration. Step classes that are not shared between stories are typically implemented as Java inner classes. The interface for Step is shown below:

```
public abstract class Step extends junit.framework.Assert {
    public abstract void runStep() throws Throwable;
}
```

StoryBook. A StoryBook contains a collection of Story and/or StoryBook objects, and is used to organize and group story tests. Story test objects are run by a utility class called the JVMStoryRunner. This class allows each Story in a StoryBook to execute with a new instance of the application under test in its own private Java virtual machine. We find that the run-time penalty for this approach is more than made up for by eliminating potentially difficult-to-debug Story interaction due to indeterminate application state when a Story executes. The interface for StoryBook is shown below:

```
public abstract class StoryBook extends
    junit.framework.TestSuite {

    public void addStory(Story s) {}
    public void addStoryBook(StoryBook b) {}
    protected abstract void stories();
}
```

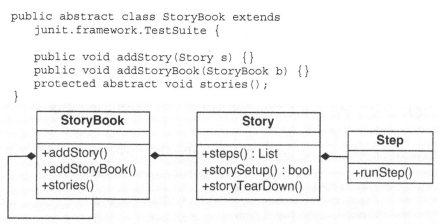

Fig. 1. Class diagram of key abstractions in Haste system test framework

2.2 Narcitecture

Unit and integration testing generally involves manipulating an object via its interface and making assertions about the state of the object to detect failures. In Java, access to the internal state of an object is easily gained by placing the test class in the same package with the class under test. In C++ the friend modifier is used for the same effect. System tests are naturally higher-level tests than unit or integration tests, and therefore assertions need to be made on multiple objects. The state of the application, rather than simply the state of a single object, needs to be evaluated in a system test.

A Java class can be a member of only a single package, limiting the use of package level access to grant a test Story access to the internal state of the application. Our convention is to place stories in packages designed only for logically grouping stories. The Haste Narcitecture was created to solve the problem of getting access to the internal state of the application.

A Narcitecture is a set of classes created for a particular application that make the internal state of the application available to Story objects. A narc class is created to reveal the internal state of a particular source class. Narc classes live in a parallel package hierarchy to the application's source classes, just like unit test classes when using JUnit. The narc exploits its package level access to a source class and makes that state available to the Story via a public interface. Narc classes can be automatically created via reflection with the NarcGenerator utility.

2.3   Pilots and Droid

Pilot interfaces wrap the complex behavior of GUI components into simpler interfaces that, together with a specific GUI manipulation toolkit, allow for test step classes to be written at a more abstract level. Complex GUI components such as combo boxes, menu trees, and file dialogs require multiple actions to do something which is conceptually simple from the user story elaboration perspective. In addition, these types of components are often platform dependent, behaving quite differently between different Java look-and-feels or operating systems. An Abstract Factory pattern is used for constructing Pilot objects. The Pilot factory insures that all Pilot objects used in a test suite are consistent with the look-and-feel or platform being tested.

Each Pilot has a one-to-one relationship with a particular class of GUI component. Pilot methods are implemented by an object from a particular GUI testing toolkit. That object manipulates the underlying GUI component to achieve the action desired in the user story elaboration. For example, the following snippet of user story

> ... the user selects a file to load...

corresponds to test step code using a JComboBoxPilot Pilot as follows:

```
PilotFactory factory = PilotFactory.getNewFactory();
JcomboBoxPilot boxPilot =
    factory.createJComboBoxPilot(fileChooser);
boxPilot.setEventDelay(50);
boxPilot.clickItem(1);
```

The clickItem() method is approximately 40 lines of code using a Droid to manipulate the fileChooser combo box. The complexity wrapped by the Pilot makes the test step simpler.

The Haste Pilot interfaces decouple system test code from any specific GUI testing toolkit. Haste includes a utility class, Droid, which extends java.awt.Robot. Robot was created to automate GUI testing. Robot is used to generate native system input events such as mouse clicks and keyboard strokes. Droid also allows for control over event timing, and for synchronization of events on the Java event queue. By driving the GUI programmatically, Droid isolates the test code from the detailed appearance of the interface. Droid is similar in approach to JFCUnit [5] and Abbot [7].

An illustrative subset of Droid's interface is shown below. Droid offers a higher-level, more convenient interface for manipulating GUI components. For example, Robot provides keyPress(int code) and mouseMove(int x, int y), while Droid builds on these to allow for typing a string or clicking a component.

```
public void typeString(String s);
public void clickComponent(Component c);
public void typeKeyShift(int k);
public static void waitOnEventQueue();
```

3   Example and Experience

Atomic Object develops custom software using XP practices. The first use of Haste was for a contract project for Burke E. Porter Machinery. We were contracted to implement the client side of a next generation, customer configurable, dynamic vehicle test (DVT) machine.

3.1   CCRT Application

Burke Porter DVTs perform the final evaluation of new vehicles at the end of an automotive assembly line, and are deployed throughout the world. The DVT has a real-time server implemented in C++ on QNX, and a platform independent, heavily multithreaded, fully internationalized Java client driving dual video displays.

With the lone exception of acceptance testing, development of the CCRT client application was done following standard XP practices. The CCRT application unit and integration test suite consists of 1,980 test methods for a source tree of 206 classes. The difficulty of automating acceptance tests for a complex application with a graphical user interface stalled us on this XP practice. Facing the first field deployment of the CCRT application in the summer of 2002, we decided we could delay no longer and needed to solve this thorny problem. Haste was born of this need.

Nine months into the project and ready for the deployment of the version 1.0 beta of the application, the customer selected the most vital functionality from among the approximately 80 story cards in the project and we created system tests with Haste. From that time forward we adopted a concurrent development strategy for system tests. As of February 2003, the CCRT acceptance test suite consists of 24 story tests. The time to develop each Story has ranged from 30 minutes to 8 hours (pair-time).

3.2   Restricted Configuration Story

An example Story from the CCRT application involves operation of the application's configuration panel. The story card reads as follows:

> *The configuration panel will only be accessible to users with sufficient privileges.*
> *Users will authenticate themselves via a login and password.*

The elaboration of this story involved more details concerning special subpanels of configuration, a multi-level access control scheme, what should happen for non-authorized users, automatic de-authentication, etc. The Story class created for this user story was called StoryRestrictedConfiguration[1]. The StoryBook named ConfigurationStories contains several related stories:

```
public class ConfigurationStories extends StoryBook {
    protected void stories() {
        addStory( new StoryRestrictedConfiguration() );
        ...
    }
```

---

[1] Atomic Object uses a convention of naming all stories by the beginning word Story, and all test steps that are shared between stories with the beginning word Step. Haste does not enforce this convention.

The Story consists of the following steps in a total of 300 lines of Java, including comments:

```java
public class StoryRestrictedConfiguration extends Story {
    Droid r2d2;
    protected boolean storySetUp() throws Throwable {
        r2d2 = new Droid();
        r2d2.setAutoDelay(50);
        return true;
    }
    protected void storyTearDown() throws Throwable {
        new StepStopApp().runStep();
    }
    protected List steps() {
        List steps = new ArrayList();
        // app starts with known preferences file
        steps.add( new StepRestoreRtcProperties() );
        // shared step for starting the application
        steps.add( new StepStartApp() );
        // user enters the configuration screen
        steps.add( new SelectConfig() );
        // non-authenticated user is denied access
        steps.add( new NotLoggedIn() );
        // authenticated user is allowed access
        steps.add( new LoggedIn() );
        // only special user can access user config panel
        steps.add( new AccessUserAdmin() );
        // confirm auto logout when the user leaves
        steps.add( new AutoLogout() );

        return steps;
    }
}
```

The source code for the AccessUserAdmin test Step is shown below:

```java
class AccessUserAdmin extends Step {

  public void runStep() throws Throwable {
    String usersButton = "users";
    Controller controller = Main.controller;

    ConfigurationManager configManager =
        controller.getGUIManager().getConfigurationManager();
    ConfigurationManagerNarc configNarc =
        new ConfigurationManagerNarc(configManager);
    String currentButton =
        configNarc.getSelectedButton();

    assertTrue("Should not already be in 'users'",
        !usersButton.equals(currentButton));

    // enter configuration panel by clicking users button
    // login dialog should display with focus
```

```
        configNarc.clickConfigButton(usersButton);

        assertTrue("Users panel visible but not authenticated",
                ! configNarc.getSelectedPanel().isVisible());
        assertTrue("Users button should be selected",
                usersButton.equals(configNarc.getSelectedButton()));
        // login with the standard login and password
        r2d2.typeString("bogus\tbogus\t ");
        assertTrue("Authenticated but users panel is not visible",
                configNarc.getSelectedPanel().isVisible());
    }
}
```

3.3   Customer Perspective

Burke E. Porter Machinery specializes in embedded real-time vehicle test software designed to verify quality and performance capability of state-of-the-art advanced vehicle systems. This specialty of testing vehicle engine control units, power train components and subsystems during the OEM design and verification phases demands total flexibility and short iterative design cycles. We employ rapid control prototyping (RCP) or the practice of testing control software with a real system as our standard development approach to solve this challenge. When we looked for a partner to implement the GUI for our new real time system, initially we chose Atomic Object due to their utilization of XP and in particular, User Stories. We are in a niche business and a big concern of ours was the time required to bring an outside contractor up to speed on the requirements for our application. The User Story approach allowed us to quickly transfer our design concept to Atomic Object and avoid the effort of compiling a static specification doomed to become "shelfware".

We quickly learned that the User Story approach was just one of the benefits to Atomic Object's approach. Since we were able to communicate our design concept in discrete User Stories, we were able to prioritize and receive them according to individual or User Story unique deadlines. The Haste Story tests were initially seen more as a method to ensure a minimum level of quality of a component in isolation. It was incorrectly seen as a type of sorting process where "bad" components were stopped prior to release. We realized, however, that we were taking delivery not of just components but of working sub-systems. As Story tests validated each additional feature, our trust and acceptance of the software grew allowing us to confidently integrate it with our real time code and not introduce bugs.

Rapid, confident iteration had many benefits for us. As embedded programming specialists, the value add we deliver to our customers is in the "black box". Traditionally, this is developed first and the user interface is developed second. This often creates the situation where the end user has to be a software engineer to understand the true state of the system. With working GUI sub-systems however, we were able to get customer feedback very early on allowing us to judge customer satisfaction and mitigate risk. Poorly understood customer requirements, desires, usability or even potential feature enhancements that could or would not have even been conceived of were made obvious by these early builds. This allowed us to adapt to these issues and take appropriate action without threat to schedule.

Lastly, the XP development process with Haste story tests provided us with a sales tool at the earliest possible point in the software development cycle. The ability to show working systems of any size is a valuable tool to demonstrate that our solutions are real and not vaporware.

4   Conclusion

Haste was built and first used in the middle of an 18 month XP project. For the CCRT application, Haste system tests satisfied the need for quality assurance in a release process, for customer buyoff, and for code maintenance via regression testing. During the release of the final 1.0 version of the application, the only bug reported in the field occurred in a related application for which no system tests had been written. We believe that the obvious system tests would have detected this bug. Haste is now used in our test-first development fashion, with system test development an integral part of working on new user stories.

Haste is available under the LGPL license. The home on the web for Haste is `http://atomicobject.com/haste`. The Haste project is maintained on Source Forge, and includes source code, test code, documentation, and sample applications.

Acknowledgements. Large projects and good ideas are rarely the sole work of the authors of a paper. We would like to acknowledge and thank the other team members of Atomic Object, namely Bill Bereza, Karlin Fox, Jeff Martin, Chris TenHarmsel, and Daniel Estrada for hard work and good ideas along the way. Burke Porter engineers, particularly the CCRT core team of Kevin Hykin, Tim Bochenek, and Brian Meinke also played an important role in the development of Haste. Paul Jorgensen made insightful comments on an early draft of the paper. Reviewer comments were helpful and much appreciated.

References

1. Jorgensen, P.: Software Testing, A Craftsman's Approach, 2nd Edition. CRC Press (2002)
2. Gold, R.: HTTPUnit: `http://httpunit.sourceforge.net/`
3. Kitiyakara, N.: Acceptance Testing HTML, Extreme Programming and Agile Methods – XP/Agile Universe 2002, Wells, D., Williams, L., Editors (2002)
4. jWebUnit: `http://jwebunit.sourceforge.net/`
5. JFCUnit: `http://jfcunit.sourceforge.net/`
6. Jemmy: `http://jemmy.netbeans.org/`
7. Abbot: `http://abbot.sourceforge.net/`
8. Marathon: `http://marathonman.sourceforge.net/`
9. Marick, B., Pettichord, B.: Workshop on agile acceptance tests, XP Universe 2002, Chicago IL, `http://www.pettichord.com/agile_workshop.html`
10. Beck, K.: Extreme Programming Explained, Addison Wesley (2000)
11. Canoo WebTest: `http://webtest.canoo.com/webtest`

Virtual Teaming: Experiments and Experiences with Distributed Pair Programming

David Stotts[1], Laurie Williams[2], Nachiappan Nagappan[2],
Prashant Baheti[2], Dennis Jen[1], and Anne Jackson[2]

[1]Dept. of Computer Science, University of North Carolina, Chapel Hill, NC 27599
{stotts,dsjen}@cs.unc.edu
[2]Dept. of Computer Science, North Carolina State University, Raleigh, NC 27695
{lawilli3,nnagapp,ppbaheti,amjackso}@unity.ncsu.edu

Abstract. Pair programming is a practice in which two programmers work together at one computer, collaborating on the same design, algorithm, code or test. Previous studies have shown that pair programmers produce higher quality code in essentially the same amount of time as solo programmers. Additional benefits include increased job satisfaction, improved team communication, and efficient tacit knowledge sharing. However, it may not always be possible for all team members to be collocated due to the rise in teleworking and geographically distributed teams. This paper analyzes the results of two distributed pair programming case studies done at UNC Chapel Hill and at NC State University. Participants used readily available off-the-shelf applications for collaborative software development. The results indicate that software development collaboratively "over the wire" is feasible, effective, and pleasant for the participants; distributed development is better done as synchronous pairs than as individuals who integrate; and distributed pairs maintain many of the advantages of collocated pairs.

1 Introduction

Distributed team projects are becoming more common in the software industry. The power of distributed development can increase an organization's opportunities to win new work by opening up a broader skill and product knowledge base, coupled with a deeper pool of potential employees [12]. Major corporations have launched global teams with the expectation that technology will make virtual collocation a feasible alternative [15]. Additionally, distance education (DE) has also come into prominence in recent years. Team projects in DE computer science courses call for distributed development. These teams need to communicate and work effectively and productively. Through the vehicle of groupware, team members can communicate with each other and complete their projects even when they are remotely located or when they work at incompatible hours.

Previous research [14,20] has indicated that pair programming is better than individual programming in a co-located environment. Do these results also apply to distributed pairs? It has been established that distance matters [15]; face-to-face pair programmers will most likely outperform distributed pair programmers in terms of sheer productivity. However, the inevitability of distributed work in industry and

F. Maurer and D. Wells (Eds.): XP/Agile Universe 2003, LNCS 2753, pp. 129–141, 2003.

education calls for research in determining how to make this type of work most effective. Additionally, Extreme Programming (XP) [3] usually has co-located pairs working in front of the same workstation, a limitation that ostensibly hinders use of XP for distributed development of software.

This paper discusses results of our research on *distributed pair programming (dPP)*. By *dPP* we mean that two members of the team (which may consist solely of these two people) synchronously collaborate on the same design or code from different locations. This means that both must view a copy of the same screen, and at least one of them should have the capability to change the contents on the screen. To be able to do this, they require technological support for sharing desktops and verbal conversation, and perhaps even video conferencing capabilities.

Our first dPP experiments have been previously reported [1,2]. This paper gives results of two other case studies done jointly between grad students[1] at the University of North Carolina at Chapel Hill (UNC-CH) and grad students at North Carolina State University (NCSU) in the spring and fall of 2002. Section 2 gives background work on virtual teams, a summary of prior dPP results, and a description of the technical infrastructure to support dPP. Sections 3 and 4 discuss the details of the two case studies. Section 5 outlines the lessons extracted from the experiments. General observations, limitations, and conclusions are presented in Section 6.

2   Background and Related Work

2.1   Virtual Teaming

Our studies involve a specific form of *virtual team*. In general, a virtual team can be defined as a group of people who work together towards a common goal but operate across time, distance, culture and organizational boundaries [8]. The members of a virtual team may be located at different work sites, or they may travel frequently and need to rely upon communication technologies to share information, collaborate, and coordinate their work efforts. As the business environment becomes more global and businesses are increasingly in search of more creative ways to reduce operating costs, the concept of virtual teams is of paramount importance [7]. In the context of this paper, the common goal of the virtual team is the development of software.

Virtual teams are also used in education. Distributed learning, or distance education, is experiencing explosive growth. "Online learning is already a $2 billion business; Gerald Odening, an analyst with Chase Bank, predicts that the figure will rise by 35% a year, reaching $9 billion by 2005" [17]. Programming students have benefited from this growth. Virtual teaming is a boon for distance education as it allows geographically remote students to participate in team projects.

Organizing and managing virtual teams is a topic of ongoing research. From our earlier studies and experiences comparing co-located solo programmers with co-

---

[1] The validity or generalizability of empirical studies with students is sometimes questioned because student projects do not deal with issues of size or scale, as is realistic in industry. Several research studies have indicated, however, that student test-beds represent ideal environments for empirical software engineering, providing sufficient realism while allowing for controlled observation of important project parameters [6,11].

located pair programmers [1,2], we surmise significant benefits for virtual teams that use dPP. Operating via dPP may help establish team trust and create a "virtual culture [13]". When programmers pair with each other, and especially when the pairs rotate among the group, they get a chance to get to know many on their team more personally. This familiarity helps to break down many communication barriers. Team members find each other much more approachable. As a result, they will struggle with questions or lack of information for less time before asking the right person a question. The rotation of team members also gives each student a broader understanding of the project through observing the work of each new partner. Additionally, they feel better about their jobs because they know their teammates on a more personal level. In short, better communication between team members leads to increased confidence levels and more effective time usage. A primary consideration, then, in virtual teaming (and so dPP) is good support for communication [10].

2.2 Prior Distributed Pair Programming Results

In the Fall 2001 semester a structured experiment was conducted in a graduate class, Object-Oriented Languages and Systems, taught by Dr Edward Gehringer at NCSU [1,2]. This course introduces students to object technology and covers object-oriented analysis and design, Smalltalk, and Java. This course has a five-week team project that was used for our experiment. A total of 132 students took this course, including 32 distance education students. For the team project, the students were divided into teams of two to four students and worked as collocated teams, collocated team with pair programming, distributed teams, and distributed team with pairs.

The results of this experiment show that distributed teams had a slightly greater productivity as compared to collocated teams but the difference was not statistically significant. Also the distributed teams outperformed the collocated teams in terms of software quality measured by the average grade obtained by the group in the project. Again, the difference was not statistically significant. Anecdotally, the co-located pairs outperformed the co-located non-pair teams, and the distributed pairs outperformed the distributed non-pairs.

Another area under study is the communication among team members. We measured this with an exit survey. The distributed pairs reported the best communication, followed by the collocated (pair and non-pair) teams. This is consistent with earlier findings on the benefits of pairing on team communication [18,20].

2.3 Technical Infrastructure Considerations for dPP

For collaborating over the Internet, we chose COTS solutions that are affordable, readily available, and easy to learn and use. One goal of our work has been to see how effective dPP can be with a simple, non-custom setup. Table 1 lists the programs and technologies used at various times and in various combinations during our two case studies and our previous experiments.

Table 1. Programs and technologies used in our studies

Technology	Capabilities	Comments from users
NetMeeting	Program Sharing, Whiteboard, Text Messaging, Voice Communication	We continued to refer to the whiteboard stored on NetMeeting.
pcAnywhere	Desktop Sharing	Some firewall issues.
WS FTP	File Transfer	
TextPad	Text Editing	
Notepad	Text Editing	
Crimson Editor	Text Editing	Color codes JSP files.
Visio	Diagram Creating Software	Used to create our web flow diagram.
Yahoo Messenger	Text messaging, File Transfer, Voice Communication	We initially used this, but stopped; MSN Messenger can start NetMeeting, while having the features of Yahoo Messenger.
MSN Messenger	Text messaging, File Transfer, Voice Communication, Start NetMeeting	
WinZip	Zip and Unzip Files	
HomeSite	HTML Editor	Used to write the meeting minutes.
CVS	File Repository and Management	It was too difficult to set up and seemed unnecessary.
Tomcat	Server	Allowed us to view JSP.
Internet	Information and Communication Medium	
Group Web Site	Web Site	Used to store meeting minutes and project documents
Internet Explorer	Web Browser	
Netscape	Web Browser	
Email	Text Communication/File Transfer	
Putty	Shell	
Eclipse	Integrated development environments (IDE)	We tested the Sangum plug-in for dPP.

We have developed systems with dPP infrastructures based on both *NetMeeting*™ (Microsoft) and *pcAnywhere* (Symantec). Some pairs have preferred one, some the other; we have recorded the various reasons given for the preferences. Both programs, though, share important functions and characteristics needed for dPP:

> *remote desktop sharing, program sharing, file transfer, session security (password login, authentication, encrypted transmissions)*

In addition, these capabilities are needed (or desirable) for dPP:

> *audio conferencing, whiteboard, text chat*

NetMeeting provides them integrally; but *pcAnywhere* requires third-party programs that are then shared with the desktop. Finally, *video* may have uses in dPP; this is a point for further research.

3   Spring 2002 Comparative Study

In Spring 2002, eight graduate students (four at NCSU, four at UNC-CH) participated in a five-week dPP/dXP experiment. We formed four distributed pairs, each having one student at UNC and one at NCSU. About 30 miles separates these locations so there was no face-to-face contact within a group, and all communication was done via the Internet connection between the campuses.

Two of the groups worked as virtual synchronous pairs (utilizing dPP); we refer here to them as "dPP pairs". The remaining two worked as more traditional virtual teams (no pair programming); we refer to them as distributed, non-paired teams, or "dNP teams". Allocation of students to groups was done randomly without regard to preferences. All four groups had to conform to the 13 XP practices (except the two dNP teams did not practice pair programming). Each group worked independently on a card game, so four separate versions of the same game were produced. The dPP pairs first tried *pcAnywhere* for desktop sharing, but they had trouble passing through each other's firewalls as they worked from different universities. Ultimately, they chose *NetMeeting* for development, but *Yahoo Messenger* was favored over *MSN Messenger* for voice communication. The dNP teams wrote their code independently and e-mailed it back and forth. All four groups had a common storage area where they could upload their code after modifications and view the other programmer's code. Programming was done in Java, and JUnit² testing was used for all projects.

The results reported here came from analysis of programmer feedback and project output throughout the experiment. The *number of test cases passed* is the metric used for program *quality*. Since all groups developed the same product, the *productivity* measure is *mean total time* for development; this frees the analysis from typical concerns with lines of code measures.

Figure 1 shows that the dNP teams took a greater amount of time (in days) compared to the dPP pairs. The dNP teams spent considerable time coordinating their activities and integrating their code. Whenever a question arose, they took more time to clear it due to the limitations of communication. The dPP pair members made "appointments" with each other for virtual collaboration sessions; the partners always

---

² See http://www.junit.org/ .

kept their commitments to these appointments and made significant progress during each session. Conversely, the dNP team members often delayed progress because they felt they were "too busy to work on the project right now". Ultimately, this caused a significant delay in project completion; one dNP team never finished the project to completion. This supports earlier findings that pairs put a positive form of "pair pressure" on each other [5,18-20]. One can easily see a parallel between the student work ethic effects of pair programming and similar effects among professional industrial programmers.

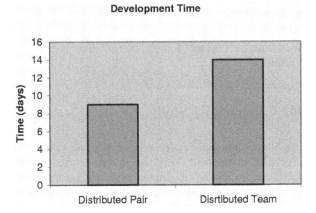

Fig. 1. Development Time (days)

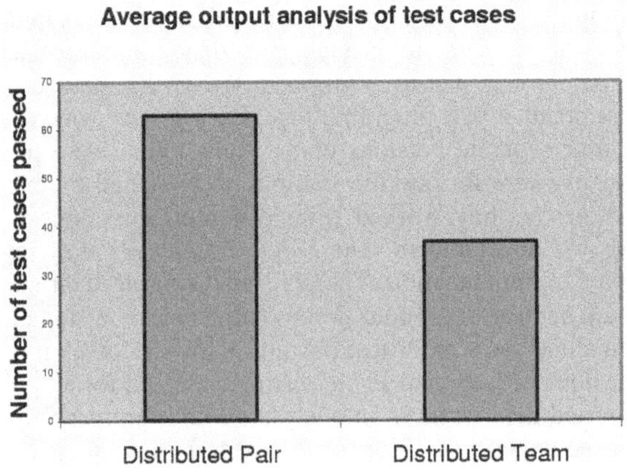

Fig. 2. Unit tests written and passed

Since programming was in Java, the groups wrote unit test cases using JUnit. Figure 2 shows the average number of test cases that were written and passed in JUnit testing. DPP pairs wrote just over 60 tests, whereas dNP teams wrote just under 40 tests. XP requires *test-driven development (TDD)*, meaning programmers write unit test cases prior to implementing code [4]. In general, we consider that groups writing more unit test cases have better tested code than groups writing fewer test cases.

Particularly with TDD, writing more test cases is associated with producing better structured code that is more likely to ultimately pass acceptance tests [9].

Figure 2 shows that dPP pairs wrote 70% more unit test cases than the dNP teams. Since the dPP pairs were working synchronously, they could concurrently decide on the flow of the code and on the test cases that could be implemented. These pairs never needed to integrate their code because they worked on the entire project together. The dNP teams needed to separately and specifically integrate their individual efforts. At times, they could not write as many test cases to fully test the integration of newly written code because their partner's code was not yet in the code base. Other significant factors include pair pressure and pair brainstorming [18]. Pairs are more likely to write a thorough set of test cases because they are continually "watching over" each other and can brainstorm more test cases by putting their brainpower together.

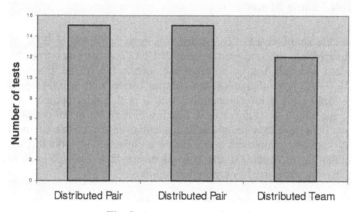

Fig. 3. Acceptance tests Passed

All four groups were required to record their user stories and the acceptance tests they performed for the software using Bryce[3], a Web-based software-process analysis system used to manage projects and to record development metrics. The results of these measures are shown in Figure 3. These results were obtained by running the code against a fixed set of 15 test cases determined before the experiment. Both the dPP pairs satisfied all the test cases. One dNP team satisfied 12 test cases, and the other did not complete the project. The sample size is too small to do a statistically significant analysis of the data.

The developers were also required to give feedback about their overall development experience and their team communication. The allowed response range was *very good, good, fair* and *poor*. As shown in Table 2, the dPP pairs reported a better experience. The main reason for this was that dNP team 2 was not able to complete the project on time due to lack of coordination between the members. Moreover, dNP team 1 experienced difficulties when there was a difference in understanding of the architectural model that took almost two days to rectify. From

---

[3] See http://bryce.csc.ncsu.edu

this case study we can say we have further suggestive evidence that the synchronous paired teams performed better than the non-paired teams.

Table 2. Qualitative Feedback

Teams	Quality of Development Experience	Communication Among Team Members
dPP pair 1	Very good	Very good
dPP pair 2	Very good	Very good
dNP team 1	Good	Good
dNP team 2	Poor	Poor

4   Fall 2002 Case Study

The second case study we have completed was done in the fall of 2002. We created one pair, distributed with one grad student at UNC and the other from NCSU. The NCSU student worked from a home office, connected to the Internet via cable modem. The UNC programmer used a campus office with a 100-megabit Internet connection. Unlike the prior comparative study, in this development there was no face-to-face meeting to start the project. Email was used for initial contacts and team organization. Four meetings online were needed over the course of the first three weeks to try various technologies and settle on a collection of tools that worked well for the computing environment the pair members had. Table 3 summarizes the computing environments used by each programmer.

Table 3. Computing Platforms used by the pair members

Property	Remote system	Host system
Net Connection	Internet II backbone, UNC office	Cable modem, home office
Communications	Headset	Speakers and microphone
Operating Sys	Windows2000	Windows 98
Ram	128 MB	384 MB
Processor Speed	400 MHZ	933 MHZ

The pair sessions were divided into two main segments: *infrastructure tests*, and *development*. The first few pair sessions were technology tests, spent trying various combinations of dPP support programs for effectiveness and to establish their preferences. The pair settled on *MSN Messenger* for voice communication and *pcAnywhere* for screen sharing. The first session after that was used to code a simple magic square program as a "development shake down", in which the pair became accustomed to the behavior patterns needed to produce working code in the dPP environment they chose. Once their dPP environment was established, the remaining sessions comprised the measured development. Each development session had six activity blocks:

1. Each person logs onto MSN Messenger.
2. One of the pair would request a voice communication.
3. Start *pcAnywhere* (UNC as remote, NCSU as host)
4. Pair programming
5. Discussion about what to do in the next meeting and confirm next day to meet.
6. Post meeting minutes to website.

The pair produced a tool to support future XP projects: a pair matcher that takes factors such as experience, personality type, and preferences into account to try to form pairs that are likely to be effective. This project ended up as a set of about 20 Java server pages with a web interface. The pair spent a total of 37.25 hours in development from 9/19/02 to 11/25/02, using 18 online sessions averaging 2.07 hours each. The longest session was 3.25 hours, and the shortest was 0.75 hours. Minutes and observations were kept of all meetings; they can be reviewed online at the project web site http://www.cs.unc.edu/~dsjen/pair/ along with user stories for the program and an architecture diagram of the system they produced.

4.1 Observations on the dPP Technical Infrastructure

The software used fir dPP must compensate as much as possible for the lack of physical contact between team members. The team in this study decided that *pcAnywhere* best emulated the co-located environment (the prior study participants used *NetMeeting*). Alternate environments, such as *NetMeeting* and *Eclipse* with a pair programming plug-in[4], also allowed the sharing of programs, but the methods for doing so were deemed less effective for the pair. The following are technical problems observed with the dPP infrastructure:

- Inability to copy and paste from one computer to another. The person connecting to the other's desktop was not able to copy and paste from his own desktop, which would have been a convenient feature.
- In *NetMeeting*, mouse locus behavior prevented use of a PC when the other pair member was driving.
- *NetMeeting* exhibited graphics problems drawing cursors that *pcAnywhere* solved.
- Network-based voice communication occasionally would break up, making hearing one's partner very difficult.
- One partner was using speakers instead of a headset, producing an audible echo in the headset of the partner (who would hear himself talking with a delay). Initially the partner found this distracting, and spoke slowly and haltingly to compensate. However, he reported becoming used to it, could ignore it, and even expected it as an indication of a live connection.
- When using *pcAnywhere*, transferring control to another is much easier.

---

[4] See http://www.industriallogic.com/software/sangam.html

- Remote machine should have a screen size slightly larger than the host machine; this allows the window showing the host PC to fit entirely on the remote, requiring no scroll bars.
- There was some lag in mouse motion and editor scrolling; however, it was minimal, easily adapted to, and not noticeable after a few initial sessions.

5 Lessons Learned

These new studies, and our earlier ones, have allowed us to gathered some observations we think characterize effective virtual team development of software with dPP using an inexpensive, COTS, easy to learn/use technical environment. These lessons include:

- At least one, but perhaps periodic, face-to-face meeting is beneficial. In the comparative study, the students used one such meeting to get to know each other and to brainstorm their initial system architecture.
- The developers have been found to work better when they strike a good rapport with their partner at a personal level. Groups in the beginning exchanged URLs to their personal Web homepages so that one developer could learn about the other.
- Using a tool that allows for the distributed teams to quickly switch between a design view, such as a class diagram, and a code view is beneficial. The *TogetherSoft Control Center*[5] has this capability.
- Distributed pair programmers absolutely must be willing to speak while they work. They must explain what they are doing as they are doing it or the navigator quickly gets lost. Programmers who are not willing to speak almost continuously should probably not try to work this way.
- Beyond the necessary basics (screen sharing, audio communications, file transfer), the appropriate technical infrastructure for dPP appears to vary with individual tastes; some teams were forced to one product or another by specific computing platform issues (firewalls, communication speeds), but overall different teams ended up selecting different combinations of *NetMeeting, pcAnywhere, MSN Messenger, and Yahoo Messenger*. All combinations worked effectively once the programmers were happy.
- Screen sharing programs used in dPP alleviate potential file duplication, data coherence and consistency problems that could occur with integrating forms of virtual teaming; one member of the pair is always the host and work is always off one project base.

5.1 Advantages of dPP over Co-located PP

In exit interviews, the participants noted they had benefited from many of the previously observed advantages of co-located pair programming, such as pair learning, pair pressure, two-brains better than one, etc. Our studies indicate that

---

[5] See http://togethersoft.com

distribution does not destroy or hinder these co-located PP advantages. In addition, distributed PP has these advantages over co-located PP:

- Visibility is improved over collocated pair programming at a single PC/monitor, since each dPP participant has a screen.
- The navigating dPP participant can use the PC to search the Web for resources
- No office changing or travel is needed to meet one's partner; work on other projects can continue until dPP appointment time.
- Although not tested, meetings are possible when on trips, out of town, etc.
- Pairs are forced to keep electronic copies and records of our work and ideas. For example, instead of drawing on a physical whiteboard, the participants used NetMeeting's whiteboard. This ensured they would be able to go back and look at earlier plans.
- Pair members are less likely to start conversations off topic; meetings are almost completely focused on the task. The computer is the medium for all exchanges, and participants can't turn away from their computers and chat one-on-one.

5.2 Disadvantages of dPP Compared to Co-located PP

The study participants observed these disadvantages of dPP over co-located PP:

- Users can't point, making it difficult to describe where a problem is; line number naming helps, but it takes a noticeable amount of time for the other to find the line number.
- A problem with one computer forces both to stop working; this theoretically doubles the MTTF over using a single computer (as in co-located PP)
- Pair members can't see facial expressions; Webcams are too small, too limited in frame rate, and too expensive in bandwidth consumption to help here.
- Passers-by often don't know a programmer is in a dPP session, and will enter an office and begin a conversation; a specific sign must be used to tell this if one does not want a shut door.
- There was a learning curve with dPP that is not present in co-located PP.
- Lack of physical proximity means large amounts of time spent on verbal explanations that could rapidly be resolved by a visual diagrams; although *NetMeeting* has a whiteboard, it is cumbersome to use and does not adequately solve this problem.

6 Conclusions and Future Work

Our experiments support these conclusions about the efficacy of distributed pair programming:

- Pair programming in virtual teams is a feasible way of developing software.
- Our earlier work found that dPP programs were equal in quality to those produced both by co-located pairs and by teams not synchronously paired; these new studies continue to uphold this as well, in that dPP pairs produced *better* programs than dNP teams.

- Effective collaborative software development is possible with a few simple, non-custom, widely-available tools (screen sharing, Internet-based audio communications)
- Feedback from the participants indicates that synchronous pairing (pair programming) engenders better teamwork and communication within a virtual distributed team.
- Distributed pairs maintain many of the benefits (pair pressure, pair learning, two brains) seen in co-located pairs

The studies have some limitations, which we seek to get beyond with further experiments. We are currently studying the following dPP and dXP issues and questions:

Sample size. We plan to repeat these case studies to build up a larger base of results.

Teams vs. pairs. We plan to run larger dPP efforts requiring more than a single pair per team.

Whiteboard, pointing, and facial expressions. As in earlier experiments, we continue to see pairs needing better capabilities for indicating areas of interest ("pointing") and whiteboard use. While *NetMeeting* has a built-in whiteboard, the participants found it limited and awkward to use, and we suspect all software whiteboard programs will be the same. The problem is size, and using wrist muscles to do drawing (not natural). The participants also indicated a desire to see facial expressions, but Webcam's were ineffective for the reasons cited above.

To investigate these problems we are doing follow-on experiments with a video-enhanced dPP environment [16]. The environment uses 2 PCs: one with the screen sharing infrastructure used here, and the other projecting a full screen image of the partner on a wall to the side of the programmer, in arm's reach. We have a whiteboard digitizer on this projection surface. Pair members can easily shift off video, then reach out and draw normally (with virtual ink); the drawings are shared and are projected at the partner's site. A button push restores video.

No "chit chat". We had one programmer make an interesting comment about the technical infrastructure and the fact that it is not as "seamless and glitchless as face-to-face conversation." This participant had developed several programs using co-located pair programming in a class at UNC. He then participated in one of the dPP developments. When asked to compare the experiences, he noted that in co-located pair programming he and his partner has spent a fair amount of time "chit chatting" and that this was not possible (or did not happen to near the same degree) in the dPP infrastructure. This comment could be taken to mean the dPP infrastructure provides a decreased capability for human, team-building interactions; his implication, however, was that the dPP infrastructure oddly enough *increased* productivity by offering slightly *less* fluid interactions. He suggested that the communications mechanisms, while adequate and effective for code development, were not smooth enough to encourage extraneous talking. We find this an interesting point for further investigation.

Acknowledgements. We gratefully acknowledge Intel for providing Webcam equipment, Symantec for providing *pcAnywhere* software, and IBM for donating PC equipment in support of our experiments. We would also like to recognize NCSU graduate student Vinay Ramachandran for developing the *Bryce* tool for recording project metrics. Our research was also partially supported by the US Environmental Protection Agency under grant # R82-795901–3.

References

[1]   Baheti, P., Gehringer, E., and Stotts, D., "Exploring the Efficacy of Distributed Pair Programming," Proceedings Extreme Programming/Agile Universe, Chicago, IL, 2002.

[2]   Baheti, P., Williams, L., Gehringer, E., and Stotts, D., "Exploring Pair Programming in Distributed Object-Oriented Team Projects," Proceedings OOPSLA Educator's Syposium, Seattle, WA, 2002.

[3]   Beck, K., *Extreme Programming Explained: Embrace Change.* Reading, Massachusetts: Addison-Wesley, 2000.

[4]   Beck, K., *Test Driven Development -- by Example.* Boston: Addison Wesley, 2003.

[5]   Cockburn, A. and Williams, L., "The Costs and Benefits of Pair Programming," in *Extreme Programming Examined*, G. Succi and M. Marchesi, Eds. Boston, MA: Addison Wesley, 2001, pp. 223–248.

[6]   Dutoit, A. H., Bruegge, Bernd, "Communication Metrics for Software Development," *IEEE Transactions on Software Engineering*, pp. 615–628, 1998.

[7]   Foley, S. P., "The Boundless Team: Virtual Teaming," Seminar in Industrial and Engineering Systems, Master of Science in Technology (MST) Graduate Program, Northern Kentucky University MST 660, July 24, 2000.

[8]   George, B. and Mansour, Y. M., "A Multidisciplinary Virtual Team," Proceedings Systemics, Cybernetics and Informatics (SCI) 2002, 2002.

[9]   George, B. and Williams, L., "An Initial Investigation of Test-Driven Development in Industry," Proceedings ACM Symposium on Applied Computing, Melbourne, FL, 2003.

[10] Gould, D., "Leading Virtual Teams," *Leader Values (Electronic)*, http://www.leader-values.com/Guests/Gould.htm, July 9, 2000.

[11] Humphrey, W. S., *A Discipline for Software Engineering.* Reading, Massachusetts: Addison Wesley Longman, Inc, 1995.

[12] McMahon, P. E., "Distributed Development: Insights, Challenges, and Solutions," *CrossTalk*, pp. http://www.stsc.hill.af.mil/CrossTalk/2001/nov/mcmahon.asp, 2001.

[13] McMahon, P. E., *Virtual Project Management: Software Solutions for Today and the Future.* Boca Raton: St. Lucie Press, 2001.

[14] Nosek, J. T., "The Case for Collaborative Programming," in *Communications of the ACM*, vol. March 1998, 1998, pp. 105–108.

[15] Olson, G. M. and Olson, J. S., "Distance Matters," Proceedings Human Computer Interaction, 2000.

[16] Stotts, D., Smith, J., and Williams, L. A., "A Video-Enhanced Environment for Distributed Extreme Programming," Department of Computer Science. Univ. of North Carolina at Chapel Hill, Chapel Hill, NC TR–02–009, March 1, 2002.

[17] Traub, J., "This Campus is Being Simulated," in *The New York Times Magazine*, 2000, pp. 88–93+.

[18] Williams, L. and Kessler, R., *Pair Programming Illuminated.* Reading, Massachusetts: Addison Wesley, 2003.

[19] Williams, L., Kessler, R., Cunningham, W., and Jeffries, R., "Strengthening the Case for Pair-Programming," in *IEEE Software*, vol. 17, 2000, pp. 19–25.

[20] Williams, L. A., "The Collaborative Software Process PhD Dissertation," in *Department of Computer Science*. Salt Lake City, UT: University of Utah, 2000.

Issues in Scaling Agile Using an Architecture-Centric Approach: A Tool-Based Solution

Kris Read and Frank Maurer

University of Calgary, Department of Computer Science
{readk,maurer}@cpsc.ucalgary.ca

Abstract. Agile software development processes are best applied to small teams on small to medium sized projects. Scaling agile methodologies is desired in order to bring the benefits of agile to larger, more complex projects. One way to scale agile methods is via an architecture-centric approach, in which a project is divided into smaller modules on which sub teams can use agile effectively. However, a problem with architecture-centric modifications to agile methods is the introduction of non-agile elements, for instance up-front design and integration difficulties. These issues are discussed and a tool-based solution is presented facilitating the adoption of the architecture-centric agile approach.

Keywords: Agile Methods, Scaling, CruiseControl, Continuous Integration, Test Driven Design, Automated Testing

1 Introduction

Martin Fowler likes to say, "Scaling agile methods is the last thing you want to do.[1]" At the Canadian Workshop on Scaling Agile Processes this generated quite a stir, but it turns out that he meant it literally. The idea is that one should examine every other alternative first, and consider scaling as a last resort. Nonetheless there is a need to scale agile methods. Large projects are out there, projects for which a small team is not ideally suited. If a team needs to deliver a lot of functionality but also has a lot of time, the team size can be quite small. Likewise the team can be small if it has not much time but can reduce the scope of the project. However, to deliver a lot of functionality in a short amount of time, the business solution is to add more people. Scaling a software development project would traditionally be accomplished through heavyweight processes and stacks of documentation. But it is desirable to reduce the project overhead in order to maximize productivity, and so the question becomes "How do we scale Agile Methods?" To improve the scalability of agile software processes, one solution is to follow a divide and conquer strategy based on architecture.

An architecture-centric strategy is nothing new – Ken Schwaber advocates using the first iteration of an agile project to have a smaller team define the project architecture, and then proposes multi-team coordination through a "Scrum of Scrums"

---

[1] Keynote address, Canadian Workshop on Scaling Agile Methods, 2003.
http://can.cpsc.ucalgary.ca/ws2003

F. Maurer and D. Wells (Eds.): XP/Agile Universe 2003, LNCS 2753, pp. 142–150, 2003.
© Springer-Verlag Berlin Heidelberg 2003

for the remainder of iterations. If the project is initially broken down into smaller modules, each module can be built using an agile approach. This plan enables the application of proven agile methodologies using small cohesive teams at a module level. Following this strategy may also enable distributed software development in an agile way. Agile depends upon co-located teams for close communication, but if a project were properly divided each sub-team could independently follow an agile process. In addition, if organizations are interested in exploiting the commonalities between its products or systems, an architecture-centric strategy may improve code re-use through the definition of modules. However, there is in fact an intrinsic contradiction between agile software development and the practice of separating a project into modules. By adopting such a strategy, will our process remain agile? Common sense says that there will be several incompatibilities between agile processes and the architecture-centric approach. These incompatibilities include up-front design, team inter-communication and module integration. This paper proposes that these problems of architecture-centric agile software development can be overcome through innovative tool support.

2   Concept

We sometimes assume that a comprehensive document is necessary for architecture-centric development, or that every team needs to know precisely how their product depends upon products developed elsewhere in order to construct it. This approach, however, is the antithesis of the maxim "Responding to Change over Following a Plan" stated in the Agile Manifesto[2]. Up-front planning can still be done in an agile way, so long as we stay focused on doing only what is required. In fact, agile projects normally have some overhead when user stories are gathered and prioritized, development tools chosen, environments configured, and so forth. Defining the system architecture can be included as one of the aforementioned startup costs, if the architecture is defined in a quick, lightweight manner that is flexible to change. The best way to assist agile developers with quickly generating such a definition is to provide a simple tool that they themselves can understand and work with.

In an ideal world, modules would work flawlessly with one another, and there would be no integration problems. Anyone who has tried integration knows that this is rarely the case. The interfaces between modules are problematic; even if these interfaces are well documented, it is possible that over time requirements changes or lack of communication between parties will result in incompatibilities. Without knowledge of exactly how outputs are going to be used, there is no guarantee that developers will be able to deliver them as expected. To address this issue, one can apply the same concept of continuous integration already utilized by agile teams.

> "An important part of any software development process is getting reliable builds of the software. Despite it's importance, we are often surprised when this isn't done. We stress a fully automated and reproducible build, including testing, that runs many times a day. This

---

[2] Agile Alliance, Manifesto Website http://www.agilemanifesto.org

allows each developer to integrate daily thus reducing integration problems." [3]

In an architecture-centric agile environment, it is not enough to simply perform an automated build and test whenever there is a change to the system. Because each module is assuming that its fellow modules will be constructed according to the architecture, tests based on the same (possibly incorrect) assumptions do not indicate the health of the system. When Jack is developing a module, it does the project little good if Jack also writes tests for his interface. Jack may be very well aware of what functionality he is providing, but likely has no knowledge of the functionality that other modules are expecting him to provide. It is thus very probable that Jill's module, which uses the module written by Jack, will have some specific need Jack knows nothing about. Conventional continuous integration should still be done for each module, but there must also be a higher level of continuous integration to ensure compatibility between modules even before they are implemented. It is therefore desirable to extend the concept of continuous integration such that some kind of quality assurance and verification of the interfaces is performed automatically with each build. The key to this continuous integration at the module level is getting the tests right.

The most effective arrangement would be for Jill to act as a customer for Jack at the module level. Jill will write tests for the functionality that she expects from Jack, and for her to do this *before* Jack writes his actual code. Jill doesn't need to test Jack's entire interface, just the features that she herself will be using. Thinking of testing before doing the development is not exclusive to agile; the "V-model" adaptation of waterfall[4] is one of the simplest examples of this, when you plan ahead to use your design documents and specification documents to verify your product. Agile processes can replace the "V-model" comparison of functional specifications to code with automated unit tests; this new concept can replace comparing an architecture specification to developed interfaces. The idea of API consumers writing tests is similar to that already discussed by Newkirk[5] for doing test first design of third party software. Newkirk asserts that in addition to writing tests before writing code, you should write tests before *using* code written by others. However in this case, the third party software itself may not have been written yet. You are tailoring the tests as much to your own requirements as to the functionality that will finally be provided.

This extension of "test first" design could have quite a few benefits. Any problems in the existing architecture would be uncovered early on in the iteration by test authors. Incompatible tests or conflicting tests will reveal problems in the architecture before more effort is wasted. Following this plan would enable an evolution of the system architecture; just as doing test first design for regular code helps you think and plan ahead better, so will doing test first design for module interfaces let you look ahead and construct your architecture. This evolution of the architecture should also involve actual customer representatives, who can make decisions about the entire deliverable system if conflicts or questions of priority arise. If a change in requirements influences the system architecture, new tests that verify the new functionality or structure can be added. The continuous integration software can

---

[3] http://cruisecontrol.sourceforge.net
[4] Daich, G: Software Test Technologies Report. 1994
[5] Newkirk, J.: A Light in a Dark Place: Test-driven Development of 3rd Party Packages. 2002

facilitate this by notifying affected teams when changes are made. Changing the architecture drastically is potentially a source of difficulty, but to address this we can recall how refactoring handles changes to code. Changing a small amount of code can sometimes have sweeping effects, but now and again we need to evaluate the cost-benefit tradeoff and make a decision. If our general strategy is to make changes little by little, and keep the architecture healthy, then flexibility is not necessarily lost. Teams will not only have access to the architecture definition describing the modules, but also to a set of tests representing the functionality that they need to implement; they can use these tests both as a knowledge sharing mechanism and as a contract between modules. Jack knows he is finished when all of Jill's tests pass. Likewise, Jill knows Jack's code will integrate with her own when the tests she provided are successfully run by Jack. In essence, the author of a test becomes a customer for the module developer. A hierarchy of customers is formed, with one or more actual on-site customers at the top. The real customers speak with some of the teams, who then define user stories and tests related to the child components. At each level the developers have their own product backlog of user stories defined by the customers with whom they interact. These user stories are complimented by the automated tests.

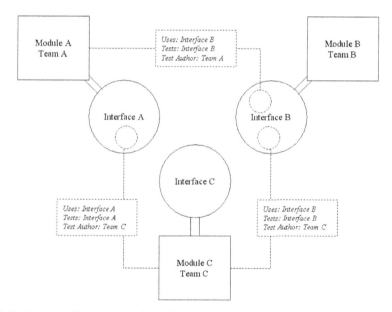

Fig. 1. Each team will do test first design for the portions of other modules' interfaces that they use. In this example, two modules depend on Interface B and one depends on Interface A. This means that three test suites will be written before development

In summary, architecture-centric software development can be combined with agile software development processes while retaining the spirit of agile by following these guidelines:

1. Design the module architecture in a quick and lightweight way
2. Provide the architecture in a format that is flexible to change
3. Require test first design at the interface level

4. Tests are written by module users not module providers
5. Test authors act as customers for dependant modules
    (in addition to real on-site customers)
6. Module teams define their own product backlog of user stories
7. Do continuous integration of the module based system

3 The Tool: COACH-IT

At the University of Calgary work is being done on a lightweight architecture planning and continuous integration tool for agile processes. **COACH-IT**, the **C**omponent **O**riented **A**gile **C**ollaborative **H**andler of **I**ntegration and **T**esting, is an effort to develop tool support for scaling agile practices using an architecture-centric approach. The sequence executed by COACH-IT is as follows:

1. Users define an architecture using the COACH-IT input web application
2. Multiple repositories are monitored for code changes in each module
3. When a change is detected the module and related modules are downloaded
4. The modules are deployed and tests are run to ensure interface compatibility
5. Teams are notified directly of any problems via electronic mail
6. The "health" of the system is available to the teams via a web page

COACH-IT combines and extends existing continuous integration technologies in order to provide an end-to-end solution for module definition and testing. The following diagram shows the interaction of COACH-IT technologies:

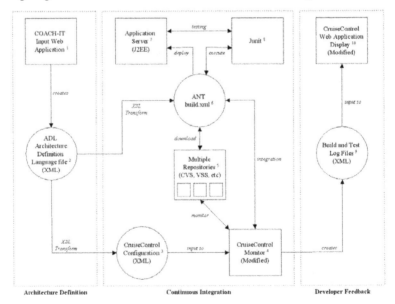

Fig. 2. Above is a conceptual drawing of how COACH-IT works. The tool has three main functions: Architecture Definition, Continuous Integration and Developer Feedback. Note: superscript references in Section 3 refer to entities in Fig. 2

The COACH-IT Input Web Application has been designed to assist agile practitioners with managing architecture definitions. In an agile project the focus is on producing value for the customer, and the architecture definition itself is not a deliverable. Using the COACH-IT tool any developer can quickly define a set of modules and assign JUnit tests to the interfaces between those modules, thus minimizing design overhead. A web application[*1] provides a simple to use, self-documenting interface with which most developers are already familiar. The same application can also load and edit current or previous architecture definitions; architecture definitions in an agile project are likely to change. Although even the minimum necessary ADL can become complex, a web interface hides this complexity and lets the developer concentrate on delivering something real.

The core of COACH-IT is the Architecture Definition Language file (ADL file)[2]. This file is a minimalist representation of the modules, interfaces and relationships in the system. Defined within this file are module names and (optionally) descriptions/annotations, module repository locations, module file locations, module interfaces, module team contact information (e-mail), module relationships (unidirectional), relationship test associations, test repository locations, test file locations and test contact information (e-mail). Only these few items are required as user input to create a simple architecture for continuous integration. The ADL file is stored as XML, which makes it both extensible and flexible. Moreover, XML is easily formatted for human viewing and is familiar to many developers. Finally, COACH-IT uses XML as its document format so that it can be integrated with existing and future tools that use XML as input and output. The core technologies underlying COACH-IT (ANT and CruiseControl) both rely heavily on XML, and therefore using XSL to generate required files makes sense. A sample COACH-IT ADL and the latest schema are available on the COACH-IT home page, but are not included here.

COACH-IT determines when modules are changed using a modified version of the CruiseControl continuous integration tool[4]. The primary modification made to CruiseControl allows the monitoring of multiple repositories, which are then monitored individually according to custom settings and schedules. Each team is thus able to configure their own repository to suit their unique needs[5]. Input to the CruiseControl monitor is via an XML file generated from the ADL using an XSL script[3]. The CruiseControl configuration file follows the standard CruiseControl format but allows multiple project definitions (one for each module). More information on CruiseControl is available at (http://crusecontrol.sourceforge.net). When COACH-IT detects a changed module it calls an ANT build file to perform the integration and testing[6]. This ANT file is likewise generated via the ADL file using XSL. Each component will have one ANT file that will download the module and any other dependant modules, deploy them on the application server[7] and run the suite(s) of associated JUnit tests[8]. Because these ANT files are generated using XSL scripts it is simple to add additional ANT tasks if required; for more information about ANT visit the Apache ANT page at (http://ant.apache.org).

COACH-IT is also able to directly notify teams and individual developers via electronic mail. In the event of a test failure or other change in system health, COACH-IT can be configured to notify any and all involved parties, such as the authors responsible for the test, the authors of the involved modules, the developers who last committed, the team leaders, or the entire teams of the failed components.

[*1...10] References to entities in Figure 2.

This direct notification is a key component to why continuous integration is effective. Alistair Cockburn has defined the concept of "information radiators" as anything that will "increase team communication without unnecessary disruption" (Cockburn, 2003). The goal of COACH-IT is partly to act as such a radiator, providing as much information as possible through everyday channels.

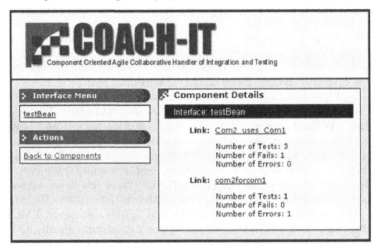

Fig. 3. Health of the system can be viewed for components, interfaces and relationships. Initially a brief summary is shown, more detail is available by clicking on the links

Output from the CruiseControl monitor is also in standard CruiseControl XML format[9]. In fact, each module creates its own logs compatible with the standard CruiseControl web application. However, COACH-IT also includes a custom web application based partially on CruiseControl that summarizes the results of tests across the entire architecture[10]. Details and contact information are provided for each test in the event of a failure. There is also a history feature that allows the user to browse through past tests and system states interactively.

4   State of Implementation

COACH-IT is being developed using JAVA, XSL and XML technologies, builds on CruiseControl and Apache ANT, and runs on a free, open-source platform. At the present time COACH-IT is able to monitor multiple J2EE components in multiple repositories, downloading, deploying and testing them as required. Our ADL file definition is stable and can be verified against an XML schema. Furthermore, the COACH-IT web interface allows simple interactive editing and creation of ADL files as well as an overall display of system health. COACH-IT is at the stage where it can be self-hosted. In fact, COACH-IT has been designed in a modular way and is therefore quite suitable for development using the previously discussed approach. If you would like to see a demo of the system, or download it for your own use, please contact the authors.

5   Future Work

Future work on COACH-IT first includes further refinements to the output web-application with the goal of constantly giving teams as much information as possible about their own component as well as the entire system. The COACH-IT system also needs to be generalized in such a way as to be applicable to non-J2EE projects. Conceptually, COACH-IT can easily be integrated with existing visual modeling (UML) tools through our XML based architecture definition. Conversion allowing users of popular industry modeling tools to directly import their component structures into COACH-IT is on the horizon. We would also like to integrate COACH-IT with MASE, a tool to support agile planning and estimation developed at the University of Calgary. MASE will facilitate developer and team communication in a non-intrusive manner.

A study of projects developed using an architecture-centric agile process with tool support is in the planning stages. This study will be collecting data to evaluate the productivity and/or satisfaction of teams using COACH-IT under the described methodology. In the future COACH-IT should also be compared with other tools used to keep track of the state of a system under development, and possibly incorporate some of the compatible features of these systems.

6   Conclusion and Potential Problems

The architecture-centric strategy is still open to some criticism. Yes, there will be some overhead in maintaining the architecture definition, even if this overhead is lessened through tool support. However, there is always a minimal amount of documentation necessary to help the developers do their work. To quote to Kent Beck, "Contrary to the claims of some of XP's detractors you do in fact invest time modeling when taking an XP approach, but only when you have no other choice. Sometimes it is significantly more productive for a developer to draw some bubbles and lines … than it is simply start hacking out code" (Beck, 2000). This approach was also designed with an object-oriented refactoring environment in mind, and so may not be applicable to other project types. Moreover, A team management process, like Scrum, is essential when working on a large or distributed agile project. COACH-IT, and the concepts proposed above, are meant to compliment existing agile processes. Lastly, there is an element of trust involved, as in many agile practices. COACH-IT does not restrict individuals from changing the architecture or tests at whim. Although this attitude may work well for some teams, there is no solid data to defend it yet. The concept and tool will undoubtedly be improved with experience, but by combining lightweight planning with an architecture-centric design strategy we hope to get the most benefit without compromising the spirit or practices of agile methods.

Acknowledgements. The COACH-IT Software is based heavily upon the CruiseControl Continuous Integration Toolkit and Apache Ant. Credit should also go to xADL, an XML-based ADL developed by the Institute for Software Research at the University of California, Irvine. The COACH-IT ADL is based roughly on the concepts and methods of xADL.

Work on implementing COACH-IT has involved the efforts of graduate students in a Distributed Software Engineering course (CPSC601.85) at the University of Calgary and the University of Alberta. In alphabetical order: Yichuan Cao, Amy Law, Tracy Li, Zhizhong Li, Anny Lin, Bill Luthi, Kris Read, Lance Titchkosky, Eileen Wang, and Fakui Wang.

References

1. Agile Alliance Home Page. Web, 2003. http://www.agilealliance.com
2. Ambler, S.: Agile Modeling: Effective Practices for Extreme Programming and the Unified Process. John Wiley & Sons, February, 2002
3. Beck, K.: eXtreme Programming Explained. Addison Wesley, 2000
4. Canadian Invited Workshop on Scaling XP/Agile Methods. Proceedings, 2003. http://can.cpsc.ucalgary.ca/ws2003/
5. COACH-IT Home Page. Web, 2003 http://pages.cpsc.ucalgary.ca/~readk/COACH-IT
6. Cockburn, A.: Crystal Clear: A Human-Powered Methodology for Small Teams. Draft, 2003. http://members.aol.com/acockburn/
7. CruiseControl Home Page. Web, 2003. http://cruisecontrol.sourceforge.net
8. Fowler, M.: Continuous Integration. Web, 2003 http://www.martinfowler.com/articles/continuousIntegration.html
9. Daich, G., Price, G., Ragland, B., Dawood, M.: Software Test Technologies Report. Software Technology Support Center, Hill Air Force Base, Utah. 1994
10. Newkirk, J.: A Light in a Dark Place: Test-driven Development of 3rd Party Packages. XP Agile Universe, 2002
11. Schwaber, K.: Agile Software Development with SCRUM. Prentice Hall, 2001
12. xADL Home Page. Web, 2003. http://www.isr.uci.edu/projects/xarchuci/

Developing a Tool Supporting XP Process

Sandro Pinna, Paolo Lorrai, Michele Marchesi, and Nicola Serra

Dipartimento di Ingegneria Elettrica ed Elettronica, Università di Cagliari
Piazza d'Armi, 09123 Cagliari, Italy
{pinnasandro,plorrai,michele,nicola.serra}@diee.unica.it

Abstract. We present the development of XPSwiki, a tool supporting the XP practices for requirement gathering and project management – user stories and the Planning Game. XPSwiki has been developed in Smalltalk using Squeak Swiki technology, and is accessed through the Internet in a user friendly, agile way. It keeps track of multiple projects, each with its releases, iterations, user stories, acceptance tests, and tasks. XPSwiki allows project tracking, and automates documentation generation and metrics collection. It is presently in use in real software development environments.

1 Introduction

Software development methodologies are usually equipped with automated tools that support the methodology, often helping its learning and adoption. Sometimes, the methodology is developed with the aim of selling the tool. More often, a successful methodology encourages firms to develop tools, in the hope of being able to make use of its popularity.

Extreme Programming (XP) is a very successful, recent methodology for software development [1]. XP developers heavily use tools supporting coding activities such as testing, refactoring, and continuous integration. X-Unit [2], the Refactoring Browser [3], and Cruise Control [4] are, respectively, examples of tools automating these activities.

As regards project planning and tracking on the other hand, XP strives to be agile and lightweight, and does not encourage the production of documentation different from the code itself. The main tools used for these activities are index cards, whiteboards, and flipcharts, which are visible to everyone and act as "information radiators" [5]. These tools are very effective as they are easy to use and maximize communication. For this reason, XP does not advocate the use of automated tools supporting the development process. While not explicitly forbidding their use, there is a strong message that "real XPers" use index cards, direct communication, and the code itself to drive and document a project.

However, many organizations are accustomed to using automated tools aiding project management and would welcome the availability of such tools. In others, management is often scared of a methodology that does not prescribe keeping written documents to track project advancement and who is in charge of what. An automated support tool could also be a powerful learning tool for beginners, who are facilitated by the structure it enforces. Moreover, when developers wishing to use XP practices

F. Maurer and D. Wells (Eds.): XP/Agile Universe 2003, LNCS 2753, pp. 151–160, 2003.

are distributed and communicate through the Internet, they need a tool to coordinate the team.

For these reasons, a number of tools supporting the XP process, or part of it, have been proposed. Among them, we may quote AutoTracker [6], Milos-ASE [7], Xplanner [8], XPCGI [9], XPWeb [10], Twiki XP Tracker [11], Iterate [12], XPPlanIt [13], and VersionOne [14].

Some of these, namely AutoTracker, XPCGI, XPWeb, and Twiki XP Tracker, are implemented using plug-ins or scripts at the top of existing servers enabling information exchange on the Web. Others are based on specifically developed servers, usually with Java technology. All these tools are Web-based, and make use of standard Internet browsers, possibly equipped with tool plug-ins.

The level of support of these tools to XP requirement gathering and planning game varies, but all support recording and estimating user stories, assigning them to iterations, tracking project advancement, and adjusting project velocity.

In this paper, we present the development of another automated tool, called XPSwiki, supporting requirement gathering using user stories, and the Planning Game (PG) for project planning. XPSwiki has been developed using XP practices, gathering its requirements with user stories and using the PG and short iterations for its development. The following are the unique characteristics of XPSwiki compared to existing tools:

- XPSwiki is implemented in Smalltalk language, and has a full object-oriented data structure, allowing it to be extended easily;
- it keeps track of project changes through a versioning system;
- it allows the production of written documentation on project advancement, to comply with the ISO 9000 quality certification manual of a software firm;
- it allows to gather process statistics, including historical, and sends them to a metrics-gathering Web Service;
- it is intended to be used after discussions and agreement with software firms, and each installation is properly adapted to the firm's needs.

XPSwiki is accessed through a Web browser and, like some of the referred tools, makes use of Wiki technology [15]. A Wiki is a tool for exchanging information on the Internet. Fundamentally, it is an open Website, where users can freely navigate through pages, add new pages, modify existing pages, and search pages by keywords.

Swiki is the Squeak implementation of a Wiki. It also enables to add structure to given pages, defining input forms for them. In this way, in a Swiki one can have both pages constrained to a given structure, that are used to hold structured information, and free-format pages, freely added to existing pages, like Post-it notes. The overall approach is very agile and user-friendly.

We focus our presentation on the requirements an automated tool must have to support the PG, and on the technology used to implement them. Section 2 presents the XP practices supported by the tool, together with their domain analysis. Section 3 deals with the requirements of a second-generation tool supporting the XP process. Section 4 presents the object structure of XPSwiki and its implementation. Section 5 presents some highlights of its use.

2   How XP Gathers Requirements and Manages the Development

In XP, requirements are gathered through user stories, which are short descriptions of interaction scenarios with the system that can be developed within one iteration. Each user story is written by the customer on an index card to make her/him be concise. User stories need not be complete, since they are an opportunity for later conversations with the customer [16]. Moreover, they are the units that drive the entire system development.

User stories are complemented with acceptance tests to check whether the story has been implemented correctly or not. Each acceptance test is written in turn on an index card. While there is usually a 1:1 relationship between user stories and acceptance tests, some stories may have zero, or more than one acceptance test, and some ATs may refer to more than one story.

The developers estimate the time to complete each story, assigning each story a number of "story points". The customer prioritizes and alters the stories, negotiating with developers, and deciding in the end which stories are allotted to each iteration. Acceptance tests are estimated and allotted as user stories. Usually, they should be implemented in the same iteration as the related stories.

System development is performed through releases. A new release is usually made available every 2-4 months, and is a major advancement compared to the previous one. Each release is made up of short iterations of 2-3 weeks.

Every iteration has a number of story points that can be implemented in its course, the so-called "project velocity". The customer decides which user stories and acceptance tests will be implemented in each iteration, with the constraint that the sum of their story points must be smaller, or equal to, the project velocity.

During the iteration, the developers write the tasks needed to implement each user story and acceptance test on index cards. Each developer freely accepts the responsibility of one or more tasks, and implements it in pair with another developer.

After each iteration, the number of story points actually implemented is recomputed, and the resulting figure is the project velocity for the next iteration. The customer is allowed to change the stories to be implemented in each iteration, depending on the stories and tests actually implemented, and on the changes in project velocity and requirements.

The key entities of the XP Planning Game exhibit a well-built tree structure:

- a project is made up of releases;
- a release is made up of iterations;
- an iteration implements user stories and acceptance tests that are related to each other;
- user stories and acceptance tests are made up of tasks;
- a team is made up of developers;
- a developer accepts responsibility of one or more tasks and usually pair-programs them with one or more developers.

Moreover, each task has one and only one responsible developer, while zero or more team members may pair-program the task together with the developer in charge.

3 Defining the Requirements of the Tool

Starting from the description of the XP process presented in section 2, the next step was to study and devise the requirements of a tool supporting the PG. The following are the main non-functional requirements needed to produce a tool that can be used not only in an academic, but also in an industrial environment:

- agility – the tool must be easy to use and easy to adapt and reconfigure;
- Web-based – the tool must be accessed through standard Web browsers;
- interoperability – the tool should be easily interfaced with other development tools;
- modularity and extensibility;
- open-source – the tool should be developed using an open-source environment.

The requirements of being Web-based and agile point to the use of Wiki technology referred to in section 1.

The requirement of being open-source, portable, modular, and extensible lead to the use of the Smalltalk language, which is still unrivaled as regards rapid development of modular and high-quality software. The chosen open-source implementation was Squeak [17], that can be used on several operating systems (Windows, Linux, Mac-OS, many Unixes), and has complete access to its source. Squeak comes equipped with a Wiki server, called Swiki.

Swiki is very powerful, and stores its pages in an XML repository, thus increasing the system's interoperability. Moreover, it enables to add structure to given Wiki pages, defining input forms and output structures for them. In this way, in a Swiki one can have both pages constrained to a given structure, which are used to hold structured information, and free-format pages that are freely added to existing pages, like Post-it notes, which can also contain uploaded documents.

These characteristics match our requirements very well, since the Web pages that hold the information related to the entities previously discussed (projects, releases, iterations, and so on) must be well structured, in order to perform computations on the project status. On the other hand, the capability of freely linking pages to the structured ones when necessary increases the agility and flexibility of the tool.

The functional requirements of the tool were given by the two of us that have more experience in XP development, in the form of 35 initial user stories and 27 acceptance tests.

XPSwiki supports:

- Team and team members' definition.
- Creation of a new project.
- Project release and iteration definition.
- User stories definition, estimation, and assignment to iterations.
- Acceptance tests definition, estimation, assignment to iterations, and relationships with user stories.
- Decomposition of stories and tests in tasks.
- Assignment of tasks to developers and task estimation, including pair programming on the task.

- Tracking of advancement and integrity computation at project, release, iteration, user story, acceptance test, and task level. This can also be made for a past date, ignoring subsequent modifications to the project.
- Pretty printing in RTF format of advancement reports at iteration, story and task level, and of acceptance test completion.
- Process metrics and statistics collection, including time-dependent process advancement.

4 The Implementation of XPSwiki

The presented tool was implemented following XP practices, and was developed with the aid of two students performing their master's thesis. Since we are not a programming team, being heavily involved in academic activities, we were only able to follow some XP practices. We were not able to use pair programming, metaphor, or refactoring consistently. Acceptance testing was applied, but since XPSwiki is Web-based, it had the problem of testing Internet applications. This kind of testing was thus mainly hand-based rather than automated.

The first version of XPSwiki was implemented using the native data structure of Swiki pages. In this implementation, the information relevant to the PG entities introduced in section 2 was simply held in the corresponding pages, and the relationships between them (for instance, the relationship between an iteration and the user stories implemented during the iteration) were recorded using the Wiki hyperlinks between pages. This allowed a quick development, but the data structure was clearly inflexible and not suitable to complex queries nor to ease further extensions.

This version however was invaluable in obtaining feedback from our internal customers. It was also installed on the site of one of our industrial partners, who evaluated it and gave us a number of suggestions on how to improve the tool.

In the second version of the development, we decided to implement a full object-oriented data structure holding all project data. An initial analysis, taking into account the experience and suggestions gathered, yielded the UML class diagram [18] shown in figure 1.

In this diagram, we introduced abstract class "Process Entity" providing data common to every entity, such as name, description, and number of story points. We also introduced the abstract class "Development Unit", superclass of both User Story and Acceptance Test, generalizing their property of being decomposed in Tasks. Another key element is class "Work Unit", which represents the work made by one developer, or by a pair, on a given task during one day. We were expressly asked this information by our industrial partner, who wished to track the daily work of its programmer pairs. This class also allows to track the code developed during the work. We expressed this information with the attribute "code", which should be considered an entry point in the configuration management system holding the code.

The object model was implemented in Squeak. Each relevant object shown here is linked with the corresponding Swiki page, and has the capability of storing and retrieving its data into and out of this page. In this way, the computations are made directly on a modular object structure, easing their implementation and extensions, while permanent data storage maintains the advantages of existing XML implementation.

The present version of XPSwiki has been implemented using this object model. The project has been tracked from the beginning using the earliest version of the tool. At present the project consists of 25 system classes and 25 test classes. It cooperates with 20 Squeak Swiki classes, including the classes holding page information in an XML repository.

It is worth noting that Swiki system logs all the changes to its pages. If needed, these changes, or a snapshot of the project status at a given time, can easily be retrieved from the logs that act as a configuration management tool.

The present status of the project has just completed its third release. XPSwiki is being used for internal purposes, and has been installed on the site of an industrial partner of ours. Almost all the requirements listed at the end of section 3 have been implemented, at least partially, while the last two (pretty printing of reports and metric collection) are the main goals of release 4. The project URL, where information can be found and where it will be possible in the future to download the tool, is: www.agilexp.org/xpswiki.

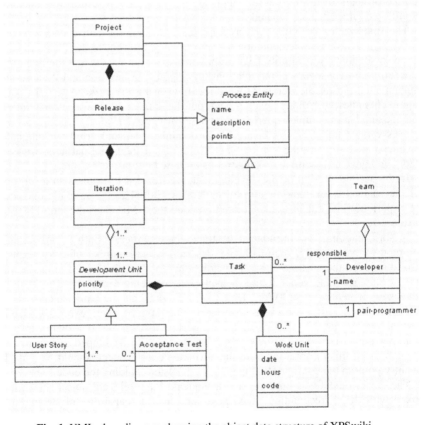

Fig. 1. UML class diagram showing the object data structure of XPSwiki.

5   Using an XPSwiki

A detailed description of XPSwiki usage has been reported elsewhere [19]. The starting page of an XPSwiki presents a list of all current projects. Clicking on one of them brings to the home page of the project (figure 2). In the upper part are the links to pages showing its team members, releases, iterations, user stories, tasks, and acceptance tests. The lower part shows the completion status of the project and the average team velocity at a glance.

The various pages holding the project process entities show a table with a list of various team members, releases, iterations, etc., respectively, with indications of their status, present velocity, possible problems and inconsistencies. Clicking on the entity name gives access to its page.

The pages of the higher-level entities of figure 1, also hold a list of their lower-level entities. In this way, releases show their iterations, iterations show their stories, and so on.

All these pages can be edited using their forms. The forms are configured through a Swiki administration tool, the Swiki Browser, and/or by direct interaction at administrator's level with the Swiki itself. This clearly separates interface from object model, allowing to increase the productivity and quality of the produced system. Fig. 3 shows the edit form of an User Story.

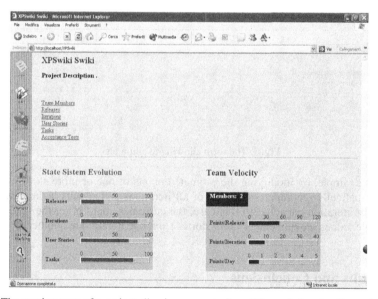

Fig. 2. The starting page of a project allowing access to its entities and showing the project completion status and average team velocity.

Figure 4 shows the page of a task. On this page, one can record in an appropriate track table the number of hours the person responsible for a task actually devoted to it. From the analysis of the data inserted in the track table, the system automatically calculates the points done for each task.

Starting from the points done for tasks, the system computes the points done for user stories, iterations and releases; it then compares them with the estimated points and calculates the points left.

These data are shown graphically and are very useful to track the project advancement and perform the necessary corrective action. In this phase, the use of XPSwiki turns out to be of great importance, as it allows to discover anomalous situations in good time and simulate corrective action.

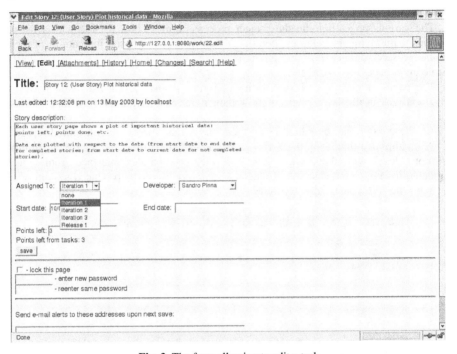

Fig. 3. The form allowing to edit a task.

As an example, by modifying the estimated points of one or more stories, the system automatically recomputes the load of all iterations and signals if the new values exceed the iteration capacity. In this case, the customer could bring the load back to acceptable values moving one or more stories from one iteration to another.

6   Results and Conclusions

We have presented the design and implementation of XPSwiki, a tool supporting the XP planning game. The tool is presently being used by our team, and by a partner software house in Sardinia, that uses it mainly to track Java development projects. We are actively gathering feedback on the tool from our partner, and are about to install the tool with other software firms. The goal is to add to XPSwiki the features needed for a fruitful and effective use in industrial environments.

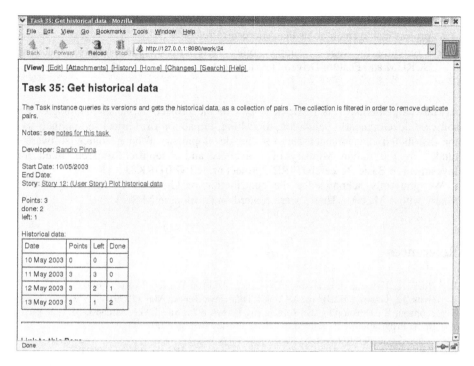

Fig. 4. The page of a task, showing task status and data. In the bottom of the page there is the track table of the task, recording the actual work performed daily on the task.

The present XPSwiki version allows project tracking and estimation. According also to our partner's report, the tool has the following advantages:

- it has been very useful for XP developers starting to learn the PG, since they were forced to use it;
- it helps keep track of project activities, keeping management satisfied, and ultimately contributing to the adoption of XP in firms.

The next version, already in development, will be provided with the process metrics collection capability. It will enable us to gather data on XP projects continuously during their life in an unobtrusive way. At given time intervals and/or upon completion of task, story, or iteration, these data will be sent through the Internet to a server devoted to metrics collection. In this way, we hope to be in a position to collect many real world data on software development, with the aim of proving (or disproving) the effectiveness of XP quantitatively.

Other future work on the tool will be entirely driven by our partners' needs. These include the following:

- Adding the capability to produce written documentation on project advancement, to comply with the ISO 9000 quality certification;
- Interface with CVS configuration management system to associate with each task the code actually written every day.

– Interface with popular development environments, such as Eclipse, and with project management tools like Microsoft Project.
– Extending the tool to support other well-defined agile processes, such as SCRUM and Feature Driven Development.

Acknowledgements. This research is part of the project "Agile methodologies for software development – validation, modelling, impact on firm organization, their use for distributed development and for the development of open source software", funded by the Italian Ministry of University and Scientific Research, Fund for Investment in Basic Research (FIRB), project nr. RBNE01JRK8.

We gratefully acknowledge the contribution of Giovanni Corriga and Simone Mauri, whose Master's Theses were centred on developing XPSwiki.

References

1. Beck, K.: Extreme Programming Explained. Addison-Wesley Boston (1999).
2. Beck, K., Gamma, E.: JUnit: A Cook's Tour. Java Report, May (1999)
3. Johnson, R.: Developing the Refactoring Browser. In: Succi, G., Marchesi, M. (eds.): Extreme Programming Examined. Addison-Wesley Boston (2001).
4. Cruise Control, http://cruisecontrol.sourceforge.net.
5. Cockburn, A.: Agile Software Development. Addison-Wesley Boston (2002).
6. Auer, K., AutoTracker, Position Paper for OOPSLA 2000 Workshop: "Refining the Practices of Extreme Programming", online at
    http://www.rolemodelsoftware.com/moreAboutUs/publications/autoTracker.php
7. Maurer, F.: Supporting Distributed Extreme Programming, in Extreme Programming and Agile Methods, D. Wells, L.A. Williams (Eds.), Proceedings of XP/Agile Universe 2002, Chicago, IL, USA, August 4-7, 2002. Lecture Notes in Computer Science 2418 Springer (2002).
8. XPlanner, http://www.xplanner.org.
9. XPCGI, http://xpcgi.sourceforge.net.
10. XPWeb, http://xpweb.sourceforge.net.
11. Twiki XP Tracker, http://twiki.org/cgi-bin/view/Plugins/XpTrackerPlugin.
12. Iterate, http://www.diamond-sky.com/products/iterate.
13. König, D., Cunningham, G.: eXtreme Programming (XP) – What is it?, online at: http://www.xpplanit.com/article.pdf.
14. VersionOne, http://www.versionone.net.
15. Bo, L. Cunningham, W: The Wiki Way. Addison-Wesley Boston (2001).
16. Jeffries, R., Anderson, A., Hendrickson, C.: Extreme Programming Installed, Addison-Wesley Boston (2001).
17. Gudzial, M.: Squeak: Object-Oriented Design with Multimedia Applications, Prentice Hall Upper Saddle River (2001).
18. Booch, G., Rumbaugh, J., Jacobson, I.: The Unified Modeling Language User Guide. Addison-Wesley Boston (1999).
19. Pinna, S., Mauri S., Lorrai P., Marchesi M., Serra N.: XPSwiki: an Agile Tool Supporting the Planning Game, in Extreme Programming and Agile Processes in Software Engineering, M. Marchesi, G. Succi (Eds.), Proceedings of XP2003, Genoa, Italy, May 25-29, 2003. Lecture Notes in Computer Science 2675 Springer (2003).

XP Agile Universe Educators Symposium Overview

Donald J. Reifer, President

Reifer Consultants, Inc.
P. O. Box 4046
Torrance, CA 90510
d.reifer@ieee.org

The Educators' Symposium brings educators together to share their experiences teaching agile methods. During the symposium, participants will be encouraged to discuss how they are incorporating XP and agile methods into their curriculum, courses and organizational training plans. Educators and trainers will hopefully network together to swap ideas and exchange course materials during the meeting.

In the conference call, we encouraged educators to submit research and experience papers. Selection for the symposium was based on clarity, originality, educational merit, and most importantly, on relevance to XP and agile method educators and trainers. We accepted the following four papers because they best met these criteria:

1. **Introducing Agile Methods in Learning Environments: Lessons Learned** – This paper by Melnik of Southern Alberta Institute of Technology and Maurer of University of Calgary summarizes the experience of introducing agile methods into four different academic programs (Diploma, Applied Bachelor's, Bachelor's and Master's) in two institutions during two years.

2. **Adapting XP to an Academic Environment by Phasing-in Practices** – This paper by Fenwick of Appalachian State University reports the experience gained using a scaled-down version of Extreme Programming developed for an academic environment.

3. **Pair Learning: With an Eye Toward Future Success** – This paper by Nagappan, Williams, Wiebe, Miller, Balik, Ferzli and Petlick of North Carolina State University reports the results of an experiment conducted over a period of a year and one half to assess the efficacy of pair programming within an introductory programming course.

4. **Adaptations for Teaching Software Development with Extreme Programming: An Experience Report** – This paper by Wainer of Southern Illinois University summarizes experience teaching a Software Design and Development course that used a development methodology based on Extreme Programming.

We were pleased that Joshua Kerievsky of Industrial Logic agreed to kick off the Symposium. His experience developing, coaching and teaching using Extreme Programming provides him with the background needed to challenge Symposium participants to do a better job in satisfying the demands of industry for graduates.

F. Maurer and D. Wells (Eds.): XP/Agile Universe 2003, LNCS 2753, p. 161, 2003.
© Springer-Verlag Berlin Heidelberg 2003

Adapting XP to an Academic Environment by Phasing-In Practices

James B. Fenwick, Jr.

Department of Computer Science
Appalachian State University,
Boone, NC 28608, USA
jbf@cs.appstate.edu

Abstract. Extreme Programming (XP) is an agile software development methodology that was originally devised for application in an industrial setting. This report presents our experience using an approach to "scale-down" XP so that it can be successfully employed in an academic setting; specifically, an upper-level software engineering course. The approach avoids overburdening students by using a series of projects that phase-in some experience with nearly all of the XP practices.

Keywords: Extreme Programming, XP, Teaching XP

1   Introduction

Appalachian State University is a mid-sized, comprehensive university offering a B.S. in computer science that requires a senior-level course in software engineering. This course is charged with introducing students to the motivations for a disciplined approach to software development; specifically, to improve the late, over-budget, and faulty condition of many software products. Additionally, the course strives to give students a practical experience applying this disciplined approach. Thus, our students learn about:

- life-cycle, process models such as waterfall, spiral, and the Unified Software Development Process (USDP);
- process improvement models (e.g., CMM);
- non execution-based testing strategies, testing criteria (utility, robustness, etc.), and execution-based testing strategies (e.g., black/white box);
- project management issues, including estimation and metrics;
- UML modeling notation;
- UML software models, including use-case, class, dynamic (state diagrams), interaction (sequence and collaboration diagrams);
- design patterns;
- CASE tool experience (e.g., Together, Rose, ArgoUML);
- working in large teams.

F. Maurer and D. Wells (Eds.): XP/Agile Universe 2003, LNCS 2753, pp. 162–171, 2003.

Unfortunately, the implementation of an introductory course such as this is immediately in a tension with its goals because the payoff of adopting a disciplined approach to software development best occurs when the scope of the project is large and complex enough to require it. (As I say in the first class, *"You don't need to engineer the 'Hello World' program."*) As has been observed by others [1,13,5,10], it is fundamentally impossible to duplicate an industrial software engineering environment in an academic setting. Some of the more prominent disparities include:

- Students are earning academic credit and not their livelihood (although both provide motivation, financial support of yourself and your family is a much stronger motivator than a final grade in a single course in a few months).
- Students will normally spend only 3-4 hours in class and 5-6 hours outside class per week on a software engineering course (compared with 40+ hours per week in industry).
- It is often difficult for student team members to meet outside of scheduled class hours (compared with the accessibility of coworkers in industry).
- The instructor usually plays the role of client, user, and system expert (compared with industry where these are separate entities).
- Students are constantly switching focus between a variety of academic activities in the course of a single day (compared with the focus on a single project in industry).
- The size and scope of the projects are in no way comparable.
- The availability of expertise in the problem domain is in no way comparable.

Educators have attempted a number of approaches to address the problems facing software engineering education. Some curricula have moved the introductory software engineering course earlier in the curriculum, typically into the sophomore year, but this jeopardizes the assimilation of the material by students who may lack sufficient software development maturity. Some schools have created a software engineering sequence in which the introductory course resembles the course described above and the second course then attempts a larger, or capstone, project. Dovetailing with this project course idea is the use of "real" projects from "real" clients. While the goal of a larger project is commendable, even these "real" projects are not usually real. In addition, because the instructor's control of these projects is greatly diminished, there can be a number of pedagogical problems associated with this approach. The "real" client's interest and/or ability to participate can wane or disappear. The location of some schools will make finding suitable "real" projects difficult. Having experienced some of these problems in recent course offerings, we conclude that the software engineering project needs to be more tightly controlled in order to guarantee each student the opportunity to practice and master crucial development skills.

The confluence of this ongoing struggle against the obstacles presented by this course and a recent, personal acceptance of the efficacy of Extreme Programming (XP) lead to a desire to use XP as the guiding methodology for this senior-level introduction to software engineering course. However, the methodology as presented by Beck and others [3,2] targets (as it should) the industrial setting.

Due to the differences between the industrial setting and the academic setting, as set forth above, XP as a viable, usable methodology was questioned. Indeed while many are questioning the ability of XP to scale up [7,2], this is requiring XP to scale *down*. After some consideration, we decided to try. It was felt that XP is an intuitive methodology that plays to the strengths of our students. Also, XP highly values communication, which includes (in our opinion) being able to express more abstract thoughts using the graphical, UML models. XP simply doesn't demand that complete, or near-complete, artifacts persist. Lastly, XP is a disciplined approach to software development.

The remainder of this paper details the pedagogical issues caused by the decision to try XP in our C++-based, senior-level software engineering course consisting of 25 students. The following section presents related work of others incorporating XP into their classrooms. Section 3 spells out the approach we used. The paper concludes with anecdotal evidence and reflections.

2   Related Work

Other educators have reported adaptations of XP to an academic setting. One way to classify these adaptations is the level of the course. Several researchers and educators report using, or considering using, XP in lower level, programming-proficiency courses (e.g., CS1 and CS2) [1,9,8,11]. Adapting XP to this level of the curriculum tends to focus on the practice of pair programming. Qualitative support of the benefits of pair programming in the introductory course is provided in [11]. The practice of test-first development is also being viewed as valuable and doable at this level. In addition, [1] as also had success with smaller release schedules and controlled refactorings in the early courses.

The other classification is upper-level students that already have developed some form of personal process and programming proficiency. In a study of the perceptions of agile processes, Melnik [8] reports that graduate students were slightly less positive in the perceived value of pair programming and test-first design. This may be due to satisfaction with their already established personal process, suggesting it may take more work to convert upper-level students. Wilson [13] reports using most of the XP practices in an upper level elective course that used a single, large project approach. This approach is an interesting one, but did experience some difficulties with adhering to the small release practice primarily due to size and scope of the project. Wilson also indicates that effective coaching is not easy. This is exacerbated if the course does not include a scheduled lab time. [5] reports a partial adoption of the XP practices in an upper level software design course. This partial adoption is their adaptation to the academic setting. One practice they did not adopt was estimating. While in agreement that student estimates are inaccurate, we believe strongly that the academic setting is precisely the time for them to begin developing this skill. Industry suffers from late software because of problems with estimating duration. Our phased-in approach using multiple projects and short release schedules gives them important feedback. The key to any success with student estimates is to break tasks down into small enough pieces, which is a good exercise in abstraction and refinement. Williams and Kessler [12] report on the value of the pair programming practice in upper level courses. Williams and Upchurch [10] focus on the efficacy of using XP practices in the software engineering course. They conclude that most of the practices are adaptable, but such a course still needs to introduce concepts and skills from more traditional methodologies, particularly modeling skills.

3 Approach

The journey to adopt XP in the required, senior-level software engineering class began with a number of concerns:

- Where in the already full semester can new material on XP be added? The methodology has a better chance of acceptance if the variables, values, principles, and steering metaphor [3] are discussed in advance.
- How will student assessment need to change, if at all?
- How to avoid overloading students too fast with new tools and practices?
- How to use enough XP practices to get their synergistic benefits?
- Will students make the time necessary for pair programming to succeed?

The method of resolving these concerns resembled a swinging pendulum. It began with goals and objectives then swung over to student assessment then back again and repeated a few more times. The result was a workable syllabus using a "phased-in approach." While not perfect, some courage and "course steering" was still necessary, it was good enough to begin.

From a student assessment perspective, the project component of the course grade increased from 25-30% for a single, "large" project to 50% for three "phased" projects as described below. The tests component increased slightly due to adding a test on XP that ensures understanding of the values, principles, and practices of XP. (The other tests focus on traditional process and UML modeling.) We eliminated quizzes and homeworks, allocating this time to the projects. A significant portion (about 25%) of the final, summative examination will consist of a demo/walkthrough of the final project that will include some presentation of the finished design using UML. In lieu of delivering a product to a real client, this mild form of "peer pressure" served as a powerful motivator. Demos of the earlier project were also given, although there was no grade associated with this.

The cornerstone of adopting XP into the course is the phased-in approach of the projects. Three projects were decided upon ranging in scope from small to medium to large. Each project adds XP practices while retaining and building upon the practices from the preceding project.

3.1 The Small Project

This project, worth 10% of the course grade, had students implement a matrix abstract data type (ADT). Clearly, this project is not difficult, which was precisely the goal. We wished students to gain confidence in their abilities and with

XP. In addition to the standard addition/multiplication (with scalars and matrices) operations, slightly more complicated operations involving inverses were requested.

The XP practice of pair programming was required. For this small project, each team consisted of a single pair. Although this team size is small, it simplified scheduling. Getting students to find time to work together is often cited as a problem in adopting XP in an academic setting [13,8,9]. Any knowledge of external, outside class, relationships was used. For example, two students known to be close friends were paired together.

The XP practice of testing first, using CppUnit in our case, was required. This practice is also cited as proving to be quite difficult for students to accept and adopt [8,5]. However, developing tests for an ADT is rather straightforward. Building on one class session devoted to a test-first coding of a complex number ADT, this small matrix ADT project allowed students to gain confidence in writing (relatively simple) tests first.

Another requirement was the use of CVS to manage source code that was now defined to include the tests. Most of the students were not accustomed to using this tool. While such a tool is not necessary for a single pair, it moved the time to learn this tool from a later, more complex, project into the small project where it was more manageable.

There was only one iteration/release, which lasted two weeks, so there was no planning or estimating. These practices were phased in later.

3.2   The Medium Project

This project, worth 15% of the course grade, had students implement a single-user library system. The instructor acted as the customer. (Actually this can be real as most instructors have accumulated a personal library of textbooks, journals, etc. that they freely loan out to people.) Indeed, this functioned nicely as the metaphor. As the customer, the instructor provided a half-dozen or so stories such as: add a book, check out a book, check in a book, report of checked out books, modify book/borrower information, report of all books. At this point in the project, only books are considered.

In addition to requiring pair programming, two pairs were joined together to make teams of four (one team of six was necessary). The teams were instructed that they can pair with anyone, but must work with more than one other person in order to spread knowledge throughout the entire team. Again, any knowledge of external relationships was used in joining pairs. The goal here was to leverage anything and everything to assist students in scheduling time with one another. Along with the additional team members, the practice of collective code ownership was employed.

Writing comprehensive unit tests using CppUnit was again required for the medium project. Conceiving of the tests was more difficult because the operations/methods were less independent than in the matrix ADT project, but we can build on the confidence gained then.

A number of new practices were introduced in the medium project, some with more focus than others. The practice of a metaphor was introduced. The system is relatively small so the metaphor's usefulness is marginal, but we've introduced the practice and so can build on it later. In terms of acceptance testing, the customer-accepted interface was a simple ASCII menu-type interface. This allows automated acceptance testing through redirection and file comparison or *expect* [6] scripts.

The medium project used two iterations/releases (each about 1.5 weeks in duration). These iterations were very short, but gave us practice playing the planning game. The customer provided the stories, which were themselves quite small. (Indeed this whole project might be a single story in industry.) In terms of estimating, each iteration was given 20 "story points." This figure was arrived at by assuming each person on the four person team could contribute five hours to the project in a week. Knowing that students' estimating skills would be weak, some margin for error was thereby included. The students were required to determine tasks and estimate them in story points (or halves of points). Then the team played the planning game with the customer (instructor).

Related to estimating is the 40-hour week practice, which in an academic setting is more accurately called the 10-hour week practice [13]. This is related to estimating because some students, in order to get an A, will underbid an estimate to ensure all stories are implemented. Then they willingly work overtime to get everything done. The key here is to promote "No death marches." Students need extra convincing that grades are determined more by playing the planning game effectively. While some were initially amiss that another group could get the same grade for doing less, it was stressed repeatedly that the team's success is dependent on the customer being happy. Ultimately, these students just want their A and give up worrying about what others get. At the other extreme, the XP-willing customer must be technically savvy enough not to be misled by a team looking for an easy way out. This team overestimates tasks in an attempt to implement less.

Continuous integration was added as a practice. The use of the CVS tool proved invaluable. We agree with Wilson's findings [13] that this practice is actually easier in an academic setting because the students work in more frequent but shorter blocks of time. The practice of integrating before leaving caused continuous integration to happen.

The practice of a "highly available" customer was included. In an academic setting, even the team is not really on-site since the whole team will rarely be together. The key was to be as available as possible. In addition to very busy office hours, email mailing lists proved helpful.

Refactoring was subtly introduced. While the term had been defined in lecture by this point, there was no active practice of it. However, a major refactoring was necessary in iteration two when several new stories were given to the team. First, periodicals were added as an element of the library. This caused a need for using inheritance. Second, a "history report" detailing every borrowing transaction (item, borrower, dates checked out and in) caused design changes.

Typically, students just have a single checked out field in the book object. This simple design must be reconsidered in light of the new story.

3.3   The Large Project

The remainder of the term was intended to be devoted to a two or three iteration large project, worth half of the overall project grade or 25%. In actuality, we used a single iteration spanning five weeks. The teams were again increased by joining together medium project teams. All prior practices remained, and while no new practices were employed, several were "turned up a few notches." Refactorings [4] were more common as the larger system evolved. Having gained some estimating experience, tracking of estimates was more feasible now. We continued to stress the 10-hour week practice.

The project had students implement an integrated restaurant system consisting of waitress stations to place/modify orders, print bills, close out orders, etc. Also included are a kitchen station to view orders and indicate when orders are prepared, and a menu creation system for the chef. Other possible subsystems include an "accounting" system to collect daily/weekly/monthly sales information, waitress tip data, etc.; and a hostess system to aid in reservations and seating.

3.4   Project Miscellany

Because student teams are not together as much as in industry, we felt that we needed to foster an increased level of communication when we were all together, which was class time. So, the beginning of each class was dedicated for a stand-up meeting. This was a highly successful strategy. It only took 5-10 minutes and was also fun as the instructor/coach/customer actually stood on the desk in order to be seen easily by everyone. One time when we didn't actually stand up, the "meeting" dragged on for 20 minutes.

In terms of project assessment, the small project grade was influenced heavily by the unit tests and effective use of CVS. The medium project was influenced heavily by how well the team defined, managed, and delivered a release (iteration). The large project also focused on the releases but also on the overall design (i.e., level of refactoring).

Enthusiasm is part of an XP-friendly environment, but the physical aspect plays a part too. Our classrooms and labs became decorated with posterboards extolling the virtues of XP. We were even allowed to rearrange the stations in the public computer lab to be more amenable to collaborative work.

4   Results

One iteration of this adaptation of XP to a senior-level software engineering course is complete and there are a number of informal items of feedback. We conducted the student survey presented in Melnik [8] after completion of the medium project. Overall, the responses concur with Melnik. Most students see the value in XP and enjoy pair programming. Regarding the test-first development questions, our students were slightly less agreeable than Melnik's. Most see the value but find it difficult to do consistently. Some see debugging test code as unproductive. Johnson and Caristi [5] attempted to observe the usefulness of the metaphor by asking for a one sentence description. We also posed this question in our survey and found that nearly all responses restated the metaphor. While this can be partly because the first two projects are not large, we are encouraged nonetheless.

More anecdotal feedback concerning the effectiveness of the phased-in projects approach, of using XP in an academic setting and as "lessons learned" are also given.

Communication is one of the XP values, and we've never had a class communicate more. There was more communication everywhere: among the students (due to pair programming), with the customer, and with the coach. We received comments from several colleagues about how many students were in and around the office. We routinely got stopped in the halls.

Overall, pair programming was successful. We concur with the observations of others that while some people take a little longer to adjust, most people grow to enjoy it. We believe our approach of keeping pairs together helps achieve this. One student confided that he normally chose to work alone even if given the opportunity to collaborate and was hesitant about being forced to pair, but he truly enjoyed the experience and felt significantly more productive when pairing. However, pairing of people with widely different abilities was problematic. The less capable person does not seem to gain confidence working with a "peer" who is more advanced; the more capable person feels completely hamstrung. A more careful matching of abilities might be warranted.

While keeping pairs together between the small and medium projects did have some benefit, it also tended to prevent pairing with other people. We needed to require that pairs break up and switch off.

We think using three distinct projects helped students keep the designs simple because they were less likely to try to anticipate additional stories. Also, it prevented merging pairs from having to merge different code bases from the earlier project when they weren't on the same team. However, it had a negative effect on the usefulness of testing. We'd like students to experience how a test written early gets broken (and discovered) by a change later. Using a single project broken into three, increasingly complex parts could be a solution.

While the small and medium projects were sized appropriately to build confidence in most of our students, some of the best students wanted to be "mavericks" [2]. In an academic setting it can be more difficult to discover this behavior, particularly in the absence of a dedicated lab session.

The 10-hour week practice was hard for some students to accept. Some students want to sink a lot of time into a project to get everything done and get a good grade. These students struggled with adhering to the planning game.

Teams tended to estimate tasks together which caused the estimates to be skewed by the more dominant (and proficient) members. Then when someone else worked on a task they didn't meet the estimate. We needed to require individual estimates first, then using these the team could agree upon a single estimate.

Students enjoyed the XP notion of sharing control of the project scope variable. Much of the communication with the customer was about scope. Again, the customer must be technically savvy enough not to be duped, but we consider this type of customer-developer communication a good thing. Most of this type of communication wasn't been about lessening scope, but rather about choosing between alternatives. Students liked negotiating for a fancier user interface, or some additional reports they felt might be useful, or even against some features they found confusing. Yet, giving student teams a part in negotiating scope can be tricky. In the small project, several groups changed the scope near midnight the morning before it was due to accommodate what they were actually going to get accomplished. A stern reminder that changing scope is a two-way negotiation seemed to correct this.

Looking back over seating charts, several pairs adjusted where they sat during class to be nearer other members of their team.

Colleagues have mentioned to us that talk of XP cross-pollinated into their project courses through students in this class. So, at least some students applied some of the practices on their own in other classes.

Time for lectures on XP came from decreasing (although not eliminating) the coverage depth of some topics presented in class. Students were instructed the first day that they must become more engaged in their own learning process through active reading of the textbook material on these topics. Then, rather than lecturing on the contents of a chapter for a week, a list of highlights of important content is presented followed by a one to two session discussion of the chapter content.

5   Conclusion

Upon reflection, we feel that the transition to XP in our senior-level software engineering course was a success. As others have observed, there are fundamental differences between an academic and an industrial software engineering environment. We adapted the XP methodology to accommodate these differences. We avoided overburdening students with too many new practices by using a series of projects that increase in complexity and phasing in new practices with new projects.

References

1. Owen Astrachan, Robert C. Duvall, and Eugene Wallingford. Bringing Extreme Programming to the Classroom. In *XP Universe*, Raleigh, NC, USA, July 2001.
2. Ken Auer and Roy Miller. *Extreme Programming Applied: Playing To Win*. The XP Series. Addison-Wesley, 2002.
3. Kent Beck. *Extreme Programming Explained: Embrace Change*. The XP Series. Addison-Wesley, 2000.
4. Martin Fowler. *Refactoring*. Addison-Wesley, 1999.
5. David H. Johnson and James Caristi. Extreme Programming and the Software Design Course. In *XP Universe*, Raleigh, NC, USA, July 2001.
6. Don Libes. *Exploring Expect: A Tcl-Based Toolkit for Automating Interactive Programs*. O'Reilly and Associates, 1995.
7. Pete McBreen. *Questioning Extreme Programming*. The XP Series. Addison-Wesley, 2003.
8. Grigori Melnik and Frank Maurer. Perceptions of Agile Practices: A Student Survey. In *XP Universe*, Chicago, IL, USA, August 2002.
9. Dean Sanders. Student Perceptions of the Suitability of Extreme and Pair Programming. In *XP Universe*, Raleigh, NC, USA, July 2001.
10. Laurie Williams and Richard Upchurch. Extreme Programming for Software Engineering Education? In *2001 Frontiers in Education*, Reno, NV, USA, October 2001.
11. Laurie Williams, Eric Wiebe, Kai Yang, Miriam Ferzli, and Carol Miller. In Support of Pair Programming in the Introductory Computer Science Course. *Computer Science Education*, September 2002.
12. Laurie A. Williams and Robert R. Kessler. Experimenting with Industry's "Pair Programming" Model in the Computer Science Classroom. *Computer Science Education*, March 2001.
13. Dwight Wilson. Teaching XP: A Case Study. In *XP Universe*, Raleigh, NC, USA, July 2001.

Introducing Agile Methods in Learning Environments: Lessons Learned

Grigori Melnik[1] and Frank Maurer[2]

[1] Department of Information and Communications Technologies
Southern Alberta Institute of Technology (SAIT)
Calgary, Canada
grigori.melnik@sait.ca
[2] Department of Computer Science
University of Calgary
Calgary, Canada
maurer@cpsc.ucalgary.ca

Abstract. This paper describes the experiences of introducing agile methods in four different academic programs (Diploma, Applied Bachelor's, Bachelor's and Master's) in two institutions during two academic years. It contains suggestions and techniques for bringing agile methods into curriculum. Based on overwhelmingly positive students' experiences this report should encourage other academics that are considering introducing agile methods in their software engineering courses.

1 Introduction

Agile methods are here. They are here to stay. As the Editor-in-Chief of Gartner Dataquest Research Group points out in her report "Business pressure on software development companies to be *agile* and *adaptable* has never been greater"[1]. Growing number of software development teams are successfully applying various agile methods in the real-world projects. How are academic institutions responding to this new wind in the software development industry?

Presently, there is a number of strong cases supporting agile practices in software engineering and computer science curricula. Williams, Kessler and Upchurch [2, 3, 11] have been evaluating pair programming for several years. The results of a recent formal experiment at North Carolina State University [4] indicated that students who practice pair programming *perform better* on programming projects and *are more likely to succeed*. Bevan, Werner and McDowell [17] discuss implementation issues of pair programming into freshman programming class at University of California at Santa Cruz and provide guidelines. We are aware of the successful effort of Dubinsky and Hazzan of integrating eXtreme Programming (XP) in the advanced Operating Systems Project course at Technion – Israel Institute of Technology [18]. Johnson and Caristi simulated the practices of XP in a Software Design upper level course at Valparaiso University [5]. The student responses and observations agree that the XP-like process resulted in *good team communication* and a *broader knowledge of the project* as a whole. They further conclude that "an XP based approach has *merit* in the con-

F. Maurer and D. Wells (Eds.): XP/Agile Universe 2003, LNCS 2753, pp. 172–184, 2003.

text of the Software Design class". Astrachan, Duval and Wallingford report on the success of adopting and adapting principles of XP (and other agile methodologies) in classroom teaching at Duke University and University of Northern Iowa [7]. Keenan also agrees with this and supports his opinion with the study of the Dundalk Institute of Technology student attitudes, which were *mostly positive* [8]. Holcombe, Gheorghe, and Macias introduced XP into fourth year term project, in which students run their own software house and carry out real projects for real business clients. "The [agile] philosophy has been adopted with *much enthusiasm* and seems to have delivered in a variety of contexts, including maintenance and new projects" [9]. Wilson reports on the success of a project-oriented course using XP at the John Hopkins University [10]. At the end the students built a significant piece of software. The instructor and the students agree that "the course was an *enjoyable experience*".

Certainly, not all innovations turn out to be completely successful. Sanders reports that the majority of senior students in software engineering class at Northwest Missouri State University were opposed to using XP, but those in an introductory programming course favored pair programming [6]. Lappo observed a group of Master's students at Brighton University who were taught XP and applied their knowledge to a 12-week project [12]. Despite the fact that the project did not go as well as planned, Lappo points out that "teaching XP should be relatively easy in a university environment". He also insists that it is important that "students come away with an understanding of why XP works", which "does not come easily as it requires plenty of practice and experience against which to compare XP". Lappo concludes *"Practice is easy to organise, but experience is harder to obtain"*.

We have been introducing agile methods in software engineering courses since fall 2001. Perceptions of broad student body on eXtreme programming in general and its individual practices were studied. Preliminary results [14] are now strengthened with additional two semesters of data and the overall perceptions are consistently positive across four semesters and four different programs.

2 Why Teach Agile Methods?

Thanks to changing requirements and technology, software changes are a fact of life. Gartner Research vice-president and research director Jim Duggan says for these kinds of projects to be successful team members need a combination of allegiance and intelligence. "The other half of the equation is *that they have to have the training*, skills, tools, and processes in place *that actually make the change able to happen*"[15]. Academic departments responsible for the development of competent software engineers are faced with this challenge. Back in 1997, Mead, Carter and Lutz in The State of Software Engineering Education and Training emphasized the fact that "many industry organization bemoan that new hires are not prepared to practice software engineering" [19]. In his talk at OOPSLA 2000 Educators' Symposium entitled "Educating for Change" Kent Beck focused on the importance of teaching collaboration skills, which is often underestimated and therefore ousted by teaching technical skills [16]. We believe in the broad approach: academic institutions should teach agile and traditional software engineering and prepare students to adapt to whatever modus operandi their future employers/teams use. The 'breadth' is the keyword and it is important to expose students to all different methodologies. We should also train them in how to adapt to changes. Of course, the faculty must be able and willing to redesign and implement curricula that not only emphasize the technical aspects of computer science, but also focuses on the practices and craftsmanship of software engineering.

Nowadays, the industry needs people who are flexible and agile. This means we, the faculty, must also "embrace the change" and must start educating students for this change.

3 Courses and Student Populations

Students of four different levels of computer science programs from the Southern Alberta Institute of Technology (SAIT) and the University of Calgary were exposed to agile methods. All individuals were knowledgeable about programming. Data was collected partially during and partially at end of the semester in which agile practices were introduced. In total, *102* students took part in the study (Table 1). Detailed program and course descriptions for the three programs we have been observing since fall 2001 are provided in the previous paper on student perceptions [14]. In addition, during the last two semesters we have been introducing agile methods to the senior undergraduate course, which we describe in more detail here.

In most courses we selectively adopted test-driven development, simple design, continuous integration, refactoring, pair programming and collective code ownership.

We studied 2nd year students of the Computer Technology Diploma program at SAIT majoring in Information Systems who were enrolled in the *Data Abstraction and Algorithms* course taught using Java as the primary language. We also studied 22 students of the Bachelor of Applied Information Systems program (BAI[1]) who were enrolled in the elective *Internet Software Techniques* course.

The senior undergraduate course on *Web-Based Systems*[2] was taught by the second author in the fall 2002 and by the first author in the winter 2003. The course includes comprehensive hands-on software development assignments (which are done in teams of 5-6 students). Students are encouraged to use pair programming, but there is no way to enforce it in the off-class time (yet student responses speak for themselves – see further in Section 5). The final exam consists of developing a small Web-based system and is done online – the students must deliver *clean code that works*.

We also studied students enrolled in a graduate course *Agile Software Processes*[3] as part of their M.Sc. program. Thirteen of the 23 students enrolled in the course had several years of software development experience (most as developers but partially also as team leads and project managers). The course is not required for completion of the M.Sc. degree.[4] At least two of the students had prior industrial experience with XP practices. The course discussed and applied agile software development methods. In the course assignment, the students were split up into two groups of 6-11 students and either developed a small Web-based system or extended an existing research proto-

---

[1] http://www.sait.ca/academic/information/programs/bai.htm

[2] http://sern.cpsc.ucalgary.ca/courses/SENG/513/F2002 and …/W2003

[3] http://sern.cpsc.ucalgary.ca/courses/SENG/609.24/F2002/

[4] Hence, students taking this course are interested in agile methods. Most of them had a positive bias while one student expressed some reservation on XP at the beginning of the course.

type. The teams were strongly encouraged to use all XP practices. Each team delivered three releases of their system over 12 weeks (one release every 4 weeks).

We would also like to point out that students do not work on a single course full time. We estimate that on average a student spends about 5-7h/week on the course assignment[5]. Hence, the effort going into a release is approximately about 20 hours per student (which is much lower than in XP or any other agile method).

4 Student Perceptions Study Overview

The intent of our descriptive study is to see what the perceptions of students of agile practices are and how they vary (if at all) depending on the programs they are enrolled in. The study focuses on agile engineering practices that are coming from XP[6]. Concretely, we are interested in perceptions on XP in general and three XP practices that we used in our classes in particular: pair programming, project planning using the planning game, and test-driven development. The subjects of the study are students on various levels of experience as described in the previous section (starting from students in the second year of their higher education up to M.Sc. graduate students who often had several years of experience in software development).

We developed a 20-question survey with both open-ended questions assessing perceptions of the agile practices and gathering suggestions on how courses can be improved and quantitative questions (on a 5 point Likert summated scale, 1 "strongly disagree" to 5"strongly agree"). These two approaches complemented each other and provided both the depth and the width of coverage on the topic.

When looking at the students' experiences, we asked a number of questions:
- Did the students enjoy agile practices?
- What worked for them?
- What problems did they encounter?
- Whether they would use agile practices in the future (if allowed) or not?
- What were their impressions of the test-driven development?
- How did XP improve their learning?

The survey was anonymous and was executed on the Web. Informal interviews and discussions were also conducted during the course of the semester to get some informal feedback on other aspects of XP that were used in the courses (continuous integration, collective code ownership, refactoring, coding standards). The use of a mix of qualitative and quantitative research methods provided an opportunity to gain a better understanding of the factors that impact students' and developers' experiences in XP.

It should be mentioned that the study performed is not intended to be a complete formal qualitative investigation.

---

[5] This estimate is based on time sheets over 10 weeks from one of the UofC groups.

[6] We are using "agile practices" to make clear that we did not use the full set of XP practices in our study.

5 Empirical Data

Considering the relative simplicity of analyses undertaken, the conclusions we report are descriptive statistics only.

Table 1. Summary of Respondents by Academic Programs

Academic program	Semester(s)	# of invitations sent out	# of respon-dents	Response rate
College-level Diploma (2 years)	Fall 2001, Winter 2002	41	22	54%
College-level Post-Diploma Applied Bachelor's Degree (2+2 years)	Winter 2002	22	15	68%
	Fall 2002	18	10	56%
University-level Under-graduate (4 years)	Fall 2002	55	19	35%
	Winter 2003	62	19	31%
University-level Graduate (4+2 years)	Winter 2002	12	9	75%
	Fall 2002	11	8	73%
Total, All Programs		**221**	**102**	**46%**

Figure 1 (answers shown by the academic program with SAIT programs combined[7]) illustrates that the overwhelming majority of all respondents (84%) either believe or strongly believe that using XP improves the productivity of small teams (mean=3.94; SD=0.97). 85% of students (mean=4.08; SD=0.82) suggested that XP improves the quality of code and 72% of all respondents (mean=3.77; SD=0.94) would recommend to the company they work for or will be working in the future, to use XP. Figure 2 shows the cumulative results on all non-open ended questions of the survey. The up-dated results are consistent with the original results reported in [14], which are over-whelmingly positive. This holds for XP in general and for individual practices. It also holds across all level of students (with M.Sc. students slightly less optimistic).

6 Lessons Learned

This is a reflection of authors based on two years of instruction of various software engineering courses using certain agile practices. It is about the effect of agile meth-ods on the way we teach and students learn as we have experienced it.

---

[7] Because the results of the survey for SAIT in fall 2001 were not differentiated by the program, but contained the answers of students of both diploma and applied degree programs.

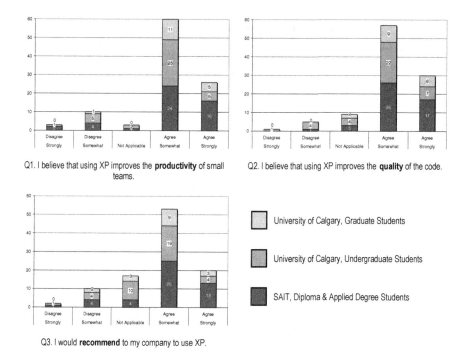

Q1. I believe that using XP improves the **productivity** of small teams.

Q2. I believe that using XP improves the **quality** of the code.

Q3. I would **recommend** to my company to use XP.

University of Calgary, Graduate Students

University of Calgary, Undergraduate Students

SAIT, Diploma & Applied Degree Students

Fig. 1. Extreme Programming Perceptions Distributed by Academic Programs.

6.1 XP in General

In our opinion it is more difficult to make XP work in the academic environment then in the industrial. This is simply because of scheduling problems (impossible to collocate students every day) and the amount of time a student can spend on the project per week (impossible to get them to work on the project every day). The logistic of the process is trickier. Both authors saw it over and over again in all four programs.

Overall, the feedback on XP and the productivity of small teams was positive:

- *"I believe that XP helps get more work done in less time and is very effective for small groups as it allows for the group members not to get stuck for extended periods of time."*

- *"Focus on results. Focus on small, fast deliverables. Focus on communication. Focus on minimalization. Focus on teamwork. I love it."*

- *"As with any technique, practice and experience lead to easier and repeatable results. What I like about XP is the managing of fast paced, chaotic project situations which is standard for real-world work."*

- *"It's the most interesting way of doing development!"*

When asked to comment on the quality of code that XP teams produce, 85% of the respondents agreed that XP improves the quality:

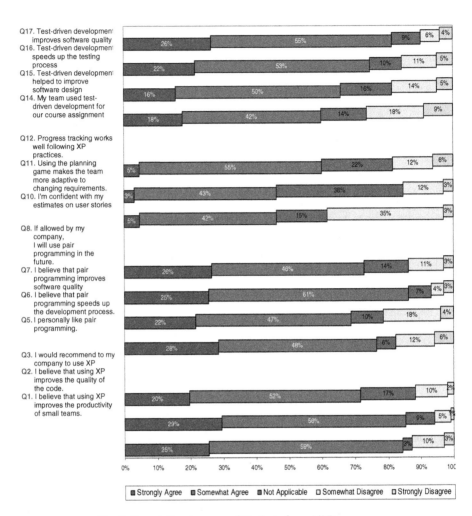

Fig. 2. Cumulative Answers of Students from All Programs.

- *"Generally by using XP the quality tends to be better as there are not as much wasted functionality implemented and what is implemented, is implemented in a superior fashion to what otherwise would be done."*

- *"Quality is built into the process (not a supporting concept but a core concept)."*

- *"Since everyone is sharing the code, everyone is constantly improving it and testing it."*

Several students indicated that XP is not a silver bullet: *"even in XP, the code quality is still highly dependent on the quality of the people writing it."* This brings us back to the notion of "superior people" discussed by DeMarco and Boehm [20].

This is not only about people's technical abilities, it is also about something Bach refers to as *"heroism"*. He defines a hero in business and engineering as "someone who takes initiative to solve ambiguous problems" [21]. There is no way to teach "heroism", but to encourage it.

We could clearly see how much the success of a group would depend on the presence of heroic software people. In student teams, we observed that having one or two exceptional developers would result in great deliverables even if no one else was contributing. Of course, this should be different in the way industrial teams work.

A true XP team (ideally) holds steady development pace and should have no spikes in delivering business value to the customer. In a student XP team, there are many spikes, normally associated with the approaching assignment deadline. The analysis of the course site visit logs (during winter 2003 semester), clearly showed the spiky nature of student involvement with the project when two days before the due date, the number of visits to the Assignments Web page would double or in some cases even triple. This is easily explained, considering the fact that students are not working on one project. Normally, they have to balance among at least five different projects assigned in different courses. Thus, students always work on the most urgent one. It was not exactly the case with the graduate students as a large part of them were part-time students, working full-time in the industry and they would only take one course at a time. However, they still had to do a similar balancing act between their day jobs and the course. Generally, agile practices oppose project interruptions for any reason. Scrum tells you that while sprint is running, there must be no interruptions. Even a CEO of the company cannot come in and pull out a member of the team to do an urgent job or a demo. But an instructor of another course can. Usually, *students serve five masters at the same time*.

We would like to emphasize another important dissimilarity between real-world and academic agile projects. In the industry, the agile projects are normally of the *"Flexible Scope-Fixed Time"* nature, while our academic projects are always *"Fixed Scope-Flexible Time"*. Academic projects break the timebox and are being evaluated against a given fixed scope. There is no such thing as a timebox for a student. If in the industry we have a pretty strong assurance that developers do not break the timebox, we cannot control how much time a student spends to complete the assignment (except during the exams – which are not considered to be a good representation of the real world development projects). Students are not being "paid" (evaluated) based on timesheets. One student may spend twice as much time as another one to do the assignment. It may depend on the amount of self-learning the assignment requires. How do you timebox learning?

If we use flexible scope projects, the problem remains: how do we evaluate students working on a flexible scope project?

In all our courses (except for CT Diploma Program at SAIT) we had emergent requirements. We would normally fix the requirements for a given iteration at the planning meeting (as recommended by XP, Scrum and other agile processes) but students were made aware that requirements may change (and they did) in the next iteration.

When asked what worked for their team and what did not, students indicated the value of good communication, responsible software engineering practices, "many eyeballs effect" for catching bugs, and expertise sharing in a pair/team. Several initially skeptical students acknowledged that it worked better than what they thought it would be. Many students reiterated the concern from the previous year about limited communication due to scheduling issues:

- *"It was very difficult to have the constant communication needed for XP. Because we all have other commitments, communication was weak within our group. As well, the less committed group members were allowed to ride along with the stronger group members who completed the majority of the work."*

In fact several studies (see [22], for example) identify a number of human issues in communications, technology, teamwork and political factors that significantly influence implementation and evolution of XP into a small software development team. As one of the students exclaimed: *"XP is about the t3am sk1llz!"* [team skills].

6.2   Practice-Specific and Implementation Lessons

Teach Software Testing Techniques Early on in the Program. The first author had an opportunity to revise the curriculum of the software engineering stream at SAIT. The main change that occurred was moving the course on Software Testing and Maintenance to the first semester. It turned out to be an extremely good decision, as students were taught unit testing, test-driven development, continuous integration, refactoring, responsible software engineering practices early on in the program. As a result, students were better equipped for the programming courses in the following semesters.

Reinforce Version Control and Test-Driven Development. We have implemented earlier deadlines for test suites, and gave a large percentage of the assignment grade to the tests. We also restricted the submission of the working projects to electronic submission of source code, tests and build scripts via cvs only. The students were informed about the "clean code that works" policy – the project that does not compile gets zero. It may have been seen a bit harsh from the very beginning, but as they were explained the values of agile methods (one of which is working software), we had no projects that would not compile. Students were encouraged to comment out the portions of the code that did not pass the tests with the marker "DIRTY" and an explanation of why it is incomplete and what they have tried to do to make it work.

Although only 60% of respondents used test-driven development, a large population believes that test-driven development helps to improve software design (mean=3.58, SD=1.14) and speeds up the testing process (mean=3.75, SD=1.14). Our evidence shows that even though students did not absorb the concept of test-driven development as enthusiastically as other practices, they do realize the importance of testing and see the benefits of finding bugs at the early stage of application design.

Encourage Electronic Communication in the Off-Class Time. Using telephone, NetMeeting or asynchronous private forums for communication can partially resolve scheduling conflicts. In one case, a group had over 100 messages in their private forum, although majority of groups would not utilize forums at all. In addition to regular office hours, the first author established online office hours, checking for messages and responding to them immediately. Furthermore, students were encouraged to post their problems, interesting findings and links to the forum and to respond to other students' inquiries. Often the solution to a problem of one team was found by another team and posted before the instructor had a chance to read it.

Direct Students to Improve Their English and Communication Skills. Normally, there is a department available on campus that provides such training to students. We also encouraged students to attend something like a toastmaster or public speaking class to gain the confidence of communicating freely. In our observations, we have noticed that more reserved students preferred to use electronic means to communicate with the group – likely because there was no time pressure to prepare the answer.

No Policing during Development. Peer pressure is strong enough motivator. The most efficient way to check whether students really worked on the projects is to give them a hands-on comprehensive online exam, where by the end of a three-hour block, they are required to produce a piece of working functionality. We have given hands-on exams to the students at SAIT and UofC and it turned out to be extremely effective to detect those who did not contribute much. The exams were of the open-book type, students were allowed to bring their past code with them and to use online reference resources. In addition to disabling certain ports, students were monitored during the exam to make sure that no instant messaging or file transfer would occur.

Establish Ground Rules. Certain rules were established by the instructor (such as accepted responsibility, collective code ownership, incremental change, simplicity, YAGNI, naming and coding conventions, all tests must pass before integration, and trust other people's code). We also advised students not to get emotionally attached to the code. Students were invited to suggest other rules for their peers that would help to create the best learning/production environment (try to solve the problem by yourself first, then ask for help; share new/interesting stuff with the group; be enthusiastic; be polite; no whining; no lame excuses).

Get a "Home Base". This worked extremely well at SAIT, where a dedicated software engineering lab was used for the specialization courses. Students felt like it was their own development area. They were allowed to post any stories, questions, solutions on the walls. Off-class access to the lab was arranged (including during evenings and weekends). Every student was given an electronic key for the room. We realize that this may not be possible in every academic environment, but providing students with a permanent working area for the duration of the course definitely helps.

Schedule Lab Time. The graduate course of UofC was originally offered as a quarter course with no scheduled lab sessions. After running it twice, it seems to be beneficial to have lab time scheduled to do at least the planning meetings together.

Do "Green-Field Development" (if Possible). We had experienced starting a course with an existing system that needed to be extended by students. The system was not originally developed in the agile way. This resulted in missing test drivers and some problems with refactoring and integrating the new functionality without breaking existing parts. In addition, understanding the existing system was already quite a task by itself and took away time from working on the new functionality.

Get a Responsive, Knowledgeable and Committed Customer or Become One. When an instructor performs the role of a customer, it is important to allot enough time for interacting with the teams outside of the classroom. The second author recalls his experience with graduate projects and the fact that he simply did not have enough time to work with the teams off-class. As a result during the final demo, the customer/instructor discovered the teams implemented some features incorrectly. An alternative solution may be to form a surrogate On-site Customer that consists of the instructor and the teaching assistants.

The first author has an experience of doing the project together with the BAI software engineering students and performing the role of the team leader/master. An outside client was recruited. Even though, the customer was not part of the development team, he was available via email and the online forum and responded to the questions within one day. Students initially met the customer for a project kickoff. They also demonstrated working components of the system to him every month. We consider this to be very useful as they actually saw the immediate reaction of the customer.

Discourage "Assumptions Disease". Agile methods encourage developers to avoid making assumptions based on partial knowledge and to get the customer answer the questions instead. Initially, students were informed of this rule and became very active interacting with the customer (both online and face-to-face). Interestingly, the analysis of the forum postings shows, what we call, *The Customer Abandonment Syndrome* – when, later during the semester students actually started making assumptions about the projects and requirements (often even without consulting with the rest of the team) instead of clarifying those with the customer. Several times during the semester the instructor had to remind the students not to make such assumptions.

Use Known Technology. If the project is chosen such that the students know the basic technology, it gives them a good boost. Otherwise, we have seen the loss of productivity and inability to do accurate estimates. Indeed, it is extremely hard to estimate how long it will take someone to learn new techniques.

Ask Students to Submit Their Estimates. This can be done on paper or electronically. The estimates must be submitted before the actual release date (assignment due date). This encourages students to think about their tasks, track their time and become better in estimating.

Encourage Responsible Software Engineering Practices. Students must learn how to take responsibility for themselves and their projects. In all courses, students were allowed to self-organize (form their own groups, choose a leader/master, agree on tasks to complete). When choosing a task, they made a commitment to ensure that it would be done right. Also, responsible software engineering practices mean that known bugs have to be fixed. Because of the nature of the course, the assignments built up one on another. If TAs discovered certain problems with the assignment submitted, it was an absolute must for the team to fix those problems in the submission of the next assignment.

7 Summary and Future Work

Our experiences introducing agile methods in the computer science curricula show that students are very enthusiastic about core agile practices. Our initial findings [14] that there are no significant differences in the perceptions of students of various levels of educational programs and experiences, were reconfirmed with additional data. The graduate students (whose majority has several years of experience) are – overall – a bit more cautious then the rest of the sampling. Overall, our results indicate that a broad range of students (although not everyone) accepts and likes agile practices. And this is in our opinion a prerequisite for their widespread adoption in industry.

In this paper, we are not trying to generalize the findings to the industrial setting. We provide a snapshot of some aspects of perceptions of agile practices and also share some thoughts that may help other faculty to introduce agile methods in their courses.

We hope that the observations made will provoke discussion and future studies on a wider selection of students and practitioners and would like to invite any interested parties (both academic and industrial) to take part in such studies.

Acknowledgements. The authors would like to thank all students from the University of Calgary and SAIT who participated in the study and provided us with their thoughtful responses. This work was partially sponsored by NSERC, ASERC, and the University of Calgary.

References

1. Correia, J. Recommendation for the Software Industry During Hard Times. *Gartner Dataquest Report*, June 6, 2002.
2. Williams, L., Kessler, R. Experimenting with Industry's "Pair-Programming" Model in the Computer Science Classroom. *Journal on Computer Science Education*, March 2001.
3. Williams, L., Kessler, R., Cunningham, W., Jeffries, R. Strengthening the Case for Pair Programming. *IEEE Software*, Vol. 17, July/August 2000, pp.19–25.
4. Williams, L., Wiebe, E., Yang, K., Ferzli, M., Miller, C. In Support of Pair Programming in the Introductory Computer Science Course. *Computer Science Education*, September 2002.
5. Johnson, D., Caristi, J. Extreme Programming and the Software Design Course. *Proc. XP Universe 2001*, July 23–25, 2001, Raleigh, NC, USA.
6. Sanders, D. Student Perceptions of the Suitability of Extreme and Pair Programming. In *Extreme Programming Perspectives*, Addison Wesley, 2002, Ch.23.
7. Astrachan, O., Duvall, R., Wallingford, E. Bringing Extreme Programming to the Classroom. In *Extreme Programming Perspectives*, Addison Wesley, 2002, Ch.21.
8. Keenan, F. Teaching and Learning XP.
    http://www.agilealliance.org/articles/articles/FrankKeenan-TeachingAndLearningXP.pdf
9. Holcombe, M., Gheorghe, M., Macias, F. Teaching XP for Real: Some Initial Observations and Plans. *Proc. XP2001 Conference*, Sardinia, Cagliari, Villasimius, Italy, May 20–23, 2001.
10. Wilson, D. Teaching XP: A Case Study.
    http://www.aanpo.org/articles/articles/TeachingXP.pdf
11. Williams, L., Upchurh, R. In Support of Student-Pair Programming. *Proc. SIGCSE Conference on Computer Science Education*, February 21–25, 2001, Charlotte, NC, USA.
12. Lappo, P. No Pain, No XP Observations on Teaching and Mentoring Extreme Programming to University Students. *Proc. XP2002 Conference*, May 26–29, 2002, Alghero, Sardinia, Italy.
13. Williams, L., Upchurch, R. Extreme Programming for Software Engineering Education. *Proc. 31ˢᵗ ASEE/IEEE Frontiers in Education 2001 Conference*, Oct. 10–13, 2001, Reno, NV, USA.

14. Melnik, G., Maurer., F. Perceptions of Agile Practices: A Student Survey. *Proc. XP/Agile Universe 2002, Lecture Notes in Computer Science*, Vol. 2418, Springer Verlag, pp.241–250.
15. Copeland, L. Extreme Programming. *ComputerWorld*, December 03, 2001.
16. Eckstein, J. Educators' Symposium Summary. *Proc. ACM OOPSLA Conference 2001*, October 14–18, 2001, Tampa Bay, FL, USA.
17. Bevan, J., Werner, L., McDowell, C. Guidelines for the Use of Pair Programming in a Freshman Programming Class. *Proc. of the 15ᵗʰ Conference on Software Engineering Education and Training*, February, 25–27, 2002, Covington, KY, USA: IEEE Computer Society Press, pp.100–107.
18. Dubinsky, Y., Hazzan, O. Agile-Training of XP-Supervising Group: A Case Study of a Project-Based Course. *Proc. Workshop on Empirical Evaluation of Agile Processes*, August 7, 2002, Chicago, IL, USA
    http://sern.ucalgary.ca/eeap/wp/Dubinsky&Hazzan_Position%20Paper.pdf
19. Mead, N., Carter, D., Lutz., M. The State of Software Engineering Education and Training, *IEEE Software*, Vol. 14, no. 6, p.24.
20. DeMarco, T., Boehm, B. The Agile Methods Fray. *IEEE Computer*, Vol. 35, no. 6, pp.90–92.
21. Bach, J. Enough about Process: What We Need are Heroes. *IEEE Software*, Vol. 12, no. 2, pp.96–98.
22. Gittins, R., Hope, S. A Study of Human Solutions in eXtreme Programming. In Kadoda, G. (Ed) *Proc. 13ᵗʰ Workshop of the Psychology of Programming Interest Group (ed. G. Kadoda)*, 2001, Bournemouth, UK, pp.41–51.
23. Johnson, D., Sutton, P., Harris, N. Extreme Programming Requires Extremely Effective Communication: Teaching Effective Communication Skills to Students in an IT Degree. *Proc. 18ᵗʰ ASCILITE 2001*, December 9–12, 2001, Melbourne, Australia, pp. 81–84.

Pair Learning: With an Eye Toward Future Success

Nachiappan Nagappan[1], Laurie Williams[1], Eric Wiebe[2], Carol Miller[1],
Suzanne Balik[1], Miriam Ferzli[2], and Julie Petlick[2]

[1] Department of Computer Science, North Carolina State University, Raleigh, NC 27695
{nnagapp,lawilli3,miller,spbalik}@unity.ncsu.edu
[2] Department of Math, Science and Technology Education, North Carolina State University,
Raleigh, NC 27695
{wiebe,mgferzli,jdhinson}@unity.ncsu.edu

Abstract. Pair programming is a practice in which two programmers work collaboratively at one computer on the same design, algorithm, or code. Prior research indicates that pair programmers produce higher quality code in essentially half the time taken by solo programmers. Pair programming is becoming increasingly popular in industry and in university curricula. An experiment was run at North Carolina State University over a period of one and a half years to assess the efficacy of pair programming as an alternative educational technique in an introductory programming course. We found that the retention rate of the students in the introductory programming courses is equal to or better than that of the students in the solo programming courses. Most students show a positive attitude towards collaborative programming, and students in paired classes continue to be successful in subsequent programming classes that require solo programming. Pair programming also leads to a reduced workload for the course staff in terms of grading, questions answered and teaching effort.

1 Introduction

In industry, software developers generally spend 30% of their time working alone, 50% of their time working with one other person, and 20% of their time working with two or more people [6]. However, most often in an academic environment, programmers must learn to program alone, and collaboration is considered cheating. This time spent working alone unfortunately conflicts with a student's future professional life in which collaboration is both encouraged and required. In addition, studies show that cooperative and collaborative pedagogies are beneficial for students [11, 12].

Research results [5, 17, 20] indicate that pair programmers produce higher quality code in about half the time when compared with solo programmers. These research results are based on experiments held at the University of Utah in a senior-level Software Engineering course. The focus of that research was the affordability of the practice of pair programming and the ability of the practice to yield higher quality code without significant increases in time/cost. However, the researchers observed educational benefits for the student pair programmers. These benefits included superior results on graded assignments, increased satisfaction, reduced frustration

F. Maurer and D. Wells (Eds.): XP/Agile Universe 2003, LNCS 2753, pp. 185–198, 2003.

from the students, increased confidence from the students on their project results, and reduced workload for the teaching staff.

These observations inspired further research directed at the use of pair programming in educating Computer Science students. Educators at the University of California-Santa Cruz (UCSC) [4, 8] and North Carolina State University (NCSU) [10, 18, 19] have reported on the use of collaborative pair programming in introductory undergraduate programming courses. The experiments were specifically designed to assess the efficacy of pair programming in an introductory Computer Science course. These researchers have found that pair programming improved the retention rates of the students. We have continued these studies and report our findings in this paper.

In our experiment, specifically aimed at the effects of pair programming on beginning students, we have examined the following four hypotheses related to the introductory course:

H1. An equal or higher percentage of students in paired labs will complete the class with a grade of C or better when compared with solo programmers.

H2. Students in paired labs will have a positive attitude towards collaborative programming settings.

H3. Doing pair programming in an introductory Computer Science course does not hamper students' performance in future solo programming courses.

H4. Student participation in pair programming will lead to a reduced workload for the course staff in terms of grading, questions answered, and teaching effort when compared with the course staff of solo sections.

In subsequent sections of this paper we provide background on this experiment and give detailed analysis of the results. Section 2 gives an overview of the previous research done in pair programming. Section 3 describes the experiment carried out at North Carolina State University. Section 4 and Section 5 present the quantitative and qualitative results. Section 6 outlines the conclusions and future work.

2 Pair Programming

Pair programming [16] refers to the practice whereby two programmers work together at one computer, collaborating on the same algorithm, code, or test. The pair is made up of the *driver,* who actively types at the computer or records a design; and the *navigator,* who watches the work of the driver and attentively identifies problems and makes suggestions. Both are also continuous brainstorming partners.

Pair programming has been practiced for a long time [16], yet only recently has much research been done on its effectiveness. One of the major factors responsible for the growth in popularity of the practice is an emerging software development methodology called Extreme Programming (XP) [3]. XP was designed for the development of small- to medium-size projects. This highly collaborative methodology reduces initial planning stages for projects and places more emphasis on customer-centric activities, adapting to their ever-changing requirements. Planning is done incrementally throughout the development cycle. XP utilizes the pair programming practice for all production code.

Research at UCSC has reported positive results in studies involving pair programming with students [4, 8]. Their studies indicate that pair programming helped increase the retention rate of students who might have otherwise dropped out of the course. They also indicate that pair programming students produce better quality code and perform comparably on exams when compared to solo programming students [9]. In addition, research done at UCSC on pairing protocol issues provide several recommendations, such as pairing students with other students within the same section; pairing students with other students with similar skill level, and having a coding standard [4]. Finally, research done at UCSC on a large sample of students (555 students) indicates that pairing bolsters the course completion and pass rates and leads to higher persistence of students in a computer related major [9]. Furthermore, students show a positive attitude towards pair programming [9].

Research done at the University of Wales [13] indicates that students with lower self-confidence enjoy pair programming the most. Students with a higher skill level report the least satisfaction when they pair program with students of lesser skill level. The researchers also found some initial evidence that students produce their best work when they are paired with a partner of equal skill and confidence level.

The research studies discussed so far involve collocated pair programmers. Additional research was done at NCSU concerning distributed pair programming, whereby the programmers are not physically collocated. An experiment was run in a graduate-level Computer Science course, Object Oriented (OO) Languages and Systems. The focus of this experiment was the performance of collocated and distributed, pair and solo programmers. The initial results indicate that distributed pair programming is a feasible technique for OO development [2]. Though there were no statistically significant results, there were three initial indications from the study. The quality of code written by the distributed pairs was comparable to collocated pairs and distributed non-pairs. There were similar productivity results (measured by the lines of code) among the collocated and distributed pairs [2]. Finally, the results also indicated that distributed pair programming fosters teamwork and communication within a virtual team.

3   Experiment

A structured empirical study was run at NCSU for three semesters (Fall 2001, Spring 2002 and Fall 2002). For these research studies, we chose an introductory programming course, Introduction to Computing – Java (CSC116). The following factors led to the choice of this course:

The course is an introductory programming course that is required of all Computer Science (CSC) majors. CSC 116 is also offered as a service course for students from other departments and for lifelong education students.

The course has compulsory closed labs, which allow for the controlled use and observation of pair programming. Closed labs are excellent for controlled use of pair programming [4]. The instructor or teaching assistant can ensure that people are, indeed, working in pairs at one computer. He or she can also monitor that the roles of driver and navigator are rotated periodically.

The course is taught with two 50-minute lectures and one three-hour lab each week. Students attend labs in groups of 24 with others in their own lecture section.

The lab period is run as a closed lab where students are given weekly assignments to complete during the allotted time. Lab assignments are "completion" assignments whereby students fill in the body of methods in a skeleton of the program prepared by the instructor. Student grades are based on two midterm exams, one final exam, lab assignments, and programming projects that are completed outside of the closed lab. The programming projects are generative, that is, the students start the project from scratch without any structure imposed by the instructor. Most students are from the College of Engineering and are either freshmen or sophomores. However, students of all undergraduate and graduate levels may take the course.

Our study is specifically aimed at the effects of pair programming on beginning students. Therefore, we analysed the results of the freshmen and sophomores only. We eliminated the lifelong education students, juniors, seniors, and graduate students from the study. We also only analysed the data from students who took the course for a grade, concluding that students who audited the class or took it for credit only were not as motivated to excel as other students.

The Fall 2001 experiment was run in two sections of the course; the same instructor taught both sections. Additionally, the midterm exams and the final exam were identical. One section had traditional, solo programming labs. In the other section, students were required to complete their lab assignments by participating in the pair programming practice. When students enrolled for the class, they had no knowledge of the experiment or if their section would have paired or solo labs. In the pair programming labs, students were randomly assigned partners based on a web-based computer program; pair assignments were not based on student preferences. Students worked with the same partner for two to three weeks. If a student's partner did not show up for a particular lab, after ten minutes, the student was assigned to another partner. If there were an odd number of students, three students worked together; no one worked alone.

In the Spring 2002 the same experiment was carried out on a much larger scale due to the increased sample size available during the semester. Two instructors handled the CSC 116 (CS1) course. The fall 2002 semester also employed the same model of operation of classes as in the previous semesters, with two instructors teaching the course. Also, in the spring semester of 2002, we analyzed the performance of students in the follow-on class (CS2) who had pair programmed in CS1 the previous fall semester. Similarly, we analyzed the performance of Fall 2002 CS2 students who has taken CS1 in Spring 202

The course also included programming projects that require work outside of the closed lab. In Fall 2001, we gave the students in both sections the option of working alone or in pairs for these projects. We modified this in Spring 2002 where only students who attained a score of 70% or better on the exams could opt to pair. At that time, we felt those who did not attain a score of 70% or above should not work with a pair on the project lest they rely too heavily on their partner to produce the project. Most students who were eligible to pair chose to pair program on projects. However, the instructors now feel that the 70% eligibility might be unfair to the students, and this practice was discontinued starting in Fall 2002. At this time, we began to assign mandatory partners; students worked on projects with the same partner assigned in labs.

4 Quantitative Results

We analyzed the quantitative data semester by semester because different instructors with different course presentation styles and different exam/project content handled the course across the three semesters. In the spring 2002 semester, we had two instructors each handling a solo and paired class and a large sample size. Therefore, the results are presented by instructor for Spring 2002.

4.1 Academic Equivalence

4.1.1 Prior Programming Experience

We wanted to determine if we had academic equivalence in our experimental groups. We assessed academic equivalence in two ways: a programming assessment (which is reflective of their prior programming experience) and the students' SAT-M scores (which are reflective of the students' mathematical ability). All students took a programming assessment questionnaire at the beginning of the semester. The questionnaire contained some very basic questions on programming. The main purpose of the assessment was to examine the differences in the programming background the students had before they took the course. This analysis helped us determine whether any section had more knowledge about programming compared to other sections before the start of the course. This assessment did not carry any weight in the grading of the course. There were eight questions in the questionnaire that covered the areas of computer arithmetic, operator precedence, selection, iteration, nested loops, arrays, encapsulation, and functions. The programming assessment was evaluated out of a total score of eight points. We tested the statistical significance of the difference in programming assessment scores by using a t-test. Table 1 shows our observations across the Fall 2001, Spring 2002, and fall 2002 semesters.

The hypotheses for the t-test are as follows:

H_0: There is no significant difference between the two sections in terms of prior programming knowledge.
H_1: There is a significant difference between the two sections in terms of prior programming knowledge.

If we get statistically significant results ($p < .05$), we accept the alternative hypotheses (H_1) else we accept the null hypotheses (H_0). Hence from the t-test results in Table 1, the two sections were equivalent in terms of their programming assessment scores for the fall 2001 semester only. Hence we further examine the students SAT-M scores to study their academic equivalence.

4.1.2 Math Skills

We use the students' SAT-M scores to form the basis of our math skill analysis. We use a one-way ANOVA test to analyze the variance between the SAT-M scores of thepaired and solo sections to investigate the academic equivalence of the two groups with respect to their math skills. As shown in Table 2, the ANOVA between SAT-M scores yielded statistically significant results ($p < .05$) in the fall semester 2001. The mean SAT-M scores are essentially equivalent across the other two semesters.

Table 1. Programming Assessment Score

Semester	Paired Mean	Paired Std Dev	Solo Mean	Solo Std Dev	Stat. Significance
Fall 2001	2.69	2.22	1.77	1.62	No, t=1.807, p<0.080
Spring 2002	2.05	2.05	1.62	1.61	Yes, t=3.51, p<0.0006
Fall 2002	2.55	1.81	1.64	1.61	Yes, t=2.08, p<0.0389

Table 2. SAT-M scores and statistical significance results

Semester	Paired Mean	Solo Mean	Statistically Significant
Fall 2001	662.10	625.43	Yes (F=5.19,p<0.018)
Spring 2002	634.88	640.25	No (F=1.101,p<0.416)
Fall 2002	639.12	640.15	No (F=1.088,p<0.395)

The statistical results in the spring 2002 and fall 2002 semesters were rejected at a very high level of confidence. We consider the level of academic equivalence in our analysis.

4.2 Success Rates

Historically, beginning Computer Science classes have a low success rate, often cited informally as about 50% nationally. Success rate is defined as students who get a C or above in the course. We chose C because it is the minimum grade required in a course to satisfy further course prerequisites. We evaluated whether pair programming could help improve the success rate of beginning students in an introductory programming course. To test the statistical significance of the difference in success rates, we performed a chi-square test. The chi-square test is designed to test for independence between two categorical variables [1].

The hypotheses for the chi-square test are as follows:

H_0: There is a statistical independence between the method of programming (solo and paired) and the success rates in the class.
H_1: There exists a statistical dependence between the method of programming (solo and paired) and the success rates in the class.

A statistically significant result (p < 0.05) indicates that pair programming impacted the student final grades. These success rates along with the results of the chi-square test are summarized below in Table 3.

Table 3. Success Rate

Semester-Section	C and above (# of students)	Below C (# of students)	Success Rate	Statistically Significance
Fall 2001[1]-Paired	30	14	68.18%	Yes $\chi^2 = 5.849$,
Fall 2001- Solo	31	38	44.93%	$p < 0.016$
Spring 2002-Paired (Inst 1)	54	28	65.85 %	No $\chi^2 = 0.000$,
Spring 2002-Solo (Inst 1)	50	26	65.79 %	$p < 0.993$
Spring 2002-Paired (Inst 2)	113	85	57.07 %	No $\chi^2 = 0.004$,
Spring 2002-Solo (Inst 2)	15	11	57.69 %	$p < 0.952$
Fall 2002-Paired	47	8	85.45 %	Yes $\chi^2 = 7.292$,
Fall 2002-Solo	72	38	65.45 %	$p < 0.007$

Hence, from the results obtained over the past three semesters we see the final course grades obtained by students working in pairs is equal or better than those working solo in two of the three semesters. Thus, two out of three semesters validate our first hypotheses that, an *equal or higher percentage of studentsin the paired labs will complete the class with a grade of C or better compared to solo programmers (H1)*.

Instructor 2 from Spring 2002 handled the Fall 2002 paired class. She attributed the increase in success rate from 57.07% in Spring 2002 to 85.45% in Fall 2002 to the following factors: a new textbook was introduced which was easier to understand from the students viewpoint; daily in-class exercises were done along with a partner; required attendance in class worth 5% of the overall grade, and written homework exercise from the book that urged the students to read the textbook.

4.3   Attitude towards Pair Programming

At the end of the semester, along with their course and instructor evaluations, students were given an optional attitude survey [15]. Using the survey, we tried to determine the students' attitudes towards pair programming. The entire survey had 63 questions. We discuss the results of only one of these questions in this paper: *If you are in a*

---

[1] The Fall 2001 semester results have previously been reported in [10, 18, 19, 21] .

paired section this semester, will you choose a paired section course in the next semester, given there is a paired section? This survey data was collected in the spring 2002 and fall 2002 semesters from students in the paired section. Students in the solo section would not have had an informed opinion on this question. Table 4 shows that in the spring 2002 semester the majority of the students (approximately 80%) did not express a preference for a solo section in future. Over 84% of the Fall 2002 students did not express a preference for a solo section in future.

Table 4. Attitude survey Results (Spring 2002-Fall 2002)

Number of Respondents (Semester)	Yes	I don't care	No
207 (Spring 2002)	124 (59.9 %)	41 (19.8 %)	42 (20.2%)
71 (Fall 2002)	46 (64.7%)	14 (19.7 %)	11 (15.4%)

Results from Table 4 support our initial hypotheses that *students in paired labs have a positive attitude towards collaborative programming settings (H2)*. A limitation of these findings is that some of these students might not have had solo programming experience, and hence their choice might have been biased towards pair programming. Similar to research results [13], we surmise that the 20% of students in the spring 2002 semester and the 15% of students in the fall 2002 semester who did not want to work in a future pair programming section might have had a higher skill level and would not have liked being "slowed" down by their partner. We will investigate this hypothesis further, as outlined in section 6.

4.4 Performance of Paired Students in Solo Programming Courses in Future Semesters

Some instructors may be concerned that in courses employing pair programming, several students get a "free ride" by passing on the entire workload to their partner and do not learn the course material. We partially addressed this problem by having students submit feedback on their partners via an effective peer evaluation system called the Peer Evaluation Tool (PET[2]). These evaluations formed a part of the grading structure, and the instructor could then judge what action needed to be taken upon identification of the problems.

To show that students who pair programmed perform satisfactorily in future programming courses and that pair programming was not detrimental to students who program in solo courses in the future, we examined students in CS1 and the follow-on class CS2. All CSC majors are required to take these courses, and CS1 is a prerequisite for taking CS2. Almost all CSC majors take CS2 the following semester after taking CS1. CS2 is "Programming Concepts – Java". During the time of this reported study, CS2 was not taught with students programming in pairs. All students had to work alone, and collaboration of any form was considered cheating.

---

[2] http://pairprogramming.csc.ncsu.edu/pairlearning/testing/mystudentlogin.jsp

4.4.1 Fall 2001-Spring 2002 Semesters

First, we analyzed students who took CS1 in Fall 2001 and CS2 in Spring 2002. We obtained the results shown in Table 5. In this table, "Paired" refers to the students in the paired section and "Solo" refers to students who worked solo in CS1 in the fall semester. In CS2, all students worked alone.

Table 5. Performance in CS2 (Spring '02) of students in CS1 (Fall '01)

Section	Percentage of A's, B's in CS2	Percentage of C's, D's, F in CS2
Paired in CS1 (N=33)	69.70% (23/33)	30.30% (10/33)
Solo in CS1 (N=29)	44.82% (13/29)	55.18% (16/29)

From Table 5, more students who paired in CS1 earned a grade of A or B. In order to statistically quantify these results, we run a chi-square test with the following hypotheses.

H_0: Performance in future programming courses are independent of programming technique employed the previous semester.
H_1: Performance in future programming courses are dependent of programming technique employed the previous semester.

The results were statistically significant, (x^2=3.921 (p < 0.048)) indicating that the performance in future programming courses is impacted by the technique employed in the previous semester.

Analyzing further, a student is said to be in a variant Group S if his/her CS2 final grades are more than one third of a grade below their CS1 grades. For example, if a student got an A in CS1 and B+ in CS2 then he or she would be placed in Group S. This same student would not belong to group S if he or she got an A in CS1 but got an A- in CS2. Table 6 summarizes these results. Only six students (21.42%) who were paired in CS1 performed worse in CS2 compared to 12 students (46.15%) in the solo class of CS1 in CS2.

Table 6. Students in Group S

Section	Group S	Variant group S's performance rate
Paired (N=28)[3]	6	21.42 %
Solo (N=26)[4]	12	46.15 %

---

[3] Five students were dropped from the analysis, thereby reducing the sample size to 29. Two of them decided to drop the course and three of them took CS2 for credit only.
[4] Three students were dropped from the analysis thereby reducing the sample size to 26 as they took CS2 for credit only.

4.4.2 Spring 2002-Fall 2002 Semester

In the fall 2002 semester we obtained the following results as shown in Table 7. Students who had programmed solo in the previous semester performed much better than students who pair programmed. A chi-square test resulted in statistically significant results (χ^2=3.934, (p<0.047), thereby revealing that there was a dependence relationship between the student performance and the technique of programming employed the previous semester. However, it must be noted that the percentage of students earning an A or B was higher than for either of the groups the prior semester (see Table 5).

Table 7. Performance in CS2 (Fall '02) of students in CS1 (Spring '02)

Section	A's, B's in CS2 (# of students)	C's, D's, F in CS2 (# of students)
Paired in CS1 (N=91)	71.43% (65/91)	28.57% (26/91)
Solo in CS1 (N=66)	85.25% (52/61)	14.75% (9/61)

Table 8 shows that approximately 26% of the students who were paired did worse in CS2 than CS1; almost 30% of the students who worked alone did worse in CS2 than CS1. Comparatively in the previous semester only 21.42% of the paired students did worse is CS2 relative to CS1.

Table 8. Students in Group S

Section	Group S	Variant group S's performance rate
Paired (N=91)	24	26.37 %
Solo (N=61)	18	29.50 %

Based on the results listed above, we can say that pair programming is not detrimental to a student's performance in future programming courses done in solo. Hence we conclude that *pair programming in an introductory Computer Science course does not hamper students' performance in future solo programming courses. (H3).*

5 Qualitative Results

Qualitative results in CSC 116 [7] were obtained by observing the CSC 116 laboratory sessions. These observations were followed up with further focus groups with the students (drawn from the entire student sample) and the Lab Instructors (LIs). Additionally, in the fall 2002 semester, we quantified some of our in-class observations. These results are presented in the following section.

5.1 Students

Students expressed a preference for being able to ask their partners questions immediately as problems arise rather than having to wait for an LI to answer them. Having someone there while working on problems seemed to help students clarify ideas, pick up on minor errors, and work on understanding conceptual knowledge.

In solo labs, most of the students had to wait for 10-30 minutes to get their questions answered, and sometimes they would not be able to get their questions answered because the LIs would be busy answering other students' questions. These students would give up and continue working, ignoring their mistakes for the time being. Comparatively, since the pairs were self-sufficient, lab instructors had more time to get around to needy students than in the unpaired sections. Paired students who needed help found it easy to get help from the LI and had little down time [18].

In the focus groups, students described "partner compatibility" as the number one problem to address in paired labs. We intend to address this compatibility issue in the following semesters. We have already carried out some compatibility research in the NCSU undergraduate Software Engineering course. We will use these results to better understand "partner compatibility." Despite their frustrations with compatibility issues, students expressed their understanding that pair programming would help them in future professional work environments where people are often randomly matched to collaborate on programming projects.

Additionally, observations were made in nine paired lab sections and seven solo lab sections [14]. Students raised their hands when they had a question. When many students need questions answered, those students waiting would often give up, leaving them with unresolved problems. These are referred to as 'Give Ups' in Table 9. As shown in Table 9, the paired lab averaged a little over one 'Give Up' every lab, while the solo labs averaged almost two and an half times more than the paired lab. This demonstrates that students are better served by the LIs in paired labs.

Table 9. 'Give Ups' statistics for Fall 2002 [14]

Section	No. of 'Give ups' Mean	No. of 'Give Ups' Standard Deviation
Paired	1.14	0.90
Solo	3.17	2.56

5.2 Lab Instructors

One benefit of pair programming is that grading is reduced by a factor of two for projects and labs. Additionally, in solo lab sections, the LIs were often overwhelmed with questions. LIs often spent a minimum of five minutes and a maximum of 20 minutes with each student. Most of the students had basic questions regarding the syntax, function passing and compilation errors. [7]

In the focus groups, the LIs also felt that the quality of questions asked by the students in the paired class were indicative of higher-order learning when compared with those of students in the solo programming class. Students in the solo programming class were always asking basic questions, for example, regarding the syntax. Paired students, spent more time discussing advanced issues with their LIs [18] For example, students in paired labs would ask the LIs how to improve their algorithm or how to apply it to another scenario. Finally LIs observed that paired students' efforts and willingness to learn seemed to surpass their "traditional" counterparts. The solo lab students needed to be taught every step of the way.

To illustrate, we report results of counting the average number of questions asked in nine paired lab sections and seven solo lab sections [14]. Students in the solo programming class asked more questions and the standard deviation also is very large, which indicates that the number of questions was widely variable between labs (see Table 10). By looking at the mean number of questions we can say that the LIs had less questions to answer in the paired labs, which ensures that the response time of the LIs to student questions was better in the paired labs.

Table 10. Statistics of questions asked (Fall 2002) [14]

Section	Total Questions Mean	Total Questions Standard Deviation
Paired	43.11	7.47
Solo	56.14	30.68

Thus from the above evidence results we can conclude that student participation in pair programming will lead to a reduced workload in terms of grading, questions answered, and teaching effort for the course staff when compared with the teaching staff for students who worked solo (**H4**). This thus validates our initial hypotheses.

6   Conclusions and Future Work

Our study provides strong results of the following findings:
- An equal or higher percentage of pair programming students completed the CS1 class with a grade of C or better when compared with solo programmers.
- Students in paired labs have a positive attitude towards collaborative programming settings.
- Students pair programming in an introductory Computer Science course does not hamper students' performance in future solo programming courses..
- Student participation in pair programming will lead to a reduced workload in terms of grading, questions answered, and teaching effort for the course staff when compared with the teaching staff for students who worked solo.

We will continue the experiment in the year 2003 and use the data to further validate our claims. Also we will further investigate pair compatibility by using personality tests like the Myers-Briggs personality test and using the skill level of students to match pairs. Already, a trial experiment has been run in the spring semester 2002 in the undergraduate Software Engineering class at NCSU to match students according to personality profiles and skill level. We will obtain similar results in the CSC 116 course. We will gather results for minority and female students to obtain meaningful results for these important groups.

Acknowledgements. We would like to thank the members of the Software Engineering reading group at NCSU for their valuable comments while reviewing this paper. We would also like to thank Dr. Matt Stallmann of the Computer Science Department, NCSU for providing us with access to the grades of the CS2 course in Spring 2002. The National Science Foundation Grant DUE CCLI 0088178 provided funding for the research in this pair programming experiment.

References

[1]   Agresti, A. and Finlay, B., *Statistical Methods for the Social Sciences*: Dellen Publishing Company, Collier Macmillan Publishers, Macmillan, Inc., 1986.

[2]   Baheti, P., Williams, L., Gehringer, E., and Stotts, D., "Exploring Pair Programming in Distributed Object-Oriented Team Projects," Proceedings OOPSLA Educator's Syposium, Seattle, WA, 2002.

[3]   Beck, K., *Extreme Programming Explained: Embrace Change.* Reading, Massachusetts: Addison-Wesley, 2000.

[4]   Bevan, J., Werner, L., and McDowell, C., "Guidelines for the User of Pair Programming in a Freshman Programming Class," Proceedings Conference on Software Engineering Education and Training, Kentucky, 2002.

[5]   Cockburn, A. and Williams, L., "The Costs and Benefits of Pair Programming," Proceedings eXtreme Programming and Flexible Processes in Software Engineering -- XP2000, Cagliari, Sardinia, Italy, 2000.

[6]   DeMarco, T. and Lister, T., *Peopleware.* New York: Dorset House Publishers, 1977.

[7]   Ferzli, M., Wiebe, E., and Williams, L., "Paired Programming Project: Focus Groups with Teaching Assistants and Students," North Carolina State University, Raleigh, NC CSC TR-2002-16, 2002.

[8]   McDowell, C., Werner, L., Bullock, H., and Fernald, J., "The Effect of Pair Programming on Performance in an Introductory Programming Course," Proceedings ACM Special Interest Group of Computer Science Educators, Kentucky, 2002.

[9]   McDowell, C., Werner, L., Bullock, H., and Fernald, J., "The Impact of Pair Programming on Student Performance of Computer Science Related Majors," Proceedings submitted to the International Conference on Software Engineering 2003, Portland, Oregon, 2003.

[10] Nagappan, N., Williams, L., Miriam Ferzli, Yang, K., Wiebe, E., Miller, C., and Balik, S., "Improving the CS1 Experience with Pair Programming," Proceedings SIGCSE 2003, 2003.

[11] Slavin, R., *Using Student Team Learning.* Boston: The Center for Social Organization of Schools, The Johns Hopkins University, 1980.

[12] Slavin, R., *Cooperative Learning: Theory, Research and Practice.* New Jersey: Prentice Hall, 1990.

[13] Thomas, L., Ratcliffe, M., and Robertson, A., "Code Warriors and Code-a-Phobes: A study in attitude and pair programming," Proceedings SIGCSE, Reno, NV, 2003.

[14] Weibe, E., Williams, L. A., Petlick, J., Nagappan, N., Balik, S., Miller, C., and Ferzli, M., "Pair Programming in Introductory Programming Labs," Proceedings Submitted to American Society for Engineering Education Annual Conference and Exposition 2003, 2003.

[15] Weibe, E., Williams, L. A., Yang, K., and Miller, C., "Computer Science Attitude Survey," North Carolina State University, Raleigh, NC CSC TR-2003-01, 2003.

[16] Williams, L. and Kessler, R., *Pair Programming Illuminated.* Reading, Massachusetts: Addison Wesley, 2003.

[17] Williams, L., Kessler, R., Cunningham, W., and Jeffries, R., "Strengthening the Case for Pair-Programming," in *IEEE Software*, vol. 17, 2000, pp. 19–25.

[18] Williams, L., Wiebe, E., Yang, K., Ferzli, M., and Miller, C., "In Support of Pair Programming in the Introductory Computer Science Course," *Computer Science Education*, vol. September, 2002.

[19] Williams, L., Yang, K., Wiebe, E., Ferzli, M., and Miller, C., "Pair Programming in an Introductory Computer Science Course: Initial Results and Recommendations," Proceedings OOPSLA Educator's Symposium, Seattle, WA, 2002.

[20] Williams, L. A., "The Collaborative Software Process PhD Dissertation," in *Department of Computer Science*. Salt Lake City, UT: University of Utah, 2000.

[21] Yang, K., "Masters Thesis: Pair learning in undergraduate computer science education," in *Computer Science*. Raleigh, NC: North Carolina State University, 2002.

Adaptations for Teaching Software Development with Extreme Programming: An Experience Report

Michael Wainer

Department of Computer Science
Southern Illinois University
Carbondale, IL 62901
wainer@cs.siu.edu

Abstract. Extreme Programming (XP) and other Agile Methods are gaining increasing attention for their ability to successfully deliver quality software on time and on budget. These methods embrace the human aspects of software development placing special value on communication and work environment. This paper explores the experience of teaching a three credit hour Software Design and Development course using a development methodology based upon Extreme Programming. Overall, Extreme Programming appears to be a good fit to the academic setting with some adjustments. Adaptations are suggested for both Extreme Programming and the typical class structure to improve the match.

1 Introduction

Our software design and development course is taught at the senior/graduate level. An important goal of the course is to give students experience in developing software in a group environment. Other goals are to give them more practice with Object-Oriented programming and to get them acquainted with key practices and terminologies of software development such as UML notations and common software patterns. A key desire is to teach as much of the material as possible through project experiences: a "learn by doing" approach.

The principles and values advanced in Extreme Programming and other Agile methods, directly consider the human aspects of software development [1,2,3,4,5]. These include the work environment, the work load and the time allocated to work. Our hypothesis is that these factors are worth considering in a similar way as we go about teaching software design and development within the context of a Computer Science program. This is not to say that these factors weren't considered in the absence of Extreme Programming but what is interesting here is the contrast between considerations derived from best practices for software development versus those which arise from course and curriculum concerns.

Certainly a case can be made for introducing various supportive practices used in Extreme Programming such as pair programming [6,7] and test driven development [8] in various places throughout the Computer Science curriculum. This is not the case described here and since students have had no prior introduction to Extreme Programming practices, some of these practices strike them as rather odd. Students

F. Maurer and D. Wells (Eds.): XP/Agile Universe 2003, LNCS 2753, pp. 199–207, 2003.

taking this course are comfortable with programming and have had some experience using an object oriented language (usually C++ but not Java).

Because of the "learn by doing" approach to teaching this course, project work incorporating best practices was considered essential. A light weight methodology such as Extreme Programming, has an advantage in that it focuses more on activities rather than on products. The goal of the course is in imparting knowledge and experience to the students rather than producing process artifacts. The activity oriented approach lets us begin very quickly with meaningful experiences rather than incur a significant learning curve in teaching artifact notations and the use of document production software. The issue of selecting, obtaining, and learning such software as part of course preparations is also minimized. Finally, Extreme Programming seems to be gaining more and more acceptance with an increasing number of books and articles describing its various aspects and regarding it as a serious software development methodology.

There were also concerns about adopting Extreme Programming methodology. The methodology considers the human aspect of how professionals come together to produce software. How does it map to students who are most likely not as skilled as professional developers and who lack the maturity, time, and work environment that their professional counterparts have? Extreme Programming relies on having very participative customers available for frequent communication with the developers. Where can suitable customers be found and what happens to the course if the customers don't live up to their commitments?

1.1 Relationship to Previous Work

The author recently became aware of other project oriented Software Design and Development courses which endeavour to use Extreme Programming as their model process [9, 10]. While we share many similar experiences, it is informative to consider the various constraints and approaches taken by each of these courses. The instructional approach described here differs from the other two in at least the following ways. Instead of the instructor acting as the primary customer we work with an outside customer who is easily accessible to our students. Our course must introduce our students to a language and development environment which they are not familiar with (We use Java which is also used by [9, 10] but from their papers, we infer that their students are already familiar with that language). Rather than devote the entire semester to one project we use a practice project in addition to the customer project. In order to begin the development experience very early, we apply XP principles to teaching Java, the development tools, and the XP process.

2 Course Description

Planning this course faces the dilemma of many computer science courses; by the time we cover all the material necessary to do an interesting project, there isn't enough time left to actually do the project. Two principles of Extreme Programming are useful here: 1. Keep it simple; 2. Iterate. Taken together it means that we can introduce enough of a concept to allow us to be productive when we need it. If the topic is needed in more detail later, a future iteration can be used to develop it further. Iterations such as this may also help students better understand the simple concepts and then see how more advanced solutions solve problems that arise as the situations become more complicated (For example, students are happy to learn about a source code control system after having had a few weeks of frustration trying to figure out how to share code using only disks or e-mails.)

The course has used multiple textbooks and many handouts. Since most of our students are not familiar with Java, a text is chosen which reviews the language and demonstrates usage of the class libraries. A text which discusses more general ideas about Software Development, UML and software patterns is also desirable. Another book is selected to explain Extreme Programming and provide some guidance and examples in that regard. Most recently [2, 11] were used as texts for this course.

The initial goal of the course is to make everyone comfortable with the development environment and the basics of Java. An introduction to software development and Extreme Programming is presented first. An extensive lab exercise (a guided tutorial demonstrating the IDE and other development tools along with the ideas of the Model-View-Controller paradigm (MVC) and Test First Development) is usually given in the second week. Presently we use the Netbeans IDE[12] along with ANT[13] and JUnit[14]. Lectures reinforce the MVC and introduce Java and elements of Java class and interface design. Based upon their backgrounds and scores on an assessment exam, students are grouped into teams of three or four and introduced to a starter project.

The starter project is designed to acquaint the students with Java and the development environment as they become familiar with their team-mates. Currently the project used during this practice period is an image based memory game. During this phase we also discuss Extreme Programming practices which students are expected to incorporate into their work activities. The project is presented as a collection of initial stories with the instructor acting as the customer. Lectures focus on topics of immediate use to the groups including Extreme Programming practices such as: use of metaphor, one simple solution for conceptualizing the system, keep it simple (YAGNI - You Ain't Gonna Need It), Coding Spikes, Test First Development, Refactoring, Pair Programming, Coding to a Standard, Collective Code Ownership, Iterative Development, and working with the customer.

The MVC paradigm is exploited to allow Java coding to start immediately even though students are not familiar with the Java class libraries. The initial code is very straightforward in its use of language features since teams begin by focusing on the model. Test first development is also stressed. Java Swing code needed to create View/ Controllers supporting graphical user interfaces (GUIs) is introduced after model testing and coding is well underway. Handouts demonstrating coding, including testing ideas and refactoring is often presented using a simple MVC examples which parallels their first project.

Approximately half of the 16 week semester will be over as students work through their practice experience. During this time they should have become comfortable with Java, the development tools and working together using Extreme Programming practices. During the end of this period, discussion begins to turn towards ideas of project planning in preparation for the customer-based project.

The second part of the class focuses on working with the customer to develop software for their needs using a methodology based upon Extreme Programming. We have been fortunate to have a cooperative on-campus customer for our projects. The class meets with the customer story tellers for an initial meeting explaining the customer's desires. Contact information is exchanged and follow-up meetings are arranged. The customers encourage our students to call or drop by anytime they have a question and we invite the customer to visit our class during lab times or for special presentations.

Iteration and release dates are announced shortly after the project is introduced. Students use their experience working together on their practice project to help form estimates for their customer project. Work for the customer project is distributed among the entire class. The original groups are maintained but as the project progresses students often need to communicate with classmates not in their original group.

Lectures are used to provide guidance, smooth over rough spots, and to generate discussion about issues which arise. Additional software engineering topics are brought up when there are no pressing needs concerning the project. These topics include UML notations and software patterns. The instructor may also introduce other project stories. For instance, requiring documentation which may include some UML diagrams and Javadoc files.

3 Extreme Programming: Difficulties and Adjustments in Applying It to the Classroom

We base our development methodology on Extreme Programming but there are aspects of Extreme Programming that are adjusted to better fit the constraints of the course. Our primary goal is to teach students about software design and development and to give them related hands-on experiences. Producing good software is a pleasant side-effect but not the overwhelming concern. We make sure that our customers understand that. Additional differences between our academic environment and a production environment include experience, hours available and work space available. Similar observations have also been made by others [9, 10].

3.1 Development Team Experience

Many of our students have not had large group projects before. While most students seem to adjust well and enjoy working as a team, there is a settling in period. As everyone starts at the same time, there are no senior members to show the new people the ropes. We strive to create an environment where everyone feels a sense of mutual benefit and responsibility to their team. Rigid positions within groups are not assigned. Groups are sometimes asked to provide someone to act in various Extreme Programming roles (tracker, facilitator) for phases of the project.

Most significantly, because of the general lack of experience, groups do not have anyone to fulfill the role of Coach. The instructor and teaching assistant provide additional guidance acting as floating pseudo members of the groups. Students are assigned to groups by the instructor to balance the diversity of skills and backgrounds among the class. The diversity among the groups seems to work well by allowing students to participate in many aspects of development as well as becoming their group's "specialist" in one or more areas.

Ambiguity which arises in determining what users want, how best to accomplish tasks, and specifically what to do next, are essential components of this course. Students are accustomed to more structured assignments and often have difficulty in using their time wisely. They have little experience with class libraries and often have difficulty in utilizing documentation effectively. The Java class libraries and development tools provide a rich environment which unfortunately can also yield many false leads, distractions and frustrations.

The instructor works with development teams and the customer to try to determine what features of the class libraries will be useful to complete needed tasks. Often examples are presented as "code spikes" to help lead the class down a productive path. Examples concerning UML notation and software patterns are often directly related to the project to aid development and make the topics more concrete to the students.

Communication, perhaps unsurprisingly, turns out to be a big issue throughout the class. Students are often too apprehensive in asking other group members, the instructor and the customers about details and concerns necessary to resolve items. Some times this is due to timidity but other times to the thought that "it doesn't matter" or to not even considering that there might be another way to do something. Communication is also hampered by the limited number of hours in a day that the group can spend with each other and the lack of a permanent workspace.

3.2 Limits of Time

Students are taking this course at the same time they are taking other upper-level or graduate courses. The credit hours available to this course (3) are the same as the other courses. Students often have additional job and family responsibilities. One commonly held rule-of thumb is that students should spend approximately 3 hours outside of class for every hour of lecture. By this rule, the students have 9 hours a week, some of which must be devoted to individual study rather than development work. The time available with group members is spread out through the week and often only on the order of an hour or two at a time. This obviously leads to a less than desirable workflow.

The lack of time together as a group undoubtedly lengthens the time it takes for the groups to gel. We arrange time for a short group meeting during almost every lecture period to assist in group communications. The lack of time, specifically together as a group, makes it much more difficult to do pair programming. We strongly encourage every student to gain experience in pair programming but find it impractical to make pair programming a requirement for all "production code". This is a violation of Extreme Programming practice which, in the absence of a strict enforcement measure, we have to make do with. Code reviews are discussed in class as another technique that can be used to reduce code defects.

Development teams use their experience during the first project to help them form estimates for later work. The quantity of work in a story point most be adjusted to be far less than an ideal 40 hour week. Groups, and then the class as a whole, come to an understanding of what a story point for our class should be. It will likely be on the order of an hour or some fraction of a day.

Extreme Programming scales nicely in this regard as we can still provide a budget of story points to our customers, calculate a velocity etc. A hierarchical story allocation scheme is used. Stories are allocated to teams rather than individuals. Within teams, stories are broken into tasks which are distributed amongst the team members.

3.3 Absence of a Permanent Workspace

Our groups have no permanent workspace available to them. We are able to reserve a lab for two one hour sessions per week. The lab is open many additional hours during the week but is in use by many other students. Setting up meeting times outside of class is often problematic for groups due to other scheduled activities. This is also a complication when trying to set up meetings with customers. Students and customers can communicate and share work over the internet. CVS [15] (a source code control system) is used by groups to share work remotely and in the lab.

4   Teaching Software Development: Adjustments to Better Fit Extreme Programming

The course format, inherited over the years, is a 3 credit hour course. Until several years ago this was scheduled as 3 hours of lecture only. A schedule change was made to allow for an additional hour per week to make scheduling group meetings easier. Our adaptation for Extreme Programming has been to meet for two hours of lecture and two hours of lab time per week. Only during those two hours do we have reserved lab space. Each group is assigned an area within the lab. Hopefully this provides some feeling of a home area. Lab and lecture time slots are each 50 minutes so class meets four days a week. Time is provided on lecture days for short group meetings. It is reasonable to assume that we may be able to increase lab time slightly within our own labs in the near future. Longer term adaptations we hope to consider as we pursue a more ideal place and format for an XP Software Development course within our curriculum follow.

Ideally, we could provide our development teams with 24 hour access to a suitable work area which would be theirs throughout the duration of the course. This would be much like the arrangement of studio space provided to architecture students. Unfortunately, this is not realistic for our department or many others.

Being more adaptable about space requirements can yield more options. If each student had access to a wireless notebook a wider range of physical locations for team meetings would exist. We hope to make some notebooks available for checkout as a partial step in this direction.

Even if suitable space for group meetings were always available, finding time slots when all group members can meet may still be a problem. Most students have many other demands on their time and coordinating with team members is extremely difficult unless the times are part of the scheduled class meeting times. Increasing scheduled hours requires a rebalancing of other degree requirements. Indeed, seniors in architecture can have 6 credit hour courses which are scheduled for 18 or more contact hours. Using the same multiplier gives us 9 contact hours for a 3 credit hour course. Distributing those hours over 3 or 4 days may be a viable way of increasing team development time.

We want to keep in mind XP's practice of "working at a sustainable pace" and not overload the students. If increased time demands are placed on students they should get credit for those hours. Some possibilities for finding additional credit hours to better support a more substantial and realistic development experience follow. Of course, these suggestions would require significant considerations and discussions before most departments would be able to implement them.

For Masters students, give the option of a Software Development Track rather than a thesis. Offer a 6 credit hour, 12 to 18 contact hour intensive software development course. This would be taught much like a studio course and would require a studio-like space for the class to meet and accomplish project work. For undergraduates, offer a variation on the standard computer science degree requiring a software development studio course along with appropriate adjustments in other requirements and electives. Alternatively, coordinate the material from several courses (i.e. Software Development, Human Computer Interaction, Database etc.) to be taught jointly as a merged capstone course where lab work is combined into a large software development lab with a large number of contact hours scheduled.

5   Impressions of Teaching Software Development Using Extreme Programming

Overall impressions of teaching software development with Extreme Programming are very good. This assessment is based upon the instructor's perception as well as student evaluations. Many of the XP practices adapt well both from the perspective of providing learning experiences for the students and also for the flexibility provided to the instructor. Starting simply and using iterations to make adjustments works well for steering the course presentation. The emphasis on communication helps make it easier to determine problem areas. Test first development helps students to create software with less bugs and gives many small "wins" during development as they see their tests pass. Team work, especially pair programming and shared code ownership helps student also learn from each other.

Many of these benefits might occur within other software courses which offer significant team projects. XP lets the class start the development process faster since the up-front planning is minimized. Since we communicate less formally, we don't have to wait until more formal types of documentation are introduced (UML diagrams and diagramming tools). UML and other topics such as software patterns can be introduced later as the project is underway. As a project gets more complex the students begin to see better how these other topics are useful and have a more personal basis of reference and stronger motivation for learning.

Finding a good project for a software development course can be very challenging. Using XP also places higher requirements on customer participation as compared to other methodologies. The risk of bad project selection, or customers who fail to commit the necessary time must be kept in mind. Using XP counters this risk by using iterations and continuous design rather than lots of up front planning. If necessary, significant changes to the project can be made; while not originally planned, this would highlight a valuable strength of the XP methodology.

While we use XP as our model methodology, we only approximate its ideal form. Given the current lack of scheduled group meeting times, it is very unlikely that our development groups actually use pair programming for all production code. The lack of time also results in fewer iterations than would be desirable and less refactoring. The general success of XP encourages us to seek out a way to expand the contact hours scheduled for the course. We can also achieve the effect of more time if students come to their senior year already having been exposed to practices such as pair programming and test first development. Pushing these practices down into lower-level courses seems to be a fruitful path to explore.

6   Summary

Teaching software design and development using a methodology based upon Extreme Programming is certainly viable and has many positive points. Others [9, 10] have also come to this favorable conclusion. Extreme Programming allows students to very quickly begin a development experience that increases their knowledge of programming, incorporates best practices in software development, and builds communication and team work skills.

Adjustments must be made to the traditional software development course format when using XP as the basis for a "learn by doing" course. In our case we switched the format to two hours of lecture and two hours of lab spread out over four days each week. The course is very much oriented around the experience of building software. Lectures are sensitive to the current needs of the students in lab. Lectures are used to provide examples (code spikes, UML diagrams, software patterns) in a way which teaches a concept and also leads the students towards concepts they need to solve their project development problems.

A shortage of time and lack of a permanent workspace affects how we try to implement XP. The notion of story points is scaled down to something on the order of an hour or so. This must be accounted for in the selection of suitable projects. Our developer groups begin with three or four students. During the final project, the class as a whole merges into one larger group (from the three or four original groups) increasing the number of story points available to the customer.

More time and access to more appropriate space would certainly better support pair programming, a practice which students now experience to only a limited degree. Communications both amongst the student developers and the customers would also be enhanced. Even so, students learn a great deal by working in groups especially about communication. The course forces them to deal with resolving ambiguity and uncertainty and allows them to feel the consequences of failures to do so.

The experience using XP so far has been positive and the promise for better results in the future are very hopeful. Introducing changes to the course format to support a more studio-like experience to increase the time and improve the work environment should be explored. Even minor changes can make significant improvements. Support for major changes should grow as XP proves that it is not a fad. As this happens, we should see more best practices from XP incorporated throughout the computer science curriculum. Additional courses such as "Test Driven Development" and "Advanced XP Software Development" are also possibilities (both would help to mix in more experienced students into project workgroups).

References

[1]   Cockburn, Alistair: Agile Software Development, Addison-Wesley (2002)
[2]   Astels, David, Miller, Granville, Novak, Miroslav: A Practical Guide to eXtreme Programming, Prentice Hall PTR (2002)
[3]   Beck, Kent, Extreme Programming Explained, Addison-Wesley (2000)
[4]   Beck, Kent, Fowler, Martin: Planning Extreme Programming, Addison-Wesley (2001)
[5]   wiki: ExtremeProgrammingCorePractices, http://c2.com/cgi/ wiki?ExtremeProgrammingCorePractices (2003)
[6]   Williams, Lauire, Upchurch, Richard: In Support of Student Pair-Programming, SIGCSE '01 Proceedings, SIGCSE Bulletin, Vol 33, No. 1, pp327–331 (2001)
[7]   Williams, Lauire, Kessler, Robert: Pair-Programming Illuminated, Addison-Wesley (2003)
[8]   Beck, Kent: Test-Driven Development by Example, Addison-Wesley (2003)
[9]   Wilson, Dwight: Teaching XP: A Case Study, 2001 XP Universe Conference Papers, http://www.xpuniverse.com/pastXpu (2001)
[10] Johnson, D., Caristi, J.:Extreme Programming and the Software Design Course, 2001 XP Universe Conference Papers, http:// www.xpuniverse.com/ pastXpu (2001)
[11] Jia, Xiaoping: Object-Oriented Software Development Using Java, 2nd Ed., Addison-Wesley (2003)
[12] netbeans.org: http://www.netbeans.org/ (2003)
[13] ant.apache.org: http://ant.apache.org/ (2003)
[14] junit.org: http://junit.org/index.htm (2003)
[15] cvshome.org: http://www.cvshome.org/ (2003)

Workshops at XP/Agile Universe 2003
Introduction

Grigori Melnik, Workshops Chair

University of Calgary
melnik@cpsc.ucalgary.ca

The goal of the workshops is to provide a forum to engage in discussions that aim to advance the state of agile software development methods. This year's workshops have two major themes. One is looking at agile methods from the perspective of creating a business value (*The Data Workshop, How to Maintain and Promote Healthy Agile Culture, Agile Best Practices for Embedded Software Development*). The other theme is the practice of agile software development which is represented by two workshops that will engage the participants in a variety of interactive activities and in actual software development (*Exploring Programmer Tests* and *XPFest*).

The workshop on *Empirical Evaluation of Agile Processes* (Grigori Melnik, Adam Geras, Laurie Williams) (blessed as "*The Data Workshop*" by Ron Jeffries) drew much interest of both academia and industry at the last year's conference. It generated a worthy debate on the notion of "business value". The intent this year is to explore it further.

The workshop on *How to Maintain and Promote Healthy Agile Culture* (David Hussman, Michael Feathers) indirectly addresses the issues that effect the business value created by agile teams, as it looks into the dynamics of agile teams and how to sustain them in the long run. Agile team integration into other cultures with potentially conflicting agendas and operational modes is an equally important topic of discussion.

The modern convergence of telecommunication, electronics and information technologies poses a great deal of new challenges to embedded systems development. *Agile Best Practices for Embedded Software Development* (James Grenning, Ward Cunningham, Dave Thomas) focuses on the issues of applying agile methods effectively to embedded software development.

Most participants from the past XPFests prized the hands-on experience provided by the workshop. During this one and a half day practicum, participants will work on a live project with a real customer. The practicum's result should be "clean code that works." Whether you are a beginner and would like to get a taste of XP or an experienced XPer, *XPFest* will allow you to learn from recognized mentors (Adam Williams, Brian Marick, Rob Mee, Roy Miller, Ward Cunningham), share ideas and have fun. Observers are also welcomed.

Exploring Programmer Tests Workshop (J.R. Rainsberger, Ron Jeffries, Rick Mugridge) focuses on test-driven development. It invites the enthusiasts to advance the art of writing programmer tests through shared experience, practical advice and new techniques.

Overall, all workshops will provide insight into future research directions and contribute to a better collective understanding of agility and wider adoption of agile methods.

F. Maurer and D. Wells (Eds.): XP/Agile Universe 2003, LNCS 2753, p. 208, 2003.
© Springer-Verlag Berlin Heidelberg 2003

Workshop on Agile Development for Embedded Software Development

Organizers
James Grenning
grenning@objectmentor.com

Ward Cunningham
ward@c2.com

Dave Thomas
dave@bedarra.com

Summary

Embedded software development suffers from many of the same problems of traditional non-embedded software. In addition embedded software has other difficulties and complexities over traditional software development, such as limited resources, critical timing constraints, late integration with target hardware and separate environments for development and target execution.

This workshop is looking to bring together developers, managers and customers with experience in embedded software that have used traditional or agile approaches for specifying, testing and developing embedded software. We are also interested in position papers that discuss perceived challenges that must be addressed by Agile methods so they can be effectively applied in embedded software development teams. We are interested in practices used by embedded systems developers to effectively develop embedded software iteratively, on-time, with high quality.

Goals

- Share experience and best practices used in the development of embedded software
- Identify embedded development issues and agile approaches to dealing with those issues
- Share experience in practices that have low overhead and contribute to successful product delivery

F. Maurer and D. Wells (Eds.): XP/Agile Universe 2003, LNCS 2753, p. 209, 2003.
© Springer-Verlag Berlin Heidelberg 2003

Workshop on How to Maintain and Promote Healthy Agile Culture

Organizers
David Hussman
david.hussman@sgfco.com

Michael Feathers
mfeathers@objectmentor.com

Summary

Though XP often works well initially, creating, maintaining, and nurturing a healthy XP environment is key to the success of any XP project. This challenge is often quite difficult as a project's culture is affected by many forces; project size, project duration, varying skills sets, egos, schedules, and external project dependencies are just a few issues that must be addressed when accessing and maintaining the health of an XP project.

Goals

- Further the importance of culture and the way in which it relates to the success of agile projects (and the growth and adoption of agile practices).
- Create a forum to identify common cultural issues associated with agile projects
- Create a collection of project health measurements and potential solutions
- Correlate the workshop findings into a publishable document

F. Maurer and D. Wells (Eds.): XP/Agile Universe 2003, LNCS 2753, p. 210, 2003.
© Springer-Verlag Berlin Heidelberg 2003

2ⁿᵈ International Workshop on Empirical Evaluation of Agile Methods ("The Data Workshop")

Organizers
Grigori Melnik, University of Calgary
melnik@cpsc.ucalgary.ca

Laurie Williams, North Carolina State University
williams@csc.ncsu.edu

Adam Geras, University of Calgary
ageras@ucalgary.ca

Imagine the benefits of knowing that an XP project expends more effort understanding software requirements than does a team using a typical traditional, or waterfall approach. Imagine the benefits of being able to predict that for this particular combination of customer, product, and project team, agile modeling is going to benefit the team more than a strict XP implementation.

As compared to last year, agile methods are increasingly closer to the mainstream. This means that more organizations require support and more detailed understanding of how agile methods will affect their development teams. In addition, these organizations want to assess the customer value that the teams deliver through agile practices. This workshop builds on the success of the 1st Workshop on Empirical Evaluation of Agile Methods at XP/Agile Universe 2002 in Chicago.

The main goal of the workshop this year is to explore, through measurement, the meaning and indicators of business value delivered by agile teams. This also means 1) providing input for software engineering decision support; 2) determining the situations when applying agile methods would be beneficial; 3) raising awareness and visibility of the competitive advantage of agile teams; and 4) planning and budgeting for a software development effort that involve agile methods. The intent is to bring together practitioners and academics who are interested in discussing the current state of ongoing empirical research efforts in agile methods.

Examples of the thematic questions that the workshop participants will discuss:
- What empirical results already exist?
- What key areas/aspects of agile methods should we be studying empirically?
- How do we measure business value delivered per unit time?
- What existing software measures and processes satisfy our data requirements?
- What is the process of collecting empirical data?
- How one remains agile while collecting data?
- Who will use the measurement results? For what purpose?

F. Maurer and D. Wells (Eds.): XP/Agile Universe 2003, LNCS 2753, p. 211, 2003.

Exploring Programmer Tests

J.B. Rainsberger[1], Ron Jeffries[2], and Rick Mugridge[3]

[1] Diaspar Software Services
jbr@diasparsoftware.com
[2] www.XProgramming.com
ronjeffries@acm.org
[3] University of Auckland, NZ
r.mugridge@auckland.ac.nz

Abstract. This workshop focusses on *Programmer Tests* as defined in Test-Driven Development and the XP literature. Such tests are written by programmers to drive the development of software, demonstrate step-by-step progress towards the completion of a task and provide a safety net for refactoring. We explore specific strategies and techniques that participants can apply in their work in addition to considering the "big picture" of testing.

1 Introduction

The spotlight on XP in 2002 and 2003 has been on testing. This began with XP/Agile Universe 2002, where one of the unofficial themes was "Where do Testers Fit in to XP?"

As programmers get better at test driving their code from the inside, skilled testers can spend more time bringing their knowledge and experience to bear on driving out obscure defects. Our interest is in exploring how programmers can improve software development and the quality of the code they deliver to skilled testers.

2 Workshop

The goal of the workshop is to advance the art of writing programmer tests through the sharing of experience, practical advice and techniques.

Enthusiasts and practitioners of test-oriented programming are invited to participate to explore issues related to programmers writing tests. Participants will share their experiences and learn through multiple group discussions on the topics that interest them most.

Possible topics include:

- The role of Programmer Tests
- Programmer Testing Strategies. Eg, selecting the next test in TDD.
- Programmer Testing Techniques. Eg, introducing tests to legacy code.
- Programmer Testing Tools and Frameworks. Eg, XUnit extensions and Fit.
- The role of testers in XP
- Programmer Tests for "non-functional" concerns: execution speed, response time, security, scalability, memory footprint, logging, etc.
- Let's write some tests!

F. Maurer and D. Wells (Eds.): XP/Agile Universe 2003, LNCS 2753, p. 212, 2003.

XPFest

Organizers
Ward Cunningham
ward@c2.com

Adam Williams
awilliams@rolemodelsoftware.com

Brian Marick
marick@testing.com

Rob Mee
robmee@ieee.org

Roy Miller
rmiller@rolemodelsoft.com

Summary

The two previous XP/Agile Universe conferences have included an XPFest, where XP practitioners and people new to XP could experience using all the practices. This tradition is continued.

This year's XPFest is similar to the ones in previous years. We will still use and explore all the practices. But our primary goal this year is to focus more on customer testing. Customer testing is a challenge for most teams, partially due to lack of understanding, partially due to lack of tools. We hope to help participants with both.

Goals

- Give those who have never tried eXtreme Programming in its entirety a chance to do just that
- Help practitioners understand customer testing and use it effectively
- Explore "the simplest customer testing tool that could possibly work" (FIT)

F. Maurer and D. Wells (Eds.): XP/Agile Universe 2003, LNCS 2753, p. 213, 2003.
© Springer-Verlag Berlin Heidelberg 2003

Author Index

Lecture Notes in Computer Science

For information about Vols. 1–2659
please contact your bookseller or Springer-Verlag

Vol. 2702: P. Brusilovsky, A. Corbett, F. de Rosis (Eds.), User Modeling 2003. Proceedings, 2003. XIV, 436 pages. 2003. (Subseries LNAI).

Vol. 2704: S.-T. Huang, T. Herman (Eds.), Self-Stabilizing Systems. Proceedings, 2003. X, 215 pages. 2003.

Vol. 2706: R. Nieuwenhuis (Ed.), Rewriting Techniques and Applications. Proceedings, 2003. XI, 515 pages. 2003.

Vol. 2707: K. Jeffay, I. Stoica, K. Wehrle (Eds.), Quality of Service – IWQoS 2003. Proceedings, 2003. XI, 517 pages. 2003.

Vol. 2708: R. Reed, J. Reed (Eds.), SDL 2003: System Design. Proceedings, 2003. XI, 405 pages. 2003.

Vol. 2709: T. Windeatt, F. Roli (Eds.), Multiple Classifier Systems. Proceedings, 2003. X, 406 pages. 2003.

Vol. 2710: Z. Ésik, Z, Fülöp (Eds.), Developments in Language Theory. Proceedings, 2003. XI, 437 pages. 2003.

Vol. 2711: T.D. Nielsen, N.L. Zhang (Eds.), Symbolic and Quantitative Approaches to Reasoning with Uncertainty. Proceedings, 2003. XII, 608 pages. 2003. (Subseries LNAI).

Vol. 2712: A. James, B. Lings, M. Younas (Eds.), New Horizons in Information Management. Proceedings, 2003. XII, 281 pages. 2003.

Vol. 2713: C.-W. Chung, C.-K. Kim, W. Kim, T.-W. Ling, K.-H. Song (Eds.), Web and Communication Technologies and Internet-Related Social Issues – HSI 2003. Proceedings, 2003. XXII, 773 pages. 2003.

Vol. 2714: O. Kaynak, E. Alpaydin, E. Oja, L. Xu (Eds.), Artificial Neural Networks and Neural Information Processing – ICANN/ICONIP 2003. Proceedings, 2003. XXII, 1188 pages. 2003.

Vol. 2715: T. Bilgiç, B. De Baets, O. Kaynak (Eds.), Fuzzy Sets and Systems – IFSA 2003. Proceedings, 2003. XV, 735 pages. 2003. (Subseries LNAI).

Vol. 2716: M.J. Voss (Ed.), OpenMP Shared Memory Parallel Programming. Proceedings, 2003. VIII, 271 pages. 2003.

Vol. 2718: P. W. H. Chung, C. Hinde, M. Ali (Eds.), Developments in Applied Artificial Intelligence. Proceedings, 2003. XIV, 817 pages. 2003. (Subseries LNAI).

Vol. 2719: J.C.M. Baeten, J.K. Lenstra, J. Parrow, G.J. Woeginger (Eds.), Automata, Languages and Programming. Proceedings, 2003. XVIII, 1199 pages. 2003.

Vol. 2720: M. Marques Freire, P. Lorenz, M.M.-O. Lee (Eds.), High-Speed Networks and Multimedia Communications. Proceedings, 2003. XIII, 582 pages. 2003.

Vol. 2721: N.J. Mamede, J. Baptista, I. Trancoso, M. das Graças Volpe Nunes (Eds.), Computational Processing of the Portuguese Language. Proceedings, 2003. XIV, 268 pages. 2003. (Subseries LNAI).

Vol. 2722: J.M. Cueva Lovelle, B.M. González Rodríguez, L. Joyanes Aguilar, J.E. Labra Gayo, M. del Puerto Paule Ruiz (Eds.), Web Engineering. Proceedings, 2003. XIX, 554 pages. 2003.

Vol. 2723: E. Cantú-Paz, J.A. Foster, K. Deb, L.D. Davis, R. Roy, U.-M. O'Reilly, H.-G. Beyer, R. Standish, G. Kendall, S. Wilson, M. Harman, J. Wegener, D. Dasgupta, M.A. Potter, A.C. Schultz, K.A. Dowsland, N. Jonoska, J. Miller (Eds.), Genetic and Evolutionary Computation – GECCO 2003. Proceedings, Part I. 2003. XLVII, 1252 pages. 2003.

Vol. 2724: E. Cantú-Paz, J.A. Foster, K. Deb, L.D. Davis, R. Roy, U.-M. O'Reilly, H.-G. Beyer, R. Standish, G. Kendall, S. Wilson, M. Harman, J. Wegener, D. Dasgupta, M.A. Potter, A.C. Schultz, K.A. Dowsland, N. Jonoska, J. Miller (Eds.), Genetic and Evolutionary Computation – GECCO 2003. Proceedings, Part II. 2003. XLVII, 1274 pages. 2003.

Vol. 2725: W.A. Hunt, Jr., F. Somenzi (Eds.), Computer Aided Verification. Proceedings, 2003. XII, 462 pages. 2003.

Vol. 2726: E. Hancock, M. Vento (Eds.), Graph Based Representations in Pattern Recognition. Proceedings, 2003. VIII, 271 pages. 2003.

Vol. 2727: R. Safavi-Naini, J. Seberry (Eds.), Information Security and Privacy. Proceedings, 2003. XII, 534 pages. 2003.

Vol. 2728: E.M. Bakker, T.S. Huang, M.S. Lew, N. Sebe, X.S. Zhou (Eds.), Image and Video Retrieval. Proceedings, 2003. XIII, 512 pages. 2003.

Vol. 2731: C.S. Calude, M.J. Dinneen, V. Vajnovszki (Eds.), Discrete Mathematics and Theoretical Computer Science. Proceedings, 2003. VIII, 301 pages. 2003.

Vol. 2732: C. Taylor, J.A. Noble (Eds.), Information Processing in Medical Imaging. Proceedings, 2003. XVI, 698 pages. 2003.

Vol. 2733: A. Butz, A. Krüger, P. Olivier (Eds.), Smart Graphics. Proceedings, 2003. XI, 261 pages. 2003.

Vol. 2734: P. Perner, A. Rosenfeld (Eds.), Machine Learning and Data Mining in Pattern Recognition. Proceedings, 2003. XII, 440 pages. 2003. (Subseries LNAI).

Vol. 2741: F. Baader (Ed.), Automated Deduction – CADE-19. Proceedings, 2003. XII, 503 pages. 2003. (Subseries LNAI).

Vol. 2743: L. Cardelli (Ed.), ECOOP 2003 – Object-Oriented Programming. Proceedings, 2003. X, 501 pages. 2003.

Vol. 2745: M. Guo, L.T. Yang (Eds.), Parallel and Distributed Processing and Applications. Proceedings, 2003. XII, 450 pages. 2003.

Vol. 2746: A. de Moor, W. Lex, B. Ganter (Eds.), Conceptual Structures for Knowledge Creation and Communication. Proceedings, 2003. XI, 405 pages. 2003. (Subseries LNAI).

Vol. 2748: F. Dehne, J.-R. Sack, M. Smid (Eds.), Algorithms and Data Structures. Proceedings, 2003. XII, 522 pages. 2003.

Vol. 2749: J. Bigun, T. Gustavsson (Eds.), Image Analysis. Proceedings, 2003. XXII, 1174 pages. 2003.

Vol. 2750: T. Hadzilacos, Y. Manolopoulos, J.F. Roddick, Y. Theodoridis (Eds.), Advances in Spatial and Temporal Databases. Proceedings, 2003. XIII, 525 pages. 2003.

Vol. 2751: A. Lingas, B.J. Nilsson (Eds.), Fundamentals of Computation Theory. Proceedings, 2003. XII, 433 pages. 2003.

Vol. 2753: F. Maurer, D. Wells (Eds.), Extreme Programming and Agile Methods – XP/Agile Universe 2003. Proceedings, 2003. XI, 215 pages. 2003.

Vol. 2759: O.H. Ibarra, Z. Dang (Eds.), Implementation and Application of Automata. Proceedings, 2003. XI, 312 pages. 2003.